Mysterious Powers

Mysterious Powers

by Colin Wilson

Aldus Books · Jupiter Books

Series Coordinator: John Mason
Design Director: Günter Radtke
Picture Editor: Peter Cook
Editor: Kit Coppard
Copy Editor: Mitzi Bales
Research: Sarah Waters
General Consultant: Beppie Harrison

SBN 490 00332 X

© 1975 Aldus Books Limited London

First published in the United Kingdom
in 1975 by Aldus Books Limited
17 Conway Street, London W1P 6BS

Distributed by Jupiter Books
167 Hermitage Road, London N4 1LZ

Printed and bound in Italy by
Amilcare Pizzi S.p.A.
Cinisello Balsamo (Milano)

**Frontispiece: Aaron changes his staff into a snake.
Above: Aleister Crowley as The Guardian of the Flame.**

EDITORIAL CONSULTANTS:

COLIN WILSON
DR. CHRISTOPHER EVANS

Most of us live our lives bounded by the ordinary physical laws. But among us are, and always have been, rare individuals who seem free of such restrictions—men and women for whom the normal laws of the universe are apparently suspended. The extent to which those of strange powers have entered popular mythology and folklore prove that they have baffled and fascinated other people for centuries. What is the source of their strange powers? "It's magic!" says the child to explain the unexplainable. As adults, we grope for more rational and scientific answers. Still we ask: what is the source of talents enabling some to bend the physical world to their will, see the unseen, hypnotize those around them? And is it possible that we all have such powers lying latent within ourselves?

1

Wild Talents

Few of us would flatly deny that the universe is a stranger place than the generally accepted natural laws can account for. Most of the time we choose not to think about it. When we discover that some people appear to have strange powers, powers that apparently enable them to ignore the normal physical laws that contain the rest of us, we prefer not to think about that either because we have no easy explanation. It makes life more complicated, and it is a subtle threat to our own sense of safety in a known world. When we do think about it we hunt for the trick, the deception, the proof that everything is as we would like it

The Israeli psychic Uri Geller. His hotly disputed control of matter by the power of his mind alone has made him the focus of a great deal of controversy and much scientific speculation.

"He asked me to transmit the thought of what I had sketched"

to be so that we can return, safely, to not thinking about it. But these wild talents tug at our sleeves, whisper in our ears. Throughout all recorded history people have been fascinated and have felt threatened by these unexplained abilities. In our recent history we have conducted complicated tests and formulated sophisticated explanations—and then a young Israeli comes along and stops clocks and bends spoons: trivial accomplishments in themselves, but how do we explain them? Then we find we have started to think about strange powers and extraordinary events.

I met the young Israeli wonder worker Uri Geller one morning in the summer of 1974 in the office of a London business tycoon. The meeting had been arranged with a view to my working on a film about Geller's life. A secretary showed me into the inner office. Uri, a good looking but seemingly quite ordinary young man, appeared to be a little nervous or preoccupied. We chatted briefly, after which the three of us went to lunch at a nearby restaurant. We sat at a table in the corner, the woman and I side by side and Uri opposite us with his back to the room. When we had ordered, he offered to try to demonstrate his powers, but said, "I don't know if it will work. Sometimes it doesn't."

We began with an experiment in *telepathy* (the transmission of thoughts by means other than the five senses). Uri handed me one of the restaurant cards on the table and, turning away from me, asked me to make a drawing on its blank side. I made a sketch of a creature I had invented some time ago to amuse my children. It took only a few seconds, as I had drawn it many times before. I glanced at Uri as I did it. He was staring out across the restaurant, and he could not have watched me without being seen to do so by the secretary beside me. When I had finished, he asked me to cover the drawing with my hand. Then he turned back to the table and took another of the cards. He asked me to concentrate hard and to try to transmit the thought of what I had sketched. A minute went by with no result. Uri shook his head. "It seems very complicated; is it a kind of amoeba?" Slowly and hesitantly he began to draw the creature's right ear—the spot where I always begin the drawing. "You've got it," I said. "Go on!" He completed the drawing quickly. I had carefully redrawn the picture in my mind as I tried to transmit it—which probably accounts for the identical starting point.

Uri then demonstrated other powers. He caused a restaurant spoon to bend by stroking it gently. He made the hands of my watch turn back two hours and the date go forward two days by stroking a coin placed over its face, explaining afterward that he derives power from metal. He had a little trouble trying to break my American Automobile Association key. Ideally, he said, the key should have more personal associations. However, he placed it against a metal radiator, and after a few seconds said, "It's starting to go." The key snapped in two.

Finally, he tried to transmit a picture to me by telepathy. I attempted to make my mind receptive, but no image came into it. Feeling rather embarrassed, I just drew the first thing that came into my head: a check mark. Uri showed me the piece of

One of Geller's favorite methods of demonstrating his mind-reading power is to reproduce a simple drawing which has just been done and then hidden from his sight, usually inside a sealed envelope. Above: an experimenter, isolated from Geller in an adjoining room, makes a rough sketch of a chair.

Left: the sketch has been hidden in two sealed envelopes, one inside the other. After he has rejoined Geller, the experimenter holds the envelopes in his hand, and Geller rests his hand on top. Concentrating intently, Geller starts to draw with his other hand.

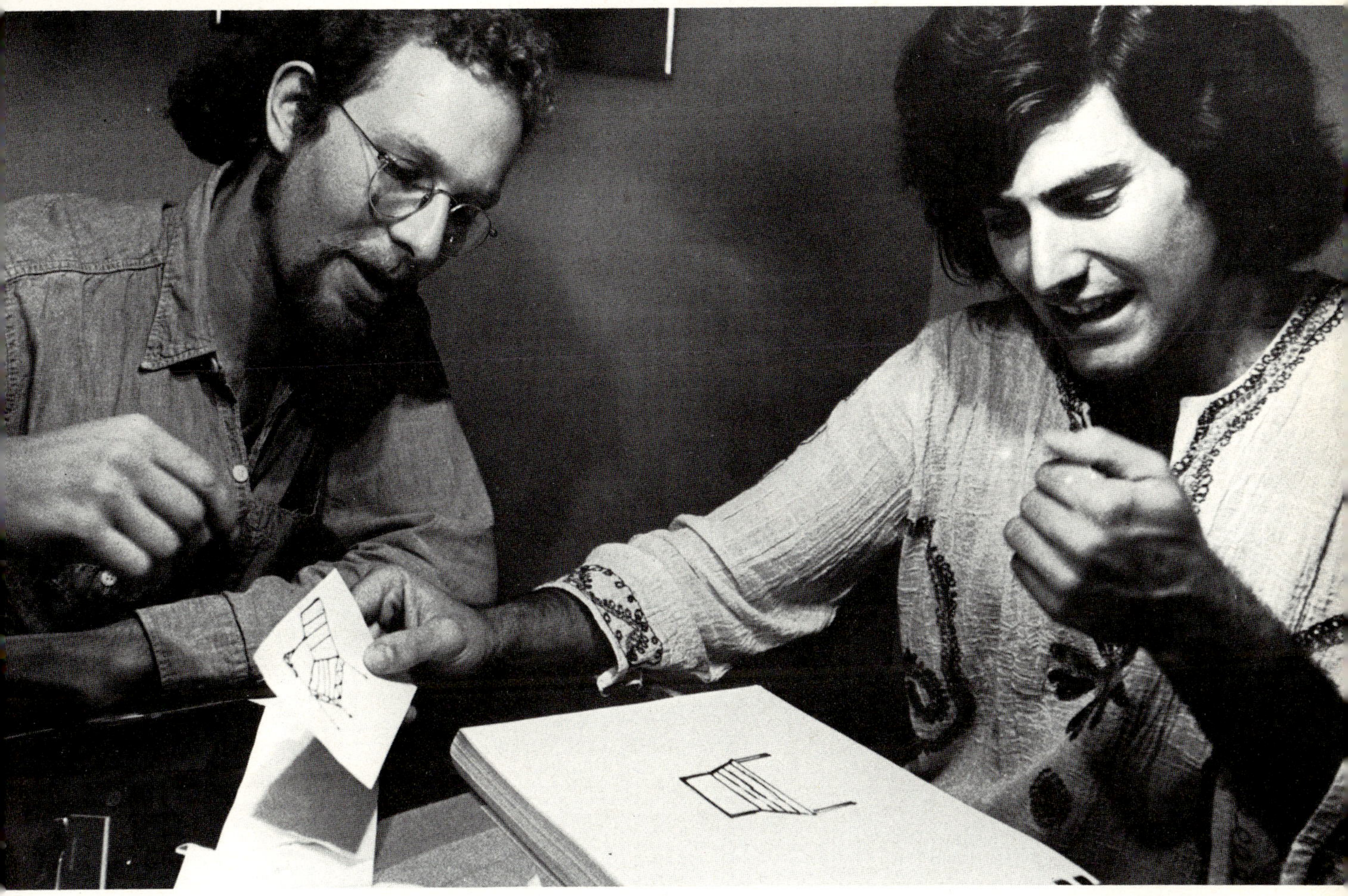

Above: comparing the two drawings. Geller has succeeded in sketching a chair very similar to the one that the experimenter had drawn.

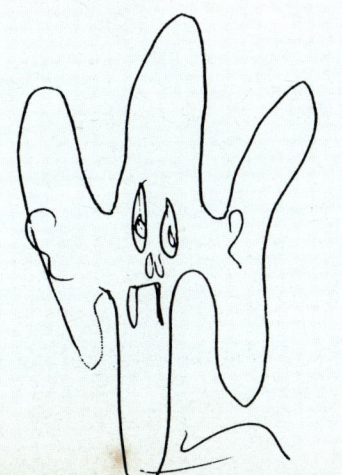

Left: the blob-like doodle that the author of this book drew, and Geller's reproduction of it, apparently by telepathy. The author's drawing is on the right.

9

paper he was holding away from me. It contained a mirror image of the symbol I had drawn. It could be significant in this connection that Uri is left-handed.

After I left Uri Geller I immediately began to sift my impressions. Only the day before, a highly skeptical scientist had warned me to watch carefully for conjuring tricks, especially as Uri had earlier been a stage conjuror. I had to admit that most of the things he had done could have been tricks. For instance, snapping the key with his fingers, and altering the hands and date on my watch with the winder would have been well within the ability of a skillful conjuror. But how could he have faked the drawing of what I had drawn? And if that feat was due to genuine telepathic powers, the other demonstrations could also be genuine.

A couple of months after this Ted Bastin, a quantum physicist, and I appeared on a television discussion show about supernormal powers—a subject about which Ted is distinctly skeptical. When I mentioned Uri Geller, however, Ted told me he had conducted extensive tests and was convinced that Uri was genuine. A few days later Ted rang me up to announce that Uri had just performed a most spectacular feat in his laboratory. He had dematerialized half a crystal that had been sealed in a metal container. Bastin said that there was no way in which Uri could have touched the crystal.

Assuming that Uri Geller possesses extraordinary powers, where do they come from? I think the answer must be from his subconscious mind. In recent years psychologists have come to the conclusion that *poltergeists* (ghosts or spirits that make noises or fling objects) originate in the subconscious minds of teenagers who have been seriously disturbed by the problems of adolescence. On the other hand, some investigators believe that poltergeists have a separate existence—that is, that they are real ghosts—but that they have to borrow energy from disturbed adolescents before they can become active. Whatever the truth of the matter, it seems probable that the subconscious mind provides the energy that causes heavy objects to rise and fly across a room or doors to open and bang shut. If this is so, it is reasonable to assume that the energy which causes spoons

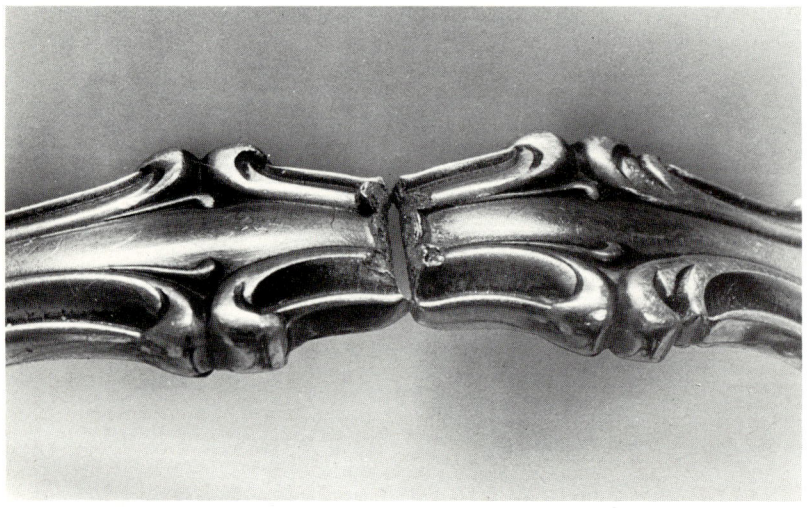

Left: the snapped handle of a spoon apparently bent by Geller. Skeptics suggest he is only a gifted conjurer who can deftly substitute a previously bent spoon (or fork, or key, or nail, or whatever) for the object he started the demonstration with. It is particularly hard for any observer to keep precise track of where things are at a given moment because Geller works best in what has been described as "rampant confusion"—moving back and forth from one experiment to another, sometimes failing, and then abruptly producing a success.

to bend and broken watches to tick originates in Uri Geller's highly active subconscious mind.

If these strange powers exist in some hidden depths of the mind, what are they doing there? Are they common to all of us, and are they available to anyone who knows how to use them? We may find part of the answer in an experience of John G. Bennett, the foremost living disciple of the remarkable Russian mystic Georgei Gurdjieff.

In 1923 Bennett was at Gurdjieff's Institute for the Harmonious Development of Man at the Prieuré in a suburb of Paris. For some days Bennett had been suffering from almost constant diarrhea, and each morning he felt weaker and found it harder to get up. One morning he woke up shaking with fever, and decided to stay in bed. But in the instant of making this decision, he found himself getting out of bed and dressing. It felt, he said, as if he was being "held together by a superior Will

Above: the power of mind over metal? Geller and the results of one of his demonstrations.

Above: J. G. Bennett in 1960. He was a disciple of Georgei Gurdjieff and attended the master's institute. Below: the lime tree grove at the Prieuré, where Gurdjieff set up his institute. It was under these trees that Bennett, while practicing the group exercises, experienced a sudden and great "influx of an immense power."

that was not my own." After a morning's work, he felt too ill to eat lunch. Nonetheless, he joined a dancing class in the afternoon. Gurdjieff's dances involved movements of great complexity, requiring tremendous concentration and physical coordination. As the exercises continued Bennett felt an immense lassitude descend on him. It became agony even to move, but he forced himself to go on. Gurdjieff introduced new exercises which were so complex that the other students began to drop out one by one. Bennett, however, felt Gurdjieff's eyes on him as if commanding him to go on, even if it killed him.

"Suddenly, I was filled with an influx of immense power. My body seemed to have turned into light. I could not feel its presence in the usual ways. There was no effort, no weariness, not even any sense of weight. . . ." When the lesson was over he decided to test the power that had entered his body. He took a spade and began to dig at a rate that would normally have exhausted him in two minutes. In spite of the summer heat, he continued digging for over an hour.

Later Bennett went for a walk toward a nearby forest where he met Gurdjieff. Without preliminaries, Gurdjieff began to talk about energies. "There is a certain energy," he said, "that is necessary for work on oneself . . . we can call it the Higher Emotional Energy. . . . There are some people in the world, but they are very rare, who are connected to the Great Reservoir or Accumulator of this energy. . . ." Gurdjieff implied that he was one of those who can tap the Great Reservoir and permit others to borrow its energy.

Bennett continued his walk in the forest, still filled with a tremendous sense of power. He recalled that Peter Ouspensky, another Russian mystic and associate of Gurdjieff's, had once said that if we wish to prove how little control we have over our emotions, we have only to try to be astonished at will. Bennett said to himself: "I will be astonished." Instantly he felt overwhelmed with amazement. "Each tree was so uniquely itself that I felt that I could walk in the forest forever and never cease from wonderment. Then the thought of 'fear' came to me. At once I was shaking with terror. Unknown horrors were menacing me on every side. I thought of 'joy,' and I felt that my heart would burst from rapture. The word 'love' came to me, and I was pervaded with such fine shades of tenderness and compassion that I saw that I had not the remotest idea of the depth and range of love. Love was everywhere and in everything. It was infinitely adaptable to every shade of need. After a time it became too much for me; it seemed that if I plunged any more deeply into the mystery of love, I would cease to exist. I wanted to be free from this power to feel whatever I chose, and at once it left me."

What is this strange power that Gurdjieff was able to evoke in his disciples? It is not as mysterious as it sounds. We are all familiar with its commonest form, which we call "second wind." In most energetic sports, such as long distance running, we force ourselves beyond the normal point of exhaustion. Then sometimes, quite suddenly, we feel a resurge of energy that enables us to continue for longer than usual. On rare occasions we can even force ourselves to continue until we get our third wind.

The American philosopher and psychologist William James wrote about this in his essay "The Energies of Man."

"Everyone is familiar with the phenomenon of feeling more or less alive on different days. Everyone knows on any given day that there are energies slumbering in him which the incitements of that day to not call forth, but which he might display if these were greater. Most of us feel as if a sort of cloud weighed upon us, keeping us below our highest notch of clearness in discernment, sureness in reasoning, or firmness in deciding. Compared with what we ought to be, we are only half awake. Our fires are damped, our drafts are checked. We are making use of only a small part of our possible mental and physical resources."

"Stating the thing broadly, the human individual thus lives unusually far within his limits; he possesses powers of various sorts which he habitually fails to use. He energizes below his *maximum,* and he behaves below his *optimum.*"

In other words, for everyday purposes human beings have certain predetermined limits. It is like the thermostat on a central heating system. When the temperature rises above a certain point it automatically switches off the heating. When our tiredness reaches a certain limit, we also switch off automatically, and allow ourselves to sink into a passive state. But if some crisis arises, we refuse to allow ourselves to remain passive. We become alert and suddenly, as our thermostat readjusts itself, we discover we have become fully alive again.

The implication seems to be that each of us contains a vast reservoir of energy. William James also asks what it is that gives a Leonardo or a Beethoven his creative energy. His answer is excitement, determination, a sense of purpose. He adds: "We live subject to arrest by degrees of fatigue which we have come only from habit to obey. Most of us may learn to push the barrier further off, and to live in perfect comfort on much higher levels of power."

This was the aim of Gurdjieff's work. He forced his students to keep pushing the barriers farther and farther back. One of his followers, Fritz Peters, has described how Gurdjieff gave him the task of mowing the lawns at the Prieuré. At first the work took Peters several days. Gradually Gurdjieff accustomed him to doing more and more in a day until finally Peters could mow all the lawns, which consisted of several acres, in one day. What Gurdjieff called his "dervish dances" were also designed to break the chain of habit. Try rubbing your stomach with one hand while patting yourself on the head with the other, or tapping the toes of one foot on the floor while rubbing the other foot back and forth like a pendulum. Most people find such movements difficult. Yet Gurdjieff trained his students to do something different with feet, arms, and head at the same time. He would also suddenly order them to break off whatever they were doing, and to freeze in some complicated attitude.

As Gurdjieff recognized, even exercises as difficult as these can become a habit. Fritz Peters tells a story which reveals that Gurdjieff himself could forget how to establish contact with his own reservoir of energy. At the end of World War II Peters, then a soldier and suffering from battle fatigue and

Above: one of Gurdjieff's dances, the Dervish Dance, performed here by Olgivanna Lloyd Wright, Mme. Galoumian and Jeanne de Salzmann. Gurdjieff's dances were designed not only for control of the body, but—by their complicated and demanding patterns—also needed unbroken mental concentration. Thus the ritual movements were meant to act on all aspects of the student's body and mind. Below: G. I. Gurdjieff as he was toward the end of his life.

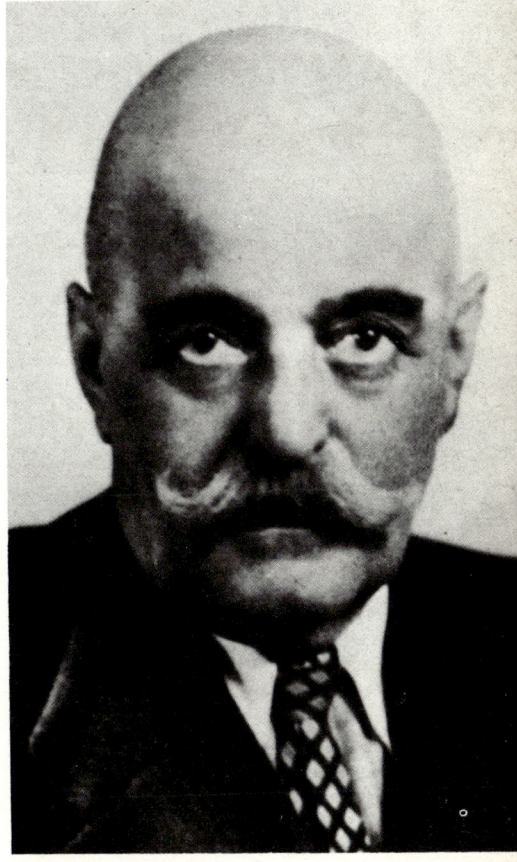

nervous strain, called on Gurdjieff at his Paris apartment. Gurdjieff was busy and asked Peters to wait for him in another room. After a minute or two alone, Peters felt so miserable and desperate that he interrupted Gurdjieff again. Gurdjieff instantly saw the seriousness of the situation, and set his work aside. As he sat with Gurdjieff, Peters experienced a sudden trickle of power flowing into him like a spring. It slowly increased until all his tiredness had vanished. But Gurdjieff himself now looked completely exhausted. Peters had no doubt that Gurdjieff had somehow given him his own energy. A crowd of people then arrived at the house, and Gurdjieff dragged himself away to entertain them. Five minutes later he returned to the kitchen radiating vitality, and remarked to Peters that the experience had been good for both of them. In other words, the effort of revitalizing Peters had awakened Gurdjieff to a recognition that he had lost touch with his own "source of power, meaning, and purpose." He promptly re-established contact, and recharged his own batteries.

Right: Olgivanna Lloyd Wright, widow of the architect Frank Lloyd Wright, carries on his work through the Taliesin Fellowship. Taliesin is a residential architectural firm and school founded by the world-famous architect. Mrs. Wright, a follower of Gurdjieff's for a time, has incorporated aspects of the Prieuré regime into the life of the community in California. They include hard manual work by all members whether students or staff, the importance of music, and the absolute authority of the leader. Below: a group portrait of the Fellowship at Taliesin West, designed by Frank Lloyd Wright. Mrs. Wright is at the far right.

There is nothing mystical or occult about this. We all have within us a robot, akin to the automatic pilot in an airplane, whose task is to simplify our lives by handling a series of routines. Learning to type or speak French or drive a car requires considerable effort and concentration, but once we have mastered it, our robot takes over and does it far more quickly and efficiently than we could do it consciously. The trouble is, the robot can become so efficient that it takes over most of our life. We begin to live like a robot. We automatically drink our martini, eat our dinner, watch TV. It takes a holiday or some sudden crisis to jar us out of this automatic living, to allow our real selves to take over from the robot.

There can be no doubt that Gurdjieff helped Bennett overcome his fatigue, just as he helped Peters. But at a certain point, Bennett's own inner dynamo took over and he wrested control from his robot. He was suddenly dazzled by vistas of possible feeling. For, like our bodies, our feelings are also controlled by the robot. We seldom experience new feeling. For the most part, we play the same old phonograph record over and over again—a record that, except in times of crisis, is full of bland harmonies. What Bennett had realized was that he could experience new intensities of feeling every day; that he could experience a compelling feeling for every tree and every blade of grass.

Our minds contain a vast unused library of "phonograph records." And not just our minds. The world around us is full of an infinite number of interesting things that the robot has been trained to ignore. This is perhaps the most important insight that arises from Bennett's description of his experience: " . . . I was pervaded with such shades of tenderness and compassion that *I saw that I had not the remotest idea of the depth and range of love.*" We accept the universe around us as stable and normal, just as a child who knew nothing about water might accept the surface of a pond as a glittering mirror, unaware that there are green depths below, teeming with innumerable forms of life. How many other things is this true of? How much mystery and complexity and reality is hidden from us by ignorance and habit?

Human beings live within arbitrary limits. Not only do we have an arbitrary idea of our powers and capabilities, but we also have an arbitrary idea of the complexity and interestingness of the world around us. Habit has confined human beings in a thoroughly stale universe.

A word of caution should be offered, however. Why should Bennett get tired of the power to see and feel more widely than ever before? Why does he say: "I wanted to be free from this power to feel whatever I chose . . . "? The reason is that these arbitrary limits to our powers are also safety limits. Our habits, which can become so oppressive, are also intended to protect us. Bennett could have achieved many of the same effects of power and perception by taking a psychedelic drug such as mescalin or LSD. These also destroy the robot and disconnect our habit mechanisms so that the world appears new and strange. Psychedelic drugs also release the capacity to feel whatever we choose—the thought of love can produce a tidal wave of love.

On the other hand, a negative thought produces equally powerful results. One man who had taken LSD under medical supervision described how the thought of death produced the hallucination that peoples' faces had become grinning skulls, and the air seemed thick with the smell of earth and decaying flesh. Some people who have had bad trips have become permanently unbalanced mentally. The power of the mind can be highly dangerous, and meddling with it simply for kicks is as irresponsible as allowing a child to drive a high-powered car. Bennett realized that it would be wiser to learn to extend the range of his consciousness step by step, and to consolidate each step before moving on rather than to take a sudden leap into powers that were beyond his understanding or ability to control.

Once we know the world is not as dull and ordinary as it may seem, we have taken a major step toward doing something about it. The real objection to habit is that it makes us lazy, paralyzing the will. Once we realize that our robot is insulating us against much that is rich and rewarding in the world around us, we can begin to organize the will to resist the power of habit.

While we know enough about second wind to understand Bennett's experience, it is altogether more difficult to grasp how Gurdjieff could have projected energy into Bennett and Peters. What is the nature of this energy? The following may throw some light on it.

In 1919 Bernard Kajinsky, a Russian electrical engineer, was awakened in the night by a ringing sound like that of a spoon hitting glass. The next day he learned that his closest friend had died of typhus. When he called on his friend's mother, he discovered that she had been about to give him a dose of medicine at the moment he died. Kajinsky, suddenly excited, asked her to show him exactly what she had done. She took a silver spoon and dropped it into a tumbler. It made the same ringing sound that had startled him awake.

Kajinsky was a scientist with no interest in telepathy or extrasensory perception. But he had no doubt that his friend had thought of him at the moment of death, and that the sound of the spoon striking glass had somehow been conveyed to him. He thereafter made an exhaustive study of telepathy and reached the conclusion that "the human nervous system is capable of reacting to stimuli whose source is not yet known."

Kajinsky's work came to the attention of a famous Russian animal trainer, Vladimir Durov, who was convinced that his animals could read his mind. Durov began to conduct experiments in association with Vladimir Bekhterev, a distinguished neurologist. Under Bekhterev's supervision, Durov gave complicated telepathic orders to his animals. Usually the animals would carry them out. For example, Bekhterev wrote instructions on a sheet of paper and handed it to Durov. Durov looked into the eyes of his German shepherd dog Mars for several seconds without speaking. Mars went into the next room, looked on three tables and, finding what Bekhterev had asked for on the third—a telephone directory—carried it to Durov in his mouth.

Many animal lovers have noticed that their pets seem to

Science is attempting to find a way to isolate and measure the elusive Psi powers. In this German experiment, target pictures are produced by a random chance generator. The sender, on the right, then tries to transmit the images telepathically to the receiver at the left. Both the target pictures and the choices made by the receiver are automatically recorded, and then evaluated by a computer.

The mysterious power that some individuals seem to possess over animals—apparently communicating directly with them and compelling obedience by the sheer force of personality—has fascinated men throughout the centuries.

Right: at the Psychical Research Foundation in Durham, North Carolina, a subject outside the room is tested on the ability to influence the movement of a cat over a numbered board.

Below: a more traditional form of animal control—a lion tamer. His power over a dangerous animal could possibly be telepathic.

possess some telepathic power. Edward Campbell, a British newspaper editor who studied this question, tells an interesting story about a German animal trainer, Hans Brick. Brick's favorite lion was a man eater named Habibi, and Brick's bond with the lion was a strange one. It was tacitly agreed between them that the lion—which was savage and unbroken—was entitled to kill Brick if it could find a moment when his attention lapsed. While Brick maintained his full attention the lion never attacked him. But on several occasions when his attention had wavered, an attack came instantly. Brick insisted it was his own fault. "I know the rules; so does he," he said.

During World War II Brick was interned in England for a while, and Habibi was looked after by a zoo. When Brick was released, a British film company asked him to supervise some wild animal sequences in a film using Habibi. A problem arose because the owner of the zoo wanted payment for having tended Habibi, and Brick could not afford the fee. According to Campbell, at six o'clock on Sunday morning Brick walked into the zoo, went to Habibi's cage on an upper floor, released the lion, and looped a whip loosely around his neck. Brick then made a mental pact with the animal: Habibi was not to attack him while they were making their escape from the zoo.

The animals in other cages were in an uproar as the lion walked out. Rabbits and peacocks were ranging freely about the floor, but Habibi made no attempt to attack them. Brick walked to the door, Habibi following. They went down a flight of stairs and into the street. The lion walked quietly behind Brick and entered a traveling cage that he had parked in the next street. In effect, Brick had told the lion telepathically: "These are special circumstances. You want to get out; I want to get you out. No tricks . . ." And the lion had kept to his side of the bargain.

So far we have been speaking of telepathy which, most investigators agree, seems to depend on some form of waves. They are generally known as *Psi* waves. (Psi is a Greek letter used in parapsychology for psychic ability or phenomenon.) At present we have no idea of the nature of such waves. We might compare Psi waves with radio waves. But radio waves can be used only to communicate, whereas when Gurdjieff used Psi power on Bennett and Peters he seems to have been doing much more than merely communicating.

In 1940, not long before the invasion of the USSR, Joseph Stalin ordered an investigation into the powers of a psychic named Wolf Messing, who appears to have possessed Psi powers to an extraordinary degree. Messing described these experiments in a Soviet science magazine. His first test was to walk into a bank, present the cashier with a note, and will him to hand over 100,000 rubles in cash. Two official witnesses went with Messing when he did this. They saw the cashier take packets of banknotes out of the safe and hand them over. Messing put them in a briefcase and left. Then, with the two witnesses he reentered the bank, and handed back the money and the note—which was in fact a sheet of blank paper. The clerk looked at it, suddenly realized what he had done—and collapsed with a heart attack.

The stories about Brick and Messing may make one conclude that Gurdjieff simply used his Psi powers to suggest certain feelings to Fritz Peters. But it is difficult to see why, in that case, the effort should have exhausted Gurdjieff—and even more difficult to see how Peters could have been so genuinely re-invigorated. For the moment, it may be best to acknowledge that we do not even begin to understand the possibilities of Psi, and leave it at that.

Psi powers are not as rare as we might suppose. In fact, there are a number of simple experiments that anyone can do to verify that they are more than merely autosuggestion. The simplest test requires four or five people. One of the group, the subject, stands in the center of the room with the others around him.

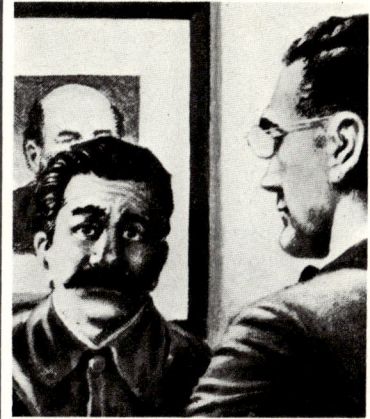

The Psychic and the Dictator

Wolf Messing was a stage mind reader who fled for his life from Poland to the Soviet Union during World War II. He had been in danger not only because he was a Jew, but also because he had predicted Hitler's death if the German dictator "turned toward the East." Hitler, a believer in fortune telling, put a price on Messing's head.

In the USSR Messing faced another dictator's challenge when Josef Stalin set a test for him. It was not an easy one. Messing was to enter Stalin's country house—a place bristling with guards and secret police—without a pass.

One day as Stalin sat working in the office of his country home, a man walked coolly into the grounds and then into the house. All the guards and servants stood back respectfully as he passed. He walked to the doorway of Stalin's study. When the dictator looked up, he was astonished. The man was Messing!

The celebrated psychic's explanation was this: by mental suggestion he had made the guards think he was Lavrenti Beria, the much-feared head of the secret police at that time. So strong were his powers that, even though Messing looked nothing like Beria, the guards were convinced he was.

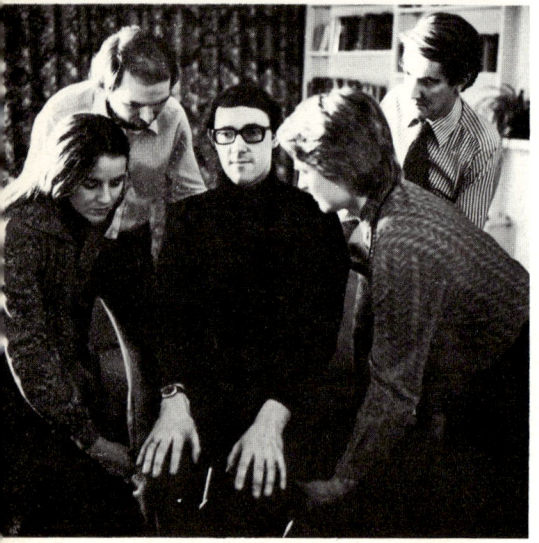

Two experiments for a group to try in applying thought pressure. Above: all stand in a circle around the subject, and place their hands on his head. Next, concentrate hard for about 20 seconds. Then, each using index fingers only, try to lift him up. Below: when the group wills the subject to move one way, she will slowly sway in that direction.

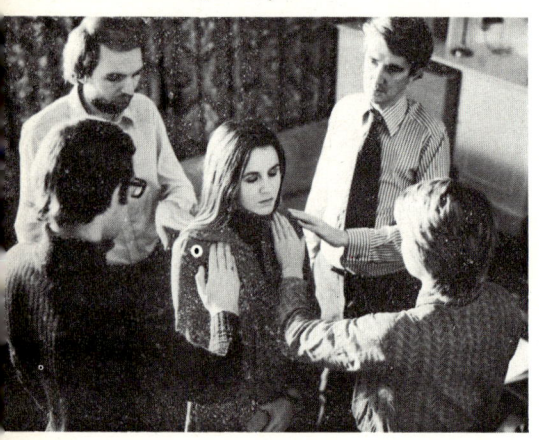

The subject closes his eyes tightly, and the others place their fingers gently against his chest, shoulders, and back making sure not to exert pressure. The aim of the experiment is to make the subject sway in a particular direction, which the others can decide upon by movement of the eyes or a nod of the head. They concentrate hard on willing the subject to sway in the chosen direction. He usually feels a force pulling him in the chosen direction, as if he were a compass needle and someone had brought a magnet close to him. It usually takes only a few seconds, depending on the suggestibility of the subject.

The second experiment, which also takes five people, is lifting a seated person using only index fingers. It is familiar to most schoolchildren. The chosen subject sits in a chair, and the other four attempt to lift him by placing a finger under his armpits and knees. It is, of course, impossible. Then the four place their hands, one on top of the other, on the head of the seated person. No person should have his own two hands next to each other. All concentrate hard for about 20 seconds. Then they quickly remove their hands from the head, place their index fingers under the subject's knees and armpits—and the seated person is lifted effortlessly into the air. The glib explanation of this is that the hands piled on the subject's head operate as a kind of Psi accumulator. The interesting question is why and how they do so—and at present we have no answer.

The third experiment can be performed with a sheet of paper about two inches square. Fold it from corner to corner, from top to bottom, and from side to side. By pinching the corner folds, it can now be turned into a kind of paper dart, its point at the intersection of the fold lines. Take a needle and stick it blunt end first into a cork. Balance the paper dart on the needle point so that it looks like a partly opened umbrella. Making sure that you do not breathe on it, try to will it to rotate about the needle point.

The first time I attempted this, nothing happened—which is what I expected. However, I kept the dart by my typewriter, and every now and then I tried to make it turn, cupping my hands around it. Eventually I stopped trying to make it move by sheer will power, and imagined that it was moving. Immediately, it began to rotate. I thought for a moment that this was due to the heat from my hands, so I tried stopping it. It stopped. Then I made it turn in the opposite direction. Once I had acquired the trick, I found it easy to make it rotate in either direction, even without my hands cupped around it.

The original paper model for this experiment was sent to me by Robert Leftwich, a water diviner who also claimed to be able to dispel clouds by concentrating on them. Although I later met Leftwich, I never saw him dispersing clouds. However, a well-authenticated experiment in cloud dispersal was filmed by a British television program in June 1956 on Hampstead Heath in London. This kind of Psi power is known as *telekinesis* (making objects or bodies move without visible force). Many experiments on this subject have been carried out by Soviet researchers.

It seems possible, then, that thought can exert some form of pressure quite distinct from powers of telepathic suggestion.

This in turn suggests that stories of the power of blessings and curses may have a foundation in fact. If Gurdjieff could make Peters feel better, he could also, presumably, have made him feel worse. Ira Levin's novel *Rosemary's Baby* has an episode in which a black magic group wills a man to death. If thought pressure is a reality, such telekinetic homicide may be possible. Donald Omand, a Church of England clergyman who has performed many exorcisms, believes that if a group of people determinedly brood on someone they dislike, they can inflict psychic damage. Directing mental forces may be as harmful as physical assault.

Gurdjieff tells this story about a station master in a small Russian town. Early every morning as he rang the bell announcing the arrival of the mail train, the station master would also shout curses. Asked why he did this, he explained that whenever he rang the bell, people all over the town woke up and invoked curses on his head. In order to fend these off, he redirected the malevolence back against the townspeople.

By the beginning of the 20th century scientists knew a great deal about the nature of light waves. One of the things they thought they knew was that light is an imponderable, that if it consisted of waves of radiation it could have no weight, and would exert no pressure. Einstein's Theory of Relativity predicted that, on the contrary, light particles have weight and should be subject to gravitation. During the 1918 eclipse of the sun he was proved spectacularly right. Measurements showed that the light rays actually bent as they passed through the sun's gravitational field. Nowadays, scientists design spaceships with "light sails" to exploit the pressure exerted by light waves.

Orthodox science has yet to accept the idea of thought pressure, and decrees that thought is supposed to be an imponderable. There are many scientists who, in the face of much evidence, decline to accept the reality of telepathy. Nevertheless, evidence has continued to accumulate until the point has now come when the only way to deny telepathy is to ignore the facts or to refuse to examine them closely. The only way to explain many of these facts is to assume that thought, like light, can exert its own kind of pressure.

A final question: if we are higher up the evolutionary ladder than other animals, why is it that Brick's lions, like many dogs and other pets, seem to possess more highly developed telepathic powers than we? The answer may be that we have allowed just as powerful faculties in us to fall into disuse. In our most primitive form our capacities may have been as highly developed as those of other animals—more highly developed, probably, or we might not have survived against predators. As we developed tools, the use of fire, and other techniques, we had less and less need for such innate powers. We needed reason and conscious awareness rather than instinct and subconscious awareness.

Humankind seems always to have been more interested in power than in inner awareness. This desire for power is the scarlet thread we shall find running through the history of men of strange powers.

2:00 p.m.

2:11 p.m.

2:14 p.m.

2:17 p.m.

Above: a demonstration of a cloud dispersal by Dr. Rolf Alexander in Ontario in September 1954. The cloud he was concentrating on has been circled. It is shown in this sequence of photography at various intervals of time—and at various stages of dispersal.

2

The Will to Power

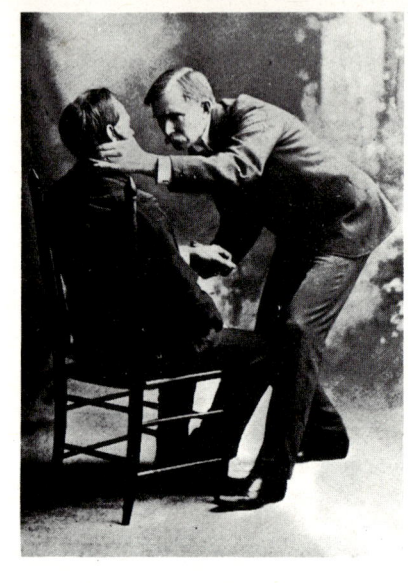

In the mid-1930s a young American psychologist named Abraham Maslow spent most of his vacation in the monkey house of New York's Bronx Zoo. The thing that impressed him most about the animals' behavior was that they all seemed to be sex maniacs. Every minute of the day, males were mounting females, males were mounting other males, females were mounting other females. It looked like a simian Sodom and Gomorrah. Maslow's first conclusion was that this behavior was proof of Sigmund Freud's view that sex is the most important of all animal urges. It was only much later that another solution dawned on

The subtle, persistent, seductive temptation of possessing power over others has caught up and mastered many otherwise genuine and important talents. Above: a picture from a mail order course of 38 lessons on Suggestive Therapeutics and Hypnotism published in 1900. It demonstrates how a practitioner, "with a very severe expression," gazes fiercely into a volunteer's eyes to draw him into a hypnotic trance as part of a stage act.

Right: the irresistible, sinister power of hypnotic eyes compells attention from the casual passer-by—in this case fulfilling its purpose as an advertising poster for a dramatic film performance.

24

"No creature is so obsessed by the will to power as man"

him: the animals were demonstrating dominance behavior.

Zoologists have grasped the full importance of the concept of dominance only in recent years. Farmers, however, have known about it for centuries. In the farmyard, the most dominant chicken can peck all the others; the second most dominant can peck all except the most dominant, and so on down to the weakest, who has no other to peck and may be pecked by all the others. The same pecking order can be seen everywhere in nature, among jackdaws, baboons, wolves, rats, mice, and other animals that live in groups.

What about human beings? Civilization has made us appear to be less obsessed with dominance, but anyone who has worked in a large office or factory knows this is untrue. The pecking order and the concern with status are still there, even if they are partly hidden by conventions of social behavior. In primitive societies the dominance hierarchy is absolutely clear, for it is part of the social structure. The ruler seems to wield a mysterious, almost divine power that is seldom if ever challenged. The young men submit themselves to all kinds of painful tests to establish their right to a place in the dominance hierarchy.

Our primitive ancestors knew all about the pecking order and the will to power, but when people began to live in cities, the old carefully graduated social structure gave way to the disorganized scramble for status. Nowadays, we refer to such a scramble as the "rat race," but this is unfair to the rats. Of all creatures, none is so obsessed by the will to power as man. From what we know of magicians, it seems likely that magic developed as an instrument of this will to power.

It seems certain that primitive man was familiar with what we have called "thought pressure." Palaeolithic cave paintings, some of them 20,000 years old, show tribal *shamans* (magician-priest-doctor) performing magical operations to aid the hunters. The anthropologist Ivar Lissner has described how modern shamans still perform these operations. The shaman makes a drawing or clay model of an animal that is to be hunted. Then, by means of spells, he summons it to a certain place. The following day the hunters go to that place—and find the animal there. In his book *Pattern of Islands* Sir Arthur Grimble describes the ceremony of "calling the porpoises,"

Below: a shaman of the Tungus in the Ural mountains of Russia as seen by an explorer in 1705. A shaman was priest, doctor, and magician for his tribe.

Right: an African witch doctor, ceremonially anonymous in his elaborate mask, preparing to work his traditional magic.

which he witnessed in the Gilbert Islands. The shaman fell asleep in his hut, and entered a trancelike state in which he invited the porpoises to a feast. When he awoke, he rushed out of the hut. All of the villagers ran into the sea, and stood there armed with clubs. Shoals of seemingly hypnotized porpoises then swam gently into shore, where they were dragged onto the beach and killed by the villagers.

Modern man finds it impossible to understand how this magic works, but it is obviously only one step away from Messing's Psi power over the bank clerk that enabled him to rob a bank unarmed. Primitive man also used magic against other human beings. We are not sure precisely when this began to happen, but we are reasonably certain that it did happen because at a certain point in history, some of our distant ancestors suddenly stopped making models and drawings of other men. Why? Because they realized that if magic was potent against deer and bison, it could be effective against people. The mind power that could lure animals to their destruction could also destroy human beings. So anybody who made a drawing or model of a person immediately became suspect. This suspicion still applies among many primitive people today. They generally refuse to be photographed in the belief that the camera is capable of stealing the soul.

Slowly, over the course of many thousands of years, the tribal shaman evolved into the modern sorcerer. That is, he ceased to be what is called a white witch—a benevolent and helpful worker of magic—and became more interested in obtaining power for himself. We can see this transformation beginning in the Old Testament prophets such as Moses, Joshua, Elijah, and Daniel. It is true that they are men of God, and that their power apparently comes from God. But it is significant how often they are engaged in magical contests in which they demonstrate their power at the expense of competing magicians. Aaron throws down his rod in front of the Pharaoh and it turns into a snake. The rival Egyptian magicians do the same thing and their rods also become snakes. But Aaron's snake eats up all the other snakes. Elijah challenges 450 priests of Baal to a test of magic in which they are to call on their god to light the fire under a sacrificial bullock. Their god fails them. Elijah, with great dramatic flair, tells his people to drench his bullock and firewood with water three times. Then he calls upon Jehovah. The God of the Jews sends down a fire that consumes the bullock, the wood, and the water. After this, Elijah orders the people to kill all the priests of Baal. The will to power swaggers through the whole story.

The desire to dominate, to assert themselves, to humiliate or destroy those who oppose them is something that can be observed again and again in the lives of the great magicians. Moreover, the magical contest—the battle with a rival—is a standard feature of the lives of the magicians. In the 1st century A.D. the Greek magician Apollonius of Tyana engaged in a contest with a rival named Euphrates. Simon Magus, the magician of Samaria referred to in the Acts of the Apostles, was supposed to have been challenged by St. Peter. The legend is that Simon conjured up huge black hounds that rushed at Peter.

The apostle held out a loaf of holy bread, and the hounds vanished into thin air. In one version of the legend, Simon then rose into the air, hovered for a moment, and flew through a window. Peter fell to his knees and prayed, whereupon Simon plummeted to the ground. He died from his injuries in this fall.

There can be no doubt that many such stories are pure invention. Others, however, are too detailed—and too widely reported—to be wholly invented. The interesting question is: What genuine powers did men such as Simon Magus possess? The account of him given in the Acts of the Apostles is, understandably, belittling. Describing himself as "some great one," Simon angered St. Peter by offering him money in exchange for the gift of the Holy Spirit. Christian documents are inclined to regard Simon as a charlatan. He claimed to be able to make himself invisible, change himself into an animal, and walk unharmed through fire. The Christians said that all this was achieved by bewitching the senses of the onlookers. Modern writers have taken this to mean that he used some form of hypnosis. For example, legend says that when Simon went to Rome, Nero ordered him to be decapitated by one of his officers. Simon, however, bewitched the officer into decapitating

Above: the fall of Simon Magus as visualized by a 15th-century Italian artist, Benozzo Gozzoli. St. Peter's prayers succeed in vanquishing the demons who, according to the legend, were supporting Simon Magus in the air. On the throne is the Roman emperor Nero, before whom the contest was supposed to have been staged.

Right: Svengali, the sinister character in a 19th-century novel, hypnotized a beautiful young artist's model into doing all he bid. His name became a synonym for evildoers who gain sway over others for their own purposes.

Below: Strindberg, the Swedish playwright and novelist, believed himself to have special psychic powers, which he exercized when he wanted to avoid an unwanted meeting with someone.

a ram instead. When he reappeared with his head still on his shoulders, Nero was so impressed by his powers that he made Simon his court magician.

But was Simon's means of control over the officer ordinary hypnosis or was it the kind of Psi·power exercised by Wolf Messing on the bank clerk? The latter is altogether more likely, because hypnosis takes the cooperation of the person about to be hypnotized. It is unlikely that Simon was able to make himself invisible or turn himself into an animal. But he certainly seemed to have command of the power of thought pressure, just as some people are born with a green thumb.

At this point, it is time to raise the question of how such a power could work. Let us look more closely at some of the recorded examples.

The poet W. B. Yeats was a member of the order of the *Golden Dawn*, one of the first and best known occult societies of late 19th century England. In his autobiography Yeats describes an incident that occurred on a walk taken by one of the other Golden Dawn members and McGregor Mathers, one of the order's founders. "Look at those sheep," said Mathers. "I am going to imagine myself a ram." The sheep immediately began to run after him.

Mathers could also use his strange powers on people, just as the Swedish playwright August Strindberg believed he himself could. Once when Strindberg was eating alone in a restaurant, he recognized two friends among some drunk people at another table. To his dismay, one of them began to approach him. Strindberg fixed his eyes on the man. At this, the friend looked bewildered and returned to his table apparently convinced that Strindberg was a stranger.

Strindberg once attempted to practice black magic, and he believed that his later suffering and bad luck was a result of this dabbling with evil forces. It was when he was separated from his second wife. He wanted desperately to bring about a reconciliation, and had to think of a way of seeing her. He decided to use his telepathic powers to make his daughter just sick enough to require a visit from him. Using a photograph of the girl, he tried to bring about her illness. When the two children of his first marriage got sick a short time later, he felt that he was responsible, and that his use of the evil eye had misfired. Strindberg dates his misfortunes from then on.

One of the most celebrated German criminal cases of 1936 concerned a hypnotist named Franz Walter, who liked to pose as a doctor. One day, boarding a train to Heidelberg, he entered a carriage occupied by a young woman. Walter talked to her, and discovered she was on her way to see a doctor about stomach pains. Walter sympathized, told her he was a doctor, and invited her to have coffee with him. She felt frightened and wanted to refuse, but when Walter took her hand, she found she could not. She later recalled that "it seemed to me as if I no longer had a will of my own." Walter had somehow hypnotized her without her consent. Later, when he wrote to her ordering her to come to him in another town, she felt strangely giddy, and immediately went to him.

Under hypnosis, she was raped by Walter, who then ordered her to become a prostitute and to give him her earnings. When she later married, he hypnotized her into making several attempts on her husband's life. The husband eventually reported her behavior to the police, and a police doctor, Ludwig Mayer, recognized some of the symptoms of hypnotism. He managed to dehypnotize her and unlock her memories of her ordeals, which Walter had ordered her to forget. Walter was tried, found guilty, and sentenced to 10 years in prison.

A mixture of hypnosis and telepathy was used in a series of experiments conducted by the Soviet scientist Leonid Vasiliev in the 1920s and 1930s. The aim of the experiments was to discover not only whether telepathic communication was possible, but also if it could be proved. In one test, Vasiliev used a hypnotist and a hypnotic subject who, the hypnotist claimed, could be made to fall asleep by telepathic suggestion. The hypnotist was placed in one room, and the subject in another. Only Vasiliev and his assistants knew precisely when the hypnotist made the mental suggestion. In repeated tests, they established that the subject fell asleep within one-and-a-half minutes of the suggestion. Later, they discovered that distance made no difference. A subject in the Crimean city of Sebastopol fell asleep at a telepathic suggestion made in Leningrad, more than 1000 miles away. Vasiliev wondered whether telepathic communication

The Singer Imprisoned by a Spell

Trilby O'Ferral in George du Maurier's 1894 novel *Trilby* was an artist's model working in Paris. Though her background was disreputable, her heart was of pure gold. Disappointed in love, she fell into the hands of Svengali, an unscrupulous Hungarian musician with strange powers.

Hypnotized by Svengali, she became a great singer: tall, elegant, with a divine voice that moved audiences to tears. When the man she truly loved saw her at a concert, he was heartbroken that she did not recognize him. Svengali, however, did recognize the young man and, in a spasm of hatred, died of a heart attack. Trilby was instantly released from the spell, with no memory of her triumphs or the ruthless training Svengali had given.

But Trilby began to fade away. Slowly she became thinner and more feeble. One day she saw a photograph of Svengali. As Trilby stared into the "big black eyes full of stern command," her smile became fixed, and she began to sing, "holy, heavenly sweetness." As she stopped singing Trilby fell back against the pillows and, whispering "Svengali, Svengali, Svengali," died.

Above: illustrations from a French medical journal of 1891 showing the reactions under hypnotism of a 23-year-old mental patient. When presented with colored sheets of glass she showed an intensely emotional response, clasping her hands as if in prayer before a blue glass, throwing up her hands in fear when she was given a red glass.

Below: a hypnotist as a social attraction in the 1850s, when the phenomenon fascinated the general public. The ladies are swept up into an ecstatic rapture, seeing only what the hypnotist suggests.

might depend upon some kind of electromagnetic radiation, and tried sealing the hypnotist up in a lead chamber. It made no difference whatever, proving that the waves involved in telepathy have nothing in common with radio waves.

There is a link between these four examples. Mathers' ability to attract the sheep is an example of the kind of telepathy that can exist between humans and animals. But Mathers was deceiving the sheep in the same sort of way that Wolf Messing deceived the bank clerk. Telepathy can also be used for a kind of hypnosis or suggestion. In the case of Strindberg and his drunk friend, the playwright projected the suggestion: "I am not Strindberg" so that the friend turned and walked away. What happened in both of these instances is consistent with the kind of telepathic suggestion that Vasiliev demonstrated so conclusively. In the Walter case, Dr. Mayer established that the hypnotist had hypnotized the young woman against her will. There can be no doubt that Walter immediately recognized her as a good hypnotic subject. It is also clear from Mayer's book

on the case that Walter was driven by a "will to power." A coarse, rather stupid man, he pretended he was a qualified doctor, and many incidents in the case reveal the pleasure he took in his power over his victim. The interesting point in this case is that Walter did not hypnotize his victim by the usual means—for example, by getting her to focus her eyes on a swinging pendulum—but he did it instantaneously by some kind of suggestion. There was some natural form of sympathy between the two, although it seems akin to the sympathy between a snake and a hypnotized rabbit.

When we look more closely at these cases, we find another interesting link. Mathers was a strange mixture of charlatan and genuine scholar. He liked to pose as a Scottish laird of distinguished ancestry while, in fact, he was the son of a clerk and was born in London. He was a quarrelsome man, intensely jealous of his status as head of the Order of the Golden Dawn. He was also driven by a restless will to power. Strindberg had a paranoid egoism that is evident in much of his work. According

Above: when presented with a series of smells, the young woman reacted equally dramatically. But the doctor making these experiments reported that words provoked no reaction at all. His work was part of the early serious medical research into hypnotism.

Below: a stage hypnotist with a woman suspended in space, from a publicity photograph of 1902. The pillars that supported the subject were so inadequately retouched on the picture that the shadowy outlines are still visible. Nonetheless, the woman was unquestionably in a state of trance: she has obviously been hypnotized into total rigidity.

Below: Faust and Mephistopheles, the Devil, from a book of 1608. The legend of the man who sold his soul to the Devil for power —and who then became a great magician as a result—is one of the most durable of all stories about black magic. The legendary Faust has been the subject of many novels, plays, and operas since the mid-16th century.

to the police doctor, Franz Walter also was an egoist driven by the craving to be admired. Mathers, Strindberg, and Walter all lacked a stable background to their lives. It would be scarcely an exaggeration to describe them as homeless wanderers. In all three we see the basic characteristics of the magician: the desire for fame, the will to power, a natural talent for using thought pressure to dominate others.

After Simon Magus, the most famous magician in European history is Faust, also known as Dr. Faustus. The Faust legend has maintained its potency for almost five centuries, and has inspired at least three great works of literature—Christopher Marlowe's *Dr. Faustus* (1604), Goethe's *Faust* (1808 and 1832), and Thomas Mann's *Doctor Faustus* (1947)—as well as many musical works. From all these, the picture that emerges of Faust is of a brilliant, proud, restless man who longs to share the secrets of the gods. But these characteristics have evolved over the centuries, and as we go backward in time we come closer to the truth about the person who called himself Faust. Thomas Mann's Faust is a great musician; Goethe's Faust is a restless scholar, chafing against the frustration of being merely human; Marlowe's Faustus is a scholar who has been led into temptation by the lust for power. The book on which all these were based is Johann Spies' *Historia von D. Johann Faustus*, which appeared in Berlin in 1587. Its hero is little more than a magical confidence trickster. Significantly, his chief gift is hypnosis—although, of course, the author does not use that word.

In a typical episode in the Spies' book, Faust goes to a Jew and offers to leave behind his arm or leg as security for a loan. The Jew accepts, and Faust appears to saw off his leg. Embarrassed and disgusted by this, the Jew later throws the leg into a river— whereupon Faust appears and demands his leg back. The Jew is forced to pay him heavy compensation. In another anecdote,

Right: one of the legendary magical feats of Faust. This story is first recorded in 1589. Taking a tour of Leipzig with some students, Faust jeers at workmen trying to get a huge barrel of wine out of a cellar. The owner offers the contents to whomever can get the barrel out. Faust goes in, mounts the barrel as if it were a horse, and rides it out. The owner has to keep his promise, and Faust and his young friends share the wine.

Faust asks a wagoner with a load of hay how much hay he will allow him to eat for a few pence. The wagoner says jokingly: "As much as you like." When Faust has eaten half the wagonload, the wagoner repents his generosity and offers Faust a gold piece on condition he leaves the rest undevoured. When he reaches home the wagoner discovers that his load is intact, "for the delusion which the doctor had raised was vanished."

Even the Faust of this original book is described as "a scholar and a gentleman." He is said to have been the son of honest German peasants, born near Weimar in 1491, but brought up by a well-to-do uncle in Wittenberg. This uncle sent him to university. Faust's "strong powers of mind" soon distinguish him, and his friends urge him to enter the Church. But Faust has greater ambitions. He begins to dabble in sorcery. He studies Chaldean, Greek, and Arabic. He takes his degree of Doctor of Divinity, and also a medical degree. In due course, he becomes a famous doctor. It is intellectual brilliance that is his downfall, "the boldness of his profane enquiries"—a quality that later generations would consider a virtue, and for which even Spies has a sneaking admiration. Faust wishes to become a great magician, and this is why he invokes the Devil. Having entered into his pact with the Devil, Faust is corrupted by the Prince of Darkness, who proceeds to fill him with greed and lust for power.

At this point, it is worth quoting the *Historia* on a subject that has some bearing on the lives of magicians. "It used to be an old saying that the magician, charm he ever so wisely for a year together, was never a sixpence richer for all his efforts." This belief that unusual powers cannot be used for financial gain is fundamental and persistent. And there seems to be some truth in it. None of the great magicians from Simon Magus to MacGregor Mathers has died rich, and most of them have died paupers. The few who have succeeded in living comfortably—Emanuel

The Man Who Pawned His Leg

When the Devil tempted Faust to make a pact with him, he promised riches as well as power. But, according to one of the early tales about Faust, the Devil did not live up to his word. Being not a penny richer, and in financial straits, Faust reproached the Devil. However, he was told that, as a magician, he could now solve his money problem.

Faust therefore went to a Jewish moneylender in the town and borrowed some money. When at a later time the moneylender wanted his money back, with the interest due, Faust said that he had none. Instead, Faust offered to cut off his leg and give it as further security, redeeming the limb on paying off the loan.

The moneylender accepted the arrangement. Faust appeared to cut off his leg, and gave it over. Later the moneylender decided that he had no use for the leg, and that Faust would not be able to replace it, so he threw it into the river.

Three days later Faust summoned the moneylender to settle the account and redeem his leg. When the man confessed what he had done, Faust demanded his leg back immediately. The unfortunate moneylender, afraid of trouble, gave Faust more money instead of collecting from him.

Left: Faust raising the Devil, from an English book on Faust published in 1830. Three hundred years after the real Faust had lived, the figure of the magician who made a pact with the Devil still had a strong grip on the popular imagination.

Right: Goethe's Faust. In his version, Faust is a serious aging scholar. Mephistopheles tempts him by giving him a vision of the most beautiful woman in the world, and offering him a potion which will return his youth and vigor so that he will be able to win her love. Faust drinks: and not only is his soul lost, but the innocent young girl who comes to love him is also lost.

Above: a 1974 performance of a well-known play about Faust. This is a scene from The Royal Shakespeare Company's production of *Dr. Faustus* by Christopher Marlowe. With Ian McKellen in the title role, the play was adapted and directed by John Barton and designed by Michael Annals. Here Faustus is shown with Mephistopheles, played by Emrys James.

Swedenborg and Gurdjieff, for example—made their money in other ways than magic.

When we pass from the Faust legends to the obscure original, as described by some of his contemporaries, we encounter exactly the sort of person that this investigation has led us to expect: a coarse, vulgar, boastful man, with some natural talent and an overmastering desire for fame. We don't know if he was named Georg Sabellicus or Johannes, but he was often called Faustus Junior. The first we hear of him is in 1507 when, through the good offices of a nobleman, he obtained a post as a teacher in a boys' school in Kreuznach near Frankfurt. Apparently he was a homosexual, for he proceeded to seduce some of his pupils, "indulging in the most dastardly kind of lewdness." When found out, he fled. In 1509, Johannes Faust was given a degree in theology in Heidelberg, some 40 miles from Kreuznach. In 1513, the canon of St. Mary's church in Gotha in what is now East Germany, recorded that he had heard Georg Faust, known as "the demigod of Heidelberg," boasting and talking nonsense in an inn in nearby Erfurt.

The alchemist Trithemius recalls a meeting with Faustus Junior as early as 1507, and dismisses him as a fool, a boaster, and a charlatan. In the few other references we have he is casting horoscopes, making prophecies, or being driven from town to town by his unsavory reputation as a sodomite and *necromancer* (one who foretells the future by communicating with the dead). From Johanne Wier, an acquaintance of Faust who wrote about him, we learn that Faust was wont to boast about "his friend the Devil"—which may have been nothing more than a typical piece of bombast. A story of Faust's malicious humor recorded by Wier describes how Faust, when a prisoner in the castle of Baron Hermann of Batenburg, offered to show the nobleman's chaplain how to remove his beard without a razor, in exchange for a bottle of wine. The chaplain was to rub his beard with the "magic formula" arsenic. The gullible chaplain did this. His beard fell out, just as Faust had prophesied—but it took most of

Above: a scene from a novel about Faust by Friedrich M. von Klinger, whose book appeared in 1791. Here Angélique is a young girl, as good as she was beautiful, whom Faust vowed he would possess. The Devil aided him by turning himself into an old man with a peepshow, showing moral scenes. Angélique gave the poor man alms, and then felt an irresistible urge to look at the wonders of the box. The moral scenes changed slowly and imperceptibly to amorous scenes in which Faust was always shown as the most seductive cavalier, performing the most magnificent deeds to win a shadow resembling herself. At last the Devil showed her some very scandalous pictures. The poor girl fled to her bedroom where Faust awaited her. She fell into his arms and, as the story says, "the scoundrel profited."

the chaplain's skin with it. Wier also tells us that Faust was a drunken wanderer who spent much of his time in low taverns, impressing the locals with conjuring tricks. Other contemporary chroniclers describe him as a liar and a "low juggler."

We do not know when Faust died—it was probably in the 1540s—but we do know how his legendary fame began. A Swiss Protestant clergyman, Johanne Gast, once dined with Faust, and was unfavorably impressed by him—perhaps because of Faust's hints at his pact with the Devil. At all events Gast later spoke of Faust in one of his sermons, declaring that he had been strangled by the Devil, and that his corpse had persisted in lying on its face, although it had been turned on its back five times. This story had the right touch of horror to appeal to the imaginations of his congregation. Soon other stories grew up. One told how the Devil had twisted Faust's head around completely so that it looked down his back. Another recounted how, toward the end of his life, Faust began to hope that he might escape the Devil's clutches—but the trembling of the house at night warned him that the end was near.

The 16th century was an age of religious persecution, a time when a man could be executed on the mere suspicion that he did not believe in the Trinity. The very idea of a man selling his soul to the Devil was enough to make Faust's contemporaries turn pale. Little wonder, then, that Spies' *Historia* became one of the most popular works of its time. Phillip Melancthon, a follower of Luther, also preached about Faust. He gilded the lily somewhat with a story that Faust had defeated and eaten a rival magician in Vienna. Luther also has two slighting references to Faust in his *Table Talk*, from which it is clear that he regarded Faust as a common charlatan rather a demonic wonder worker. The only powers that some of Faust's educated contemporaries were willing to grant him were the gifts of casting accurate horoscopes and of foretelling the future. In 1535, for instance, Faust correctly predicted that the Bishop of Munster would recapture the city, and in 1540 he foretold the defeat of the European armies in Venezuela.

Legend has made Faust the most famous figure in the history of necromancy. But when we peer through the legendary mist, what do we find? Most of the more sensational stories about the man as told by people who knew him, tell of feats that have been more or less duplicated by other men of strange powers down the ages. It is difficult to decide whether this helps to support or to discredit Faust's credentials as a magician. When we try to sift fact from legend, it becomes clear that Faust knew something about hypnosis. It may be that he also knew how to conjure poltergeists. The priest Gast claimed that when Faust was angered by the poor hospitality offered to him by some monks, he sent a poltergeist to trouble them. Apparently the rattling spirit created such a furore that the monks had to abandon their monastery. Accounts made it plain that Faust was stupid, boastful, and malicious. The same is true of many men of strange powers. As we shall see, Faust's restless egoism, his desire to impress, his need to bend nature to his will are characteristic of many of the best-known magicians from Simon Magus onward. Magicians are not comfortable people to know.

Below: von Klinger's Devil, whom he called Leviathan, finally returns to his true and monstrous form and seizes Faust, who makes a magnificent speech of defiance. Leviathan gives a mocking laugh that shakes the world, then tears Fausts body into pieces, scornfully throws the limbs away, and carries his soul off to hell.

Above: the temptations of Faust from von Klinger's novel. The Devil offers him worldly wealth and power—symbolized here by the crown, the jewels, and the bishop's mitre—and lovely women.

3

The wise men of the East, with strange power over the material world—like this Muslim Sufi gliding across a river on his prayer mat—have attracted curious Westerners for hundreds of years.

Wonder-workers

When Louis Jacolliot, an eminent French lawyer and later a chief justice, went to India in the early 1860s, he was a free-thinker with a profound skepticism about religion. However, when his servant announced one morning that a fakir (Hindu holy man) wished to see him, his curiosity got the better of him and he decided to see the man. Jacolliot opened the conversation by saying that he had heard that fakirs possess the power to move objects without touching them—a power that is now called psychokinesis. The fakir—a thin bony little man—replied that he himself possessed no such power, but that spirits lent him their

"The fakir asked Jacolliot if he would like to ask a question of the spirits"

aid. The Frenchman asked if he might see a demonstration of these powers. The Hindu said that he would demonstrate and requested seven flowerpots filled with earth, seven thin wooden rods each a yard long, and seven large leaves from any tree in the garden.

The wooden rods were stuck in the flowerpots so that they were upright. Then a hole was made in the center of each leaf, and the leaves were impaled on each rod so that they fell down and covered the flowerpots. The fakir stood up, joined his hands above his head, and intoned a Hindu prayer. After that he seemed to go into a state of ecstasy, his hands outstretched toward the flowerpots. Suddenly, Jacolliot felt a breeze on his face. During the next 10 minutes, it blew several times. Slowly and gently the leaves began to rise up the wooden rods, then to float downward again. Jacolliot went closer to see if the Hindu could somehow be causing them to move by a trick. But the leaves continued to rise and fall undisturbed as Jacolliot passed between them and the fakir. For the remainder of that morning Jacolliot tried different tests to discover if the fakir used trickery. He arranged the flowerpots and rods himself in case of collusion between his servant and the fakir. He had the rods fixed into holes bored in a plank. It made no difference; the leaves still rose and fell as before.

Finally, the fakir asked Jacolliot if he would like to ask a question of the spirits. In doing so, Jacolliot used an alphabet of brass letters with which he printed his name in his books. Thinking of a dead friend, he began to take letters out of their bag one by one. When he pulled out the letter "A," the leaves moved. He returned the letter to the bag and repeated the process. This time the leaves moved when he pulled out the letter "L." By this process the leaves slowly spelled out the message: "Albain Brunier died at Bourg-en-Bresse January 3, 1856." This was the friend Jacolliot had been thinking of.

Jacolliot concluded that the Hindu had simply read his mind. He thought of a way to test this suspicion and tried it with the fakir next day. As he held the bag containing the letters, he concentrated on changing the name to "Halbin Pruniet." The leaves spelled out "Halbin Pruniet" instead of "Albain Brunier;" but no amount of concentration could change the date of Brunier's death, or the name of the city in which he died.

Jacolliot had experiences in psychokinesis with other fakirs,

Above: another traditional Indian miracle. The fakir—an Indian mystic—plants a seed, places it in a vessel, covers it with a light muslin sheet, and goes into a deep trance. Within hours the seed germinates, the plant grows, and fruit—in this case, mangoes—appear on the plant as if conjured up by sorcery.

In Zen archery, or kyudo, each movement has its own importance, and the entire performance, from moving into position with the bow to watching the arrow fly to the target, is ideally an expression of the archer's perfect mental serenity. When the center of the target is hit, it is taken to be proof of his mastery of himself. Hitting the target, therefore, is secondary: the attitude of mental calm is the main purpose of such archery. Each step, as shown here, has its own name, and there are precise instructions for mastering every aspect so that the whole exercise flows with grace and simplicity.

Stepping into place and setting the torso in the right position, then breathing deeply.

Setting the bow in place. It is held in the left hand.

Lifting up the bow. This is done in two stages with pauses.

Drawing the bow. The correct shooting position is attained.

Taking aim. The archer concentrates on the right form.

Releasing the arrow and remaining in position. The archer lets fly at the target, watches the arrow, and listens to the string twang till it stops.

one of whom was able to hold down a small table so firmly that Jacolliot's attempts to move it only tore off one of its folding leaves. The same fakir dropped a papaw seed into a pot filled with damp earth, went into a trance for two hours, and caused the seed to sprout into an eight-inch-tall plant. Jacolliot's most startling experience was when a fakir named Covindasamy caused a phosphorescent cloud to form in the air. After a moment, white hands appeared in the cloud. One of them held Jacolliot's hand for a moment. At his request, it plucked a flower from a bowl and dropped it at his feet. Next, the fakir conjured up the shade of an old Brahmin priest. When Jacolliot asked it whether it was once alive on earth, the word "Am" (yes) appeared on its breast in glowing letters as if written with phosphorus. Finally, the fakir materialized another shade that moved around the room playing a flute. When the apparition vanished, it left the flute on the ground. It was a flute that Jacolliot had borrowed from a rajah and that he had had in his locked house.

What is so impressive about these stories is that Jacolliot does not write as an occultist. The book in which they appear is a sober study of Hinduism, and these stories of his experiments are added almost as an afterthought. He is merely interested in recording inexplicable events to which he attaches no undue importance. Not being concerned with psychical research, which in the 1860s had not yet attracted much attention, he does not attempt to classify the phenomena as the products of extrasensory perception, telepathy, or psychokinesis. He puts it that, "What we call spirit force is called by the Hindus *artahancarasya* or the force of I." It seems clear that he is referring to what we have called Psi power. The fakirs themselves believe that all such phenomena spring from the same source—the spirits. The fact that Jacolliot actually saw entities that appeared to be spirits suggests that this idea cannot be wholly dismissed.

Most Hindus find nothing strange about such marvels. The ancient Hindu scriptures—the Vedic hymns, the *Upanishads*, the *Bhagavad Gita*—all teach that the human soul, the Atman, is

identical with the godhead, Brahman. Thus, if one could penetrate through all a man's outer layers to the very depth of his being, one would find Brahman. Stripped of its religious essence, this echoes the central conviction of occult philosophers: the deeper we penetrate our innermost being, the closer we approach the strange powers that all men possess, but that few can tap or consciously use.

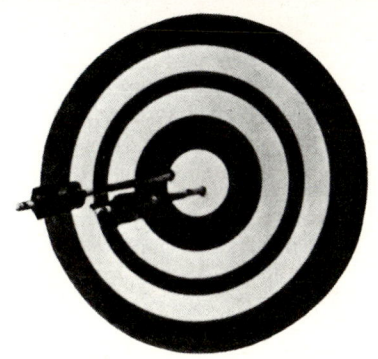

The science of yoga, which is basically a system of meditation, is intended to enable man to gain control over his body and emotions, and to move inward toward the "source of power, meaning, and purpose." A yogi assumes one of the traditional yoga postures, withdraws deep into himself, concentrates his gaze, and attempts to still his mind. The aim is total inner serenity. In attempting yoga, many westerners make the mistake of simply suspending the mind, as if sitting in church. Consequently they find it difficult to prevent it from wandering. The more experienced practitioner soon realizes that, although the posture suggests absolute rest, the mind is actually in gear, concentrating with a certain earnestness as if engaged in some difficult and dangerous operation. In the imagery of the Buddhist scriptures, the mind is like a pond, and the aim is to still the pond until it becomes a perfect mirror reflecting the moon, man's basic divinity. Great importance is attached to *prana* (breathing) because the breath is identified with life, or the spirit.

Eugen Herrigel, a German professor who taught in Japan for many years, determined to attempt to master the secrets of Zen, the peculiarly Japanese form of Buddhism. A central aim of Zen studies is the total integration of one's mental and physical powers. One of Herrigel's spiritual exercises directed toward this end was learning how to draw an archer's bow correctly. He watched his Zen master draw the bow without effort and release the arrow casually. It flew to the center of the target. When Herrigel tried it, he found it almost impossible even to draw the string of the massive bow.

After a long period of frustration, Herrigel was told by the Zen master that he was not breathing correctly. "Press your breath down gently after breathing in so that the abdominal wall is tightly stretched, and hold it there for a while. Then breathe out as slowly and evenly as possible and, after a short pause, draw a quick breath of air again—out and in continually in a rhythm that will gradually settle itself. If it is done properly, you will feel the shooting becoming easier every day. For through this breathing you will not only discover the source of all spiritual strength, but will also cause this source to flow more abundantly, and to pour more easily through your limbs the more relaxed you are." It took Herrigel a year to succeed in drawing the bow with this perfect ease. Then came another long struggle, this time to release the arrow without a jerk, "as if the bow string had cut through the thumb that held it."

What Herrigel had to learn so painfully was to use his whole being, his subconscious as well as his conscious mind, in drawing and releasing the bow. Once this was learned, he had also learned the basic secret of Zen. This union of every part of one's self also enables men and women to begin to grasp the perfect truth about Being. For Zen Buddhism holds that our central problem is that we have become too self-conscious, or rather, that we have developed what the novelist D. H. Lawrence called "head consciousness."

We are all familiar with the sensation of doing some simple physical activity badly because we are thinking about it. For instance, if we are aware of someone staring at the way we walk, we begin to walk awkwardly. If something makes us self-conscious about our accent, we begin to trip over words. According to the mystical tradition, this awkwardness has reached deep into human consciousness so that most of our powers are tied in a knot and unable to find expression. To some extent, relaxation can help to release these powers. For example, the fashionable cult of Transcendental Meditation is basically a kind of self-hypnosis that brings deep relaxation, leading to the release of hidden powers. We are out of tune with ourselves. We oppose ourselves like clumsy adolescents tripping over our own feet. All spiritual disciplines aim at removing this self-division. But, as Zen recognizes, the basic problem is how to arouse our "true will."

All the mystical traditions, Western as well as Eastern, recognize that the awakening of the true will can occur in a single flash. That is why the Zen master may sometimes kick his disciple violently. In one of the Zen stories, the disciple is awakened to a state of total enlightenment by such a kick. Similarly, there is a story told of the 19th-century Hindu saint Ramakrishna. When he was a young priest, Ramakrishna became deeply depressed because he seemed unable either to escape from the boredom of everyday existence or to catch a glimpse of Brahman. One day in despair he seized a sword, and was about to plunge it into himself. Suddenly the Divine Mother revealed herself to him. Ramakrishna was filled with a vision of an endless sea of vitality and self-knowledge, and with such deep ecstasy that he became unconscious. Undoubtedly the threat of death aroused his true will—showed him, as it were, the trick of

Above: like the pious biographies of saints of Christianity, the holy writings of Hinduism are full of miracles. Here a poor Brahmin, a friend of Krishna, the incarnation of the god Vishnu, is urged by his wife to ask Krishna's help. After much arguing, he sets out with only a handful of rice as an offering. Krishna greets him graciously, and the Brahmin is too ashamed to ask for aid. Returning home, he finds that his hovel has been transformed into a golden palace.

Left: the fakir Sri Ramakrishna.

Left: the yogi Paramahansa Yogananda. Living as he did for more than 30 years in the West, he was the first great master of India to present the philosophy and spiritual discipline of yoga to thousands of Westerners.

Above: an attempt in 1935 to scientifically assess the well-known yoga feat, the fire walk. A young Indian named Kuda Bux agreed to perform the fire walk for a group of scientists from the University of London Council for Psychical Investigation. An 11-foot trench was filled nine inches deep with red-hot embers, with a temperature of 430°C (806°F) at the surface. Swabs were taken of Bux's feet just before the walk and proved they were unprotected. He stepped into the pit and took a total of four steps. He was reported to have walked steadily and deliberately but quickly, the entire walk lasting just over four seconds. When his feet were examined after the walk, there was no sign of injury. An Englishman attempted to duplicate the walk, but jumped out after two steps; his feet blistered badly.

parting the curtain of everyday existence that obstructs our view of reality.

According to Ramakrishna, such powers as Jacolliot's fakir exhibited are merely the first consequences of this deeper knowledge of reality, and are utterly without value. Again and again he insists on the triviality of the feats that are traditionally ascribed to yogis and fakirs—for example, walking on water, moving objects without touching them, and climbing a rope that hangs unsupported in the air. The yogi who wants to do such things, says Ramakrishna, is at a rudimentary level of spiritual progress. The yogi who has tasted *samadhi*—the moment of absolute union with Brahman, the moment in which he realizes that his own soul is Brahman—cares only to strive for continual union. The conjuring tricks he regards with contempt.

Yet these examples of strange powers, called conjuring tricks by Ramakrishna, are a vital part of the Hindu tradition. One of the most extraordinary spiritual autobiographies of this century is Paramhansa Yogananda's *Autobiography of a Yogi*, to which the eminent orientalist W. Y. Evans-Wentz wrote an introduction that vouched for its authenticity. The book breathes the essential spirit of the Hindu religion, yet it is so full of tales of miracles that the skeptical Westerner's first reaction is to dismiss it as a pack of lies. At the age of eight, Yogananda was dangerously ill with cholera. He was told by his mother to bow mentally, being too weak to move physically, to a picture of a great yogi on the wall of his room. As he did so, the room seemed to glow with light, and his fever disappeared. Shortly after this, he quarreled with his sister about some ointment she was using to cure a boil. He told her that the following day her boil would be twice as large, and that he would have a boil on his forearm. Both things turned out as he said, and his sister accused him of being a sorcerer.

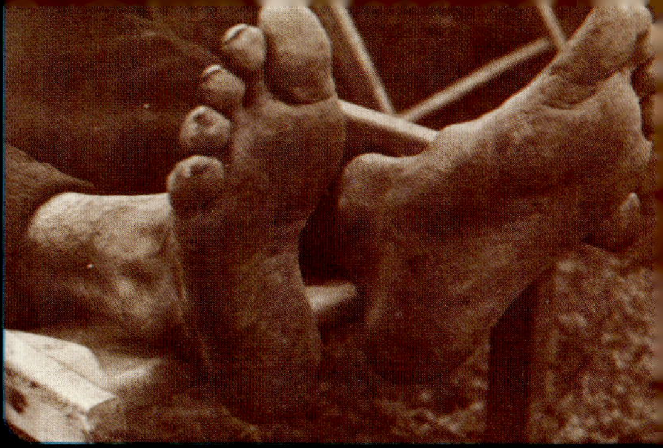

From this point on the stories become ever more incredible. Yogananda tells of visiting a yogi named Pranabananda. The yogi told him that a certain friend of his was on his way. At exactly the moment foretold, the friend arrived. Yogananda asked him how he had come to be there. The friend explained that Pranabananda had approached him in the street, and told him that Yogananda was waiting in his room. Then the yogi had vanished into the crowd. What baffled Yogananda and his friend was that Pranabananda had been with Yogananda throughout the previous hour. It seems, then, that Pranabananda had been able to project his astral body—the spiritual second body.

Pranabananda's feat may not be as unusual as it seems. G. N. M. Tyrell, a member of the British Society for Psychical Research, has documented many cases in which experimenters have deliberately set out to project themselves elsewhere. According to one such experimenter: "On Friday, December 1st 1882 at 9:30 p.m. I went into a room alone and sat by the fireside, and endeavored so strongly to fix my mind on the interior of a house at Kew . . . in which resided Miss V. and her two sisters, that I seemed to be actually in the house. During this experiment I must have fallen into a mesmeric sleep, for although I was

Below: this yogi is wired up for tests as he sits on a bed of nails. The experimenter is a doctor from the Menninger Foundation, a respected psychiatric center in Kansas. The Foundation was investigating psychic phenomena in India.

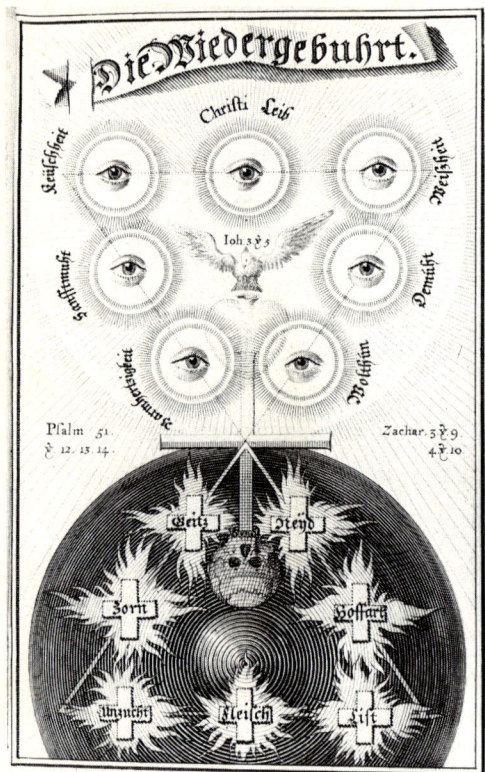

conscious, I could not move my limbs. . . ." She then went on:

"On the next day, Saturday, I went to Kew to spend the evening, and met a married sister of Miss V. In the course of conversation (although I did not think for a moment of asking her any questions on such a subject), she told me that on the previous night she had seen me distinctly on two occasions."

The interesting point is that the experimenter, a woman, had not tried to appear to this married sister, apparently not even knowing that she was in the house at the time. The apparition had not merely appeared to the married sister; it had stroked her hair, taken her hand, and looked intently at the palm. Unlike Pranabananda's projection, however, this apparition did not speak.

In another chapter of his autobiography Yogananda describes visiting the "perfume saint," a yogi able to induce the smell of any perfume. At Yogananda's request, the yogi caused a scentless flower to smell of jasmine. When Yogananda arrived home, his sister was also able to smell the scent of jasmine on the flower, thus allaying any suspicion that the yogi had managed merely to suggest the perfume to Yogananda.

Some of the most incredible of Yogananda's stories are about Babaji, the 19th-century "Yogi-Christ." One tells of how he allowed a disciple to hurl himself from a high crag, and then resurrected him. Another recounts how he materialized an immense golden palace in the Himalayas. Yogananda tells these stories at second hand, and it may be that he intended them to be accepted as myths or parables rather than as literal truth. But the stories he tells of his own *guru* (religious teacher or spiritual adviser) Sri Yukteswar, are almost as astonishing. Yukteswar also appears simultaneously in two places, Calcutta and Serampore. One day when his disciples are about to attend a festival in stifling heat, Yukteswar assures them that a cooling umbrella of cloud will be sent to help them. As he said, the sky clouds over and a gentle rain falls during the festival. However, Yukteswar did not claim to have conjured up the rain himself.

The climax of Yogananda's book is the description of the death and resurrection of Yukteswar. He predicted the time of his death, and died exactly when he had foretold. After his death, he appeared to Yogananda in a hotel room in Bombay, and Yogananda insists that he was there in the flesh. Before vanishing, Yukteswar explained to his disciple at length that his task was

Above: St. Joseph of Copertino flying in a religious rapture. This picture was published in a book in 1735. St. Joseph was even said to have lifted others into the air with him in his ecstasies.

now to serve as a savior on an astral plane, or another dimension of the world.

It is possible, of course, to dismiss the whole of Yogananda's book as the invention of a religious crank. But before doing so, it is well to bear in mind that most of the strange powers described in it have been observed and vouched for many times in the records of the reputable Society for Psychical Research. Moreover, we know that many yogis and fakirs have remarkable control over their bodies. Some have survived after being buried alive for some time—a feat that is beyond the understanding of most of us. Until we have a more systematic knowledge of the possibilities of higher states of consciousness, it may be as well to keep an open mind.

How, for example, do we account for the apparently ghastly self-mutilations of the Muslim holy men called the dervishes? Gurdjieff's disciple John G. Bennett has described a Moslem dervish ceremony that he witnessed twice in Istanbul. The dervishes knelt on the floor, swaying as they chanted the name of Allah. At a certain point of intense emotion, they began to drive spikes and skewers through their cheeks and arms. One old man lay down on the ground and placed a sharp sword, edge downward, across his stomach. Another man stepped onto the sword, balancing himself by holding the hands of two men on either side. When the man stepped down, the old dervish raised the sword from his body and revealed that it had not even made a mark. Bennett examined the sword after the ceremony. It was as sharp as a razor and bore no trace of blood.

The Western temperament is more given to intellectual speculation and is less mystical than the Eastern—which partly explains why the technological advances of the West have been so much greater than those of the East. All the same, the West has produced many great mystics who believe that certain kinds of truth are reached not through logical reasoning or the experiences of the senses, but through some kind of spiritual intuition. The father of Western mysticism was the Greek philosopher Plato, who lived in the 5th century B.C. In his *Symposium*, Plato writes about the teachings of his mentor Socrates. The older philosopher explains how the lover begins by desiring attractive bodies, then learns to admire beautiful souls, and ends by loving the beauty of the universe itself. This, says he, is the true aim of all love.

Socrates' insistence on the love of the impersonal has remained the central theme of Western mysticism ever since. The Greek philosopher Plotinus, who taught in Rome in the 3rd century A.D., described the aim of the mystic as "the flight of the Alone to the Alone." Later, Christian mystics often used words such as "darkness" and "emptiness" to describe the God of the true mystic. In the Middle Ages, when alchemy began to fascinate those of a philosophical turn of mind, mysticism and magic became oddly mixed up together. The alchemist sought the Philosopher's Stone, a substance believed capable of turning base metals into gold, and the elixir of everlasting life. The mystic sought union with God. For many thinkers, the two kinds of search became identical.

One of the most remarkable of these mystical alchemists was

The Friar Who Flew

St. Joseph of Copertino became known as the "flying monk" because of the way he levitated during ecstatic states. Born Giuseppe Desa in 1603, he was a strange and sickly child. As a teenager with strong religious tendencies—and later as a monk—he tortured himself for penance. But in moments of rapturous joy, usually inspired by religious feeling, Joseph rose in the air with loud shouts and, sometimes, wild movements.

At the age of 22 Joseph became a Franciscan monk in the district of Copertino in southern Italy. He became known to the neighboring people for his kindness and holiness, even though his noisy levitations disturbed his fellow friars. In fact, he was not allowed to join the rest of his brothers in the choir. One day he went away from the others into an obscure corner of the chapel to pray by himself. Suddenly he cried out with special intensity, rose straight up into the air and—to the astonishment of all present—flew to the altar. With another cry, he flew back to his corner in a kneeling position, and then began to whirl around in song and dance

Joseph was investigated by the Church, but was acquitted of the charge of practicing deception by false miracles.

the German shoemaker Jakob Boehme, born in Gorlitz, Silesia—now part of East Germany. At the age of 25 in 1600 Boehme had his first experience of mystical insight. He found himself staring at a pewter dish whose polished surface reflected the sunlight. Gazing into it, Boehme found himself drifting into a kind of ecstasy. He had the sensation of being able to see into the heart of all nature. He walked out to the fields, and it seemed to him that the trees and grass were transparent, and lit by a kind of flame from within.

How can we explain such mystical ecstasies? They seem to be due to the release of a flood of emotional energy—a flood so powerful that it overwhelms the senses. Many people have experienced something of the kind—perhaps when listening to music or looking at magnificent scenery—so we are inclined to dismiss such experiences as mere emotion. But we fail to understand the possibilities of mere emotion. Boehme's mystical intensities carried him into a realm in which he seemed to see into the heart of the universe. He wrote of a later ecstasy that "the Gate was opened to me, so that in a quarter of an hour I knew more than if I had been many years at a university." He tried to express this insight in a number of strange works. His first book caused him a great deal of trouble: the local clergyman denounced him as a false prophet, and the magistrates ordered him to stop writing. Fortunately he ignored them, and he produced a number of strange and difficult masterpieces full of the language of the alchemists, attempting to describe the soul's relation to God. Although he died in relative obscurity, his fame afterward

Above: Emanuel Swedenborg, the Swedish mystic. Although his visions did not begin until he was in his fifties, he writes about himself that "from my fourth to my tenth year I was constantly engaged in thought upon God."

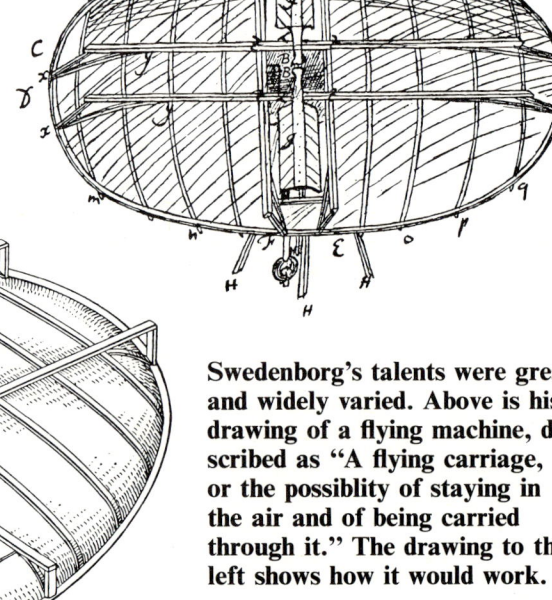

Swedenborg's talents were great and widely varied. Above is his drawing of a flying machine, described as "A flying carriage, or the possiblity of staying in the air and of being carried through it." The drawing to the left shows how it would work.

spread all over Europe. He influenced another great visionary, the English poet and painter William Blake, whose work vibrates with the same feeling of strange hidden realities lying behind the curtain of the everyday world.

The state of ecstasy can produce remarkable effects. There is reliable evidence that it caused a devoutly religious monk to rise into the air and fly. Giuseppe Desa was born at Apulia, Italy, in 1603. He was feeble and sickly as a child. At the age of 22 he joined the Franciscan order, and soon became well known for his prayers and fasting. One day after Mass, he suddenly rose into the air, floated above the congregation, and hovered over the altar. The candle flames did not burn him. From this time on Father Joseph as he was now known, often levitated and flew considerable distances. Many eminent contemporaries witnessed this strange feat, including the great German philosopher Leibniz. There are so many apparently reliable records of his flights that it seems probable they were not faked. Significantly, when a hostile and envious superior started to bully and humiliate him, Father Joseph ceased to fly. He recovered his spirits, however, and afterward flew through the air and embraced the statue of the virgin above the altar. A century after his death, he was canonized as St. Joseph of Copertino.

Science cannot explain levitation, although there are thousands of well-authenticated cases on record, particularly from India. But then, neither can science explain how John G. Bennett, seriously weakened after a three-day attack of dysentery, could dig furiously for an hour without collapsing. We know little about the powers of the mind because in most of us they are undeveloped. If we lived in a world in which there was only the moon and no sun, no one would believe that light could cause sunburn or make forests burst into flames. We know the universe only to the extent of our as yet feeble attempts to perceive and measure it, and the results are often absurd and contradictory.

One of the most eminent Protestant mystics was also a distinguished scientist and engineer. Emanuel Swedenborg was born in Stockholm in 1688 and began his career as a mathematician. He also studied watchmaking, carpentry, and music. Later he became Assessor of the Swedish board of mines, and demonstrated his engineering skill when he transported five ships overland for 15 miles during his country's war with Denmark.

In 1744 when he was 56, Swedenborg had an overpowering dream in which a roaring wind flung him on his face. Then Jesus appeared and spoke the words: "Well then, do it!" From this time onward, Swedenborg began to go into ecstatic trances and to see visions. His books contain vivid descriptions of journeys he claimed to have made through heaven and hell under the guidance of angelic spirits.

One's first reaction to this is to conclude that Swedenborg must have gone mad. But people who met him and expected to find a lunatic were surprised by his sanity and good humor. Moreover, his powers of clairvoyance were witnessed by many. One night when about to sit down to dinner in Gothenburg, he suddenly turned pale and announced that a great fire had just broken out in Stockholm 250 miles away. It was threatening his

Jean-Marie-Baptiste Vianney, the curé of Ars, was a parish priest who spent his life fighting the temptation to retire to the solitude of a monastery. He was such a perceptive confessor that the faithful flocked from all over France to seek his counsel. He said little, but what he said was always precisely to the point— so much so that many thought he was able to look into their minds.

own house, he said. For the next two hours he was in a state of agitation. Then he said with relief: "Thank heavens, the fire is under control. It had almost reached my doorstep." The next day he wrote a detailed description of the fire to the governor of Gothenburg, and the day after that, a letter arrived confirming to the last detail all that Swedenborg had said.

One day when Swedenborg was at the royal court, the queen asked him perhaps mockingly if he had seen her deceased brother on his visits to heaven. Swedenborg replied gravely that he had not. The queen then remarked that, if Swedenborg met him, perhaps he would give him her greeting. The next time Swedenborg came to court, he told the queen that he had seen her brother and had given him her message. The brother, he said, sent his apologies for not having answered her last letter to him before he died, but he would now do so through Swedenborg. The scientist then repeated her brother's reply to various points in her letter. The queen was dumbfounded as she declared "No one but God knows this secret."

About this time the Dutch ambassador to the Swedish court died. When his widow afterward received an invoice for a silver tea service, she was convinced that her husband had paid for it shortly before his death. But she could not find the receipt. She asked Swedenborg for help. A few days later as she sat with friends, Swedenborg told her: "Your husband says the receipt is in the bureau upstairs." "Impossible," said the widow, "I have searched it." Swedenborg said that there was a secret drawer, which he described. The widow went to the bureau, found the secret drawer, and opened it. The receipt was inside.

Many of Swedenborg's contemporaries believed that these remarkable demonstrations proved that his visions of heaven and hell must be true. We should be more cautious. One of his books contains a description of Mars and its inhabitants that is wholly nonsensical in the light of our present knowledge of the planet. We can only conclude that if Swedenborg had visions—as he almost certainly did—then some of them were false ones.

Of the more modern European wonder workers, perhaps the most interesting is Jean-Marie-Baptiste Vianney, the curé (parish priest) of Ars. In 1818 at the age of 34, Vianney was appointed to the parish of Ars near Lyon. He was a simple man, not particularly intelligent, and generally narrow-minded. Yet his piety and reported understanding of the human soul soon spread his reputation far afield. He had mystical visions, although he would say little about them—and many seriously ill people who came to see him were cured. His most famous miracle took place during a year of famine when there were only a few cupfuls of wheat left in the village granary. Vianney prayed all night. The next morning when a girl tried to enter the granary, she found the door blocked. Forcing it open, she found the place full of grain—enough to feed most of the parish for months.

This story was not investigated by an independent observer, and one hardly needs to be a skeptic to be suspicious of it. But, even allowing for the credulity of the more devoted members of his flock, Vianney seems to have possessed special powers, particularly of telepathy. As his fame spread, people came from far and wide to attend services at his church.

Right: *The Lord Answering Job Out of The Whirlwind*, a watercolor by William Blake. Blake intended his illustrations to the *Book of Job*—22 in all—to be more than illustrations alone: they were to be a prophetic vision, a personal and spiritual testimony.

Right: Vincent Van Gogh's *The Starry Night*. (Collection, The Museum of Modern Art, New York, acquired through the Lillie P. Bliss Bequest). The stars swirling across the mysterious, radiant sky glow like so many mystic suns.

Powerful religious feelings sometimes seem able to release deep and hidden forces in the human soul. But it is important to realize that many of these powers are little more than by-products of our inner evolution. What is impressive about all the mystics, from Boehme to Yogananda, is not the wonders or visions. It is the sense they all share that the everyday world conceals some tremendous reality that all are capable of seeing if they can discover how to look. We feel something of this kind in the paintings and poetry of William Blake. We feel it in Vincent Van Gogh's evocative painting *Starry Night*, which the artist painted with candles tied around his hat so that he could see the canvas in the dark. Works such as these suggest something of the ecstatic intensity experienced by Boehme when he found himself looking "into the heart of nature," or by Ramakrishna when he was overwhelmed by the vision of the Divine Mother. They give us a glimpse of the source of power, meaning, and purpose that lies deep inside all human beings.

4

The Magicians

It was a windy, chilly evening in March, 1865, and most of the inhabitants of the French village of Solliés-Farliede were indoors. A limping man approached the cottage of a workman and knocked on the door. The girl who opened it shrank back when she saw the unkempt stranger, whose beard was as tangled as a bird's nest. The man pointed to his mouth, then to his ears, and shook his head, indicating that he was deaf-mute. The girl's father came to the door and, after the kindly fashion of country people, invited the tramp in for a meal. The girl, Josephine, kept house for her father. The only other occupant of the

Above: Franz Anton Mesmer, the Austrian doctor who discovered the kind of suggestion first known as "mesmerism," from his name, and now called hypnotism. He used the power of suggestion to rouse a patient's subconscious to throw off symptoms of disease. Mesmer himself thought that his cures came about through his use of magnets, which rearranged the patient's "vital fluids" flowing like the tides through the body.

Right: Mesmer treating a patient.

"The tramp had deprived the girl of her will..."

small country cottage was Josephine's 15-year-old brother.

From the first moment, Josephine felt terrified of the ugly stranger. His manners were eccentric and uncouth. Instead of filling his glass with wine, he poured in a little at a time, putting the bottle down several times. He made the sign of the cross over his glass before drinking, as if afraid the Devil was in it. After the meal, the girl's father questioned the man by means of pencil and paper. They learned that his name was Timotheus Castellan, that he had been a cork cutter, and that he had had to abandon the trade after an injury to his hand. Now, he said, he traveled around the country making a living as a healer and water diviner. Curious neighbors came in to see the magician, and all were impressed. That night, the tramp slept in a haystack. Josephine lay on her bed, fully dressed, her mind full of foreboding.

The next day her father and brother went off to work, and Castellan went with them. Shortly afterward, however, he returned to the cottage. Josephine let him in, and went about her housework. Several neighbors called in at the cottage, having heard about the wonder worker, and brought him presents of food. One of them saw Castellan making strange signs in the air behind Josephine's back.

At lunchtime, the two ate together. Suddenly, Castellan stretched out his hand, pointing two fingers at Josephine. She immediately became unconscious. When she woke up, Castellan was sprinkling water on her face. Then he picked her up, carried her into the bedroom, and raped her. Although she was fully conscious, she was unable to move. At one point a neighbor knocked on the door and called her name, but she found herself unable to reply.

Later that afternoon Castellan left the cottage, and beckoned to her. In a state of confusion she followed him. Neighbors asked her where she was going, but though she answered, her words were unintelligible.

That night the couple stayed at a farmhouse and slept together. The next day they persuaded a farmer at the nearby village of La Cappelude to give them a bed. The farmer and his household were baffled by Josephine's behavior. Sometimes she seemed like an infatuated newlywed, kissing and caressing the ugly deaf-mute; then suddenly she would turn away, as if nauseated. During the evening she managed to talk to a girl who lived nearby and asked her if she could stay with her overnight. Castellan overheard their conversation, however, and ordered Josephine to remain with him. He made a sign with his hand. She collapsed in his arms and remained in a trance for an hour.

Two days later the distraught girl succeeded in giving Castellan the slip. She approached a group of men and asked them to take her home. A search for the tramp began immediately, but it turned out later that soon after the girl's escape he had been arrested for vagrancy. Two doctors examined Josephine and pronounced that the tramp had deprived the girl of her will by "magnetism" (hypnosis). A court sentenced him to 12 years' hard labor.

What are we to make of this sinister beggar? He was undoubtedly a confidence man and a liar. Josephine declared that she had escaped while he was in conversation with a band of hunters; evidently he could speak and hear normally. It seems clear that Castellan's intention in hypnotizing Josephine was not only to obtain a mistress, but also to get a companion whose attractions would persuade country people to provide him with meals and a bed. Yet his powers were certainly genuine. He was a water diviner, healer, and hypnotist of remarkable ability. He was, in short, both a genuine magician and a charlatan—a mixture we have already found in Simon Magus and Faust, and will encounter again and again in the history of magic.

The Castellan case, which is well documented, underlines something we should not forget: that magical powers are not confined to a few famous names in history. In every age there are thousands of such men and women, and their powers are of many kinds. Timotheus Castellan evidently recognized Josephine as an easy hypnotic subject as soon as he saw her— just as Franz Walter earmarked his victim on the train. What is more interesting is that Josephine undoubtedly recognized Castellan as a man who might gain power over her. Moreover, if the evidence of the neighbor is to be believed, Castellan did not hypnotize Josephine by the usual methods. He made passes in the air when her back was turned. This suggests that he was exercising some form of thought pressure.

It is a curious fact that the careers of most magicians seem to follow a definite pattern: a spectacular rise to power or fame, followed by a long slow downfall. Timotheus Castellan's downfall obviously began when he mesmerised Josephine. We do not know enough of the historical Faust to know when his career took the downward plunge; but the fact that we know nothing about his later years or his death suggests that his fame evaporated before he was 40 years old.

Faust and Castellan had another interesting thing in common: both were black magicians. This term may seem quaint in our scientific age, but it is less absurd than it sounds. The black magician is, quite simply, a man who wants power for himself, for self-aggrandizement. He wants to be able to vent his spite on enemies, and to satisfy all his desires. Black magicians are usually defined as those who have made a pact with the Devil, but this is not necessarily the case. A magician may summon the Devil or one of his demons and remain a white magician so long as his purpose is benevolent. On the other hand, a magician may have no interest in the Devil or may even deny his existence, but if his intentions are malicious and self-centered, he is a black magician.

Faust was not the most celebrated magician of his age. He had two remarkable contemporaries, Cornelius Agrippa and Paracelsus, whose fame greatly and deservedly surpassed his own, and who were undoubtedly white magicians. Agrippa and Paracelsus were both students of that strange mystical system of knowledge called the Cabala, whose purpose is to show the fallen man his way back to Paradise and the godhead. The two works that contain the essence of cabalistic teaching— the *Sefer Yetsirah*, Book of Creation, and the *Zohar*, Book

of Splendor—are of such profound importance in the history of magic that we must say a few words about them here.

The Book of Creation dates from the 2nd century A.D. The Book of Splendor appeared in an Aramaic manuscript written by a student named Moses de Léon in the late 13th century. It is, however, a tradition that the teachings of both books date from the beginning of human history, when angels taught Adam the secret of how to recover his lost bliss. Cabalists think of man as a being who is tied up and enveloped in a complicated straitjacket—like Houdini before one of his celebrated escapes—and whose problem is to discover how to untie all the knots. Most men do not even realize that they are tied up. The cabalist not only knows it: he knows also that man's highest state is total freedom.

According to the Cabala, when Adam sinned he fell from a state of union with God. He fell down through 10 lower states of consciousness into a state of amnesia, in which he totally forgot his divine origin, his true identity. Man's task, therefore, is to clamber back until he once more attains his highest state. The journey is long and hard. It is not simply a matter of climbing, like Jack clambering up the beanstalk, because the "beanstalk" passes through 10 different "realms." But even that image is too simple: the beanstalk does not pass straight upward, like a fireman's pole, but wanders from side to side.

The image of the beanstalk is apt because the Cabala is essentially the study of a sacred tree—the Tree of Life. At the top of the tree is God the Creator, who is called Kether (the crown). The nine other branches of the tree are wisdom, beauty, power, understanding, love, endurance, majesty, foundation, and kingdom. These are known collectively as the Sefiroth—emanations, or potencies, and it is they that constitute the realms through which the beanstalk passes. There is a further complication. The traditional picture of the Tree of Life looks rather like a diagram of a chemical molecule, in which the atoms are connected to each other by lines. These lines correspond to the 22 paths of the Cabala that connect the realms.

The Tree of Life no longer grows on earth. How, then, does the aspirant set about climbing it? There are three main ways. First, one may explore the realms on the astral plane. Another way to explore the realms of the Cabala is through inner vision—that is, by achieving a semitrancelike or visionary state in which the realms appear before the inner eye. A third way is the obvious one: study of the Cabala itself. It is, however, perhaps the most difficult way of all, because its revelations of man's consciousness and destiny are not spoken of directly, but lie hidden in an enormously complex system of symbols.

The realms of the Sefiroth, however, are not themselves symbols. According to the Cabala, they are real worlds. For instance, if the wandering astral body finds itself in a realm containing doves and spotted leopards, a land bursting with an almost overwhelming glory of life, it is almost certainly in the realm of Netshah, or Venus—symbol of endurance and victory.

The doctrines of the Cabala were probably far above the head of a charlatan such as Faust. But Cornelius Agrippa and

Above: the Tree of Life of the Cabala. The center circle at the top represents God the Creator. Each of the other circles are ways in which God manifests himself, and through which the soul returning to God must pass.

Above: the scholar-magician **Cornelius Agrippa**, whose book *The Occult Philosophy*, is still regarded as one of the greatest magical texts. Brilliant and headstrong, Agrippa's career was marked by flamboyant failures.

Below: a drawing from *The Occult Philosophy* shows the proportion and harmony of the human body.

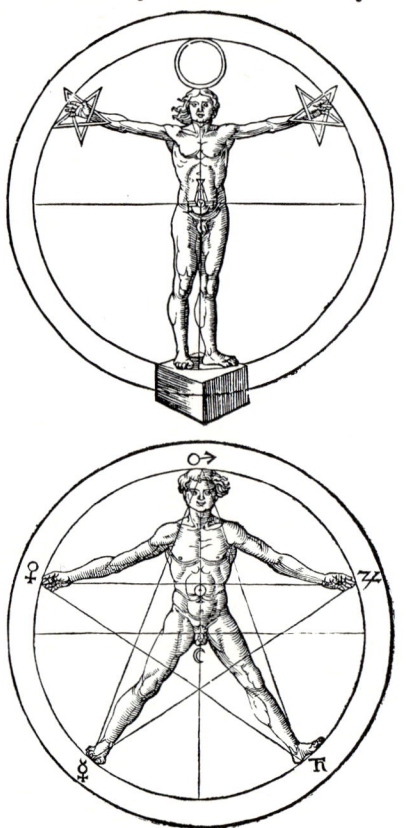

Above: another drawing from the same book, which demonstrates how a man's body can be measured in a circle to form a pentagram.

Paracelsus were not charlatans. They regarded themselves as scientists and philosophers, and they were far more intelligent than Faust. Yet both of them were flawed by the defects we have come to realize are characteristic of so many magicians: a craving to be admired, and a crude will to power. When these ambitions are frustrated, even men of genuine powers will often misuse their powers like a charlatan.

Like Faust, Cornelius Agrippa became the subject of many remarkable legends. What was the truth behind such incredible tales? Cornelius Agrippa—whose real name was Heinrich Cornelis—was born in Cologne in 1486. His parents were sufficiently well-off to send him to the recently founded university of Cologne, where he proved to be a brilliant scholar. It was an exciting time for young intellectuals. Gutenberg had invented the printing press some 50 years before Agrippa was born, and the printed book had created the same kind of revolution as radio and television were to do five centuries later. Agrippa read everything he could lay his hands on. One day he discovered the Cabala, and it at once appealed to something deep within him. A magician was made.

At the age of 20 Agrippa became a court secretary to the Holy Roman Emperor, and a distinguished career seemed assured for him. But Agrippa was a divided man. Part of him, as we have said, craved celebrity and power; but he loathed the world of diplomacy and courtly intrigue by which such success could be achieved. By now he was also obsessed by the ultimate other world of the Cabala.

At about this time, he attended the University of Paris where he studied mysticism and philosophy. There he met a Spaniard named Gerona, who had recently been forced to flee from his estate in Catalonia after a peasants' revolt. Agrippa offered to help him, sensing that if their mission succeeded, Gerona's gratitude might enable Agrippa to settle in Spain and devote his life to study of the Cabala. They went to Catalonia, and Agrippa devised a brilliant plan that enabled them to capture a stronghold from the rebels. But they were later besieged, Agrippa was forced to flee, and Gerona was captured and probably murdered. The episode was typical of the bad luck that was to pursue Agrippa for the rest of his life.

He returned to his job as court secretary, but he felt so frustrated that he left after a few months and began wandering around Europe. Within a year or two he had acquired a reputation as a black magician, and it was to cause him a great deal of trouble. In 1509 he taught in Dôle, France under the patronage of Queen Margaret of Austria. The local monks became jealous of this patronage, however, and plotted against him. When one of them preached against him in the presence of the queen, Agrippa decided it was time to move on. In 1515 he was knighted on a battlefield in Italy, and became Cornelius Agrippa von Nettesheim—a name taken from that of a small village near Cologne.

He was granted a pension by King Francis I of France, but this was revoked when Agrippa refused to cast horoscopes for the king's mother. Agrippa was later made official historian by Queen Margaret, but was unwise enough to publish a work in which he attempted to demonstrate that all knowledge is useless. This so enraged his academic colleagues that he lost his job. Soon he was imprisoned for debt. Agrippa certainly lacked tact, for after this he again made the mistake of speaking his mind about Queen Margaret, for which he was thrown into prison and tortured. His health broken, he died in 1535 at the age of 49. Legend says that, as he lay on his deathbed, he cursed his wasted life and the black arts that had seduced him. Whereupon his black dog rushed out of the house and threw itself into a river—clearly proving thereby that it was a demon in disguise.

These biographical snippets, however richly spiced with legends, hardly add up to a man of strange powers. The certainty that Agrippa was indeed a magician, however, lies in the three volumes of his treatise *The Occult Philosophy*, which is regarded as one of the great magical texts. The book makes it clear that Agrippa knew all about thought pressure. Magic, he insists, is a faculty that springs from the power of the mind and imagination. There are mysterious relations between the human body and the universe, and between the earth on which we live and higher spiritual worlds. Thus, he argued, a stone can teach us about the nature of the stars. Agrippa believed that all nature is bound together by a kind of vast spider's web. Most human beings never learn to use their innate magical powers because they believe that they are cut off from the rest of nature. The magician, on the contrary, knows that his thought, if properly directed, can set the web vibrating and cause effects in far distant places.

Agrippa wrote his extraordinary masterwork when he was only 23 years old. It shows that, even at this early age, his study of the Cabala had given him some profound insights. Because he was always in danger of being burned as a black magician, he was careful to insist in his book that his knowledge is of a kind that any serious student can acquire from study of the great philosophers and mystics. But he also admits that he has successfully practiced divination and foretelling the future. For example, he describes two methods by which he claims to have detected the identity of thieves. One method is to pivot a sieve on forceps held between the index fingers of two students. The sieve will begin to swing like a pendulum when the name of the guilty person is mentioned. Similarly, if the sieve is pivoted so that it can be made to spin, it will stop spinning when the thief's name is spoken.

Agrippa insists that the success of these and other magical techniques are due to spirits—similar, presumably, to the spirits that help fakirs to perform their wonders. The overwhelming impression that emerges from the book is that Agrippa was a sensitive—born with the gifts of precognition, telepathy, and the ability to influence events by using the power of his mind. His belief that mind is more powerful than matter runs like a thread through the book. *The Occult Philosophy* is the work of a young man—full of vitality and brilliance— and of a dreamer who peered into a world that few of us have the gift to see.

The case of Paracelsus is even more tantalizing than that of

The Ill-fated Magician's Apprentice

Once, the stories go, a student of the magician Agrippa managed to get into his master's study when the magician was away. The student found Agrippa's book of spells and started reading it. There was a knock on the door; but the student, engrossed in his reading, ignored it. The knock sounded again loudly. Then the door flew open and a demon leaped in. Demanding to know why it had been summoned, the evil fiend caught the terrified student by the throat and strangled him. Not long afterward Agrippa returned. Horrified by what might happen if a dead body —especially that of one of his students—were discovered in his house, Agrippa ordered the demon to restore the student to life long enough to be seen in the busy marketplace.

The demon did as Agrippa bid. The student, apparently alive and in good health, left Agrippa's house and walked through town. After a little while he dropped dead. The townspeople were at first convinced that the unfortunate youth's death was completely natural. But when the body was examined closely, the telltale marks of the strangler's fingers were clear on his throat. Agrippa fled town to avoid scandal.

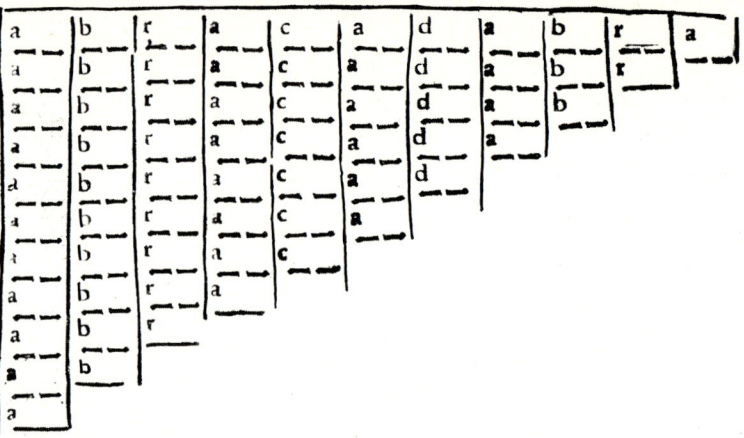

Agrippa. His writings prove him to have been a more remarkable man—a great scientist as well as a magician. But, again, seeking the truth about him is like groping about in a fog, so obscured is his life with myth and legend.

He was born as Theophrastus Bombastus von Hohenheim in 1493, the son of an impoverished Swiss nobleman who had become a doctor. He studied medicine in Basel and completed his education at universities in Italy and Germany. His gifts as a physician were immediately apparent, and a series of remarkable cures soon earned him a formidable reputation. In 1524, when he was only 29 years old, he was appointed professor of medicine at Basel University. In nine years he had become one of the great names in medicine in Europe.

It was at this point that his career, so rich in both achievement and promise, was undermined by the same kind of character defects that brought ruin to Agrippa, and that seem to be hallmarks of so many magicians. He was vainglorious. He chose the pseudonym "Paracelsus" because it implied that he was greater than Celsus, the famous physician of ancient Rome. He was a heavy drinker, and was prey to sudden violent tempers. One of his first acts as professor at Basel University was to order his students to hold a public burning of the books of Avicenna, Galen, and other famous doctors of the past. This enraged his colleagues, who condemned him as an exhibitionist and a charlatan. When they plotted against him, Paracelsus compounded his unpopularity by calling them names—like many paranoid people he had a powerful gift for invective. For a while his reputation held his enemies at bay and when he cured the publisher Frobenius of an infected leg that other doctors had decided to amputate, it seemed that he had become invulnerable to attack. Soon after this, however, a patient declined to pay his bill and Paracelsus took him to court. Owing to the plots of his enemies, he lost the case, whereupon he rained such violent abuse on the heads of the judges that a warrant was issued for his arrest. He was forced to flee Basel—and his long soul-destroying downfall had begun.

For the remainder of his life Paracelsus wandered all over Europe as an itinerant doctor, writing book after book of which few were published in his lifetime, and pouring scorn and invective on his enemies. Fourteen years of wandering and

Below: Agrippa as the bogeyman disciplinarian of naughty boys, from the English version of a famous 19th-century German picture book for children *Struwwelpeter*. Three boys are jeering at a black man, and the great sorcerer first sternly rebukes them. When they ignore him, he seizes them and dips them, wriggling, into his magic inkstand. When they emerge, they have been made as black as crows.

Right: Theophrastus Bombast von Hohenheim, the physician who took for himself the name Paracelsus. He chose this name because *para* means beyond in Greek, and it so indicated that he was greater than Celsus, the greatest Roman Doctor.

Above: one of the illustrations from Paracelsus' complicated work *Prognosticatio*, emphasizing the futility of man's own efforts, and the necessity of humility under the powerful hand of God. For Paracelsus, theology was an essential part of medicine because a doctor should also treat the soul.

disappointment wore him out. In 1541, when he was 48 years old, he was invited by the Prince Palatine to settle at his seat in Salzburg. At last he might have found contentment in a quiet life of study. But he continued to drink too much, and six months later he rolled down a hill in a drunken stupor, and died of his injuries.

Then, ironically, his books began to be published, and they spread his fame over Europe once more. They have a range and boldness of imagination that is reminiscent of Leonardo da Vinci's notebooks. Paracelsus immediately became a kind of patron saint of occultism—a position he maintains even today, with his writings being studied by a new generation of occultists.

As with Agrippa, it is difficult to discover four centuries later what genuine powers lay behind the many legends of Paracelsus's magical prowess. One thing is clear: most of the stories concern remarkable cures, and this suggests that he was primarily gifted with seemingly magical powers of healing. For example, we are told that he cured an innkeeper's daughter who since birth had been paralyzed from the waist down. The medicine he gave her was probably saltpeter in teaspoonfulls of wine. This would obviously have had no effect, but it seems that the hypnotic force of his personality and his natural healing power brought about a cure. We are also again confronted by the paradox of the split personality: a man who was bad-tempered, thin-skinned, and boastful, yet who could be taken over by some strange power that rose from his subconscious depths and made him a great healer.

So we reach the odd conclusion that the contemporaries of Agrippa and Paracelsus were probably right when they called them charlatans—but that, at the same time, both men possessed genuine powers. It would be another four centuries before the great Swiss psychologist Carl Jung attempted to explain these powers scientifically in terms of that vast reservoir of energy known as the subconscious mind.

In the 16th century it was still dangerous for a man of knowledge to gain a reputation as a wizard or sorcerer. The witch hunting craze was spreading across Europe, and many people were being burned for being in league with the Devil. This no doubt explains why we know so little of the lives of the alchemists who followed in the footsteps of Agrippa and Paracelsus. That remarkable 16th-century French physician and prophet Nostradamus took care to hide his visions in verse of such obscurity that even nowadays we cannot be certain what most of them mean.

The tide turned in the 17th and 18th centuries—the age of scientists such as Newton, Huygens, and Harvey—and the seeker after forbidden knowledge once again became respectable, at least in Protestant countries. Sir Isaac Newton—one of the greatest names in science and philosophy—spent as much time in his alchemical laboratory as at his telescope.

In 1734 was born one of those remarkable pioneers to whom the modern world owes much, but to whom it pays little attention: Franz Anton Mesmer. He was the discoverer of what came to be called mesmerism and later hypnotism. Mesmer, whose parents were Swiss, studied medicine at the

Above: an illustration for a medical work by Paracelsus, which shows the doctor treating one of his patients. Paracelsus said that since man contains all the elements, and needs them for the curing of his illnesses, a good physician must understand all physical sciences plus alchemy.

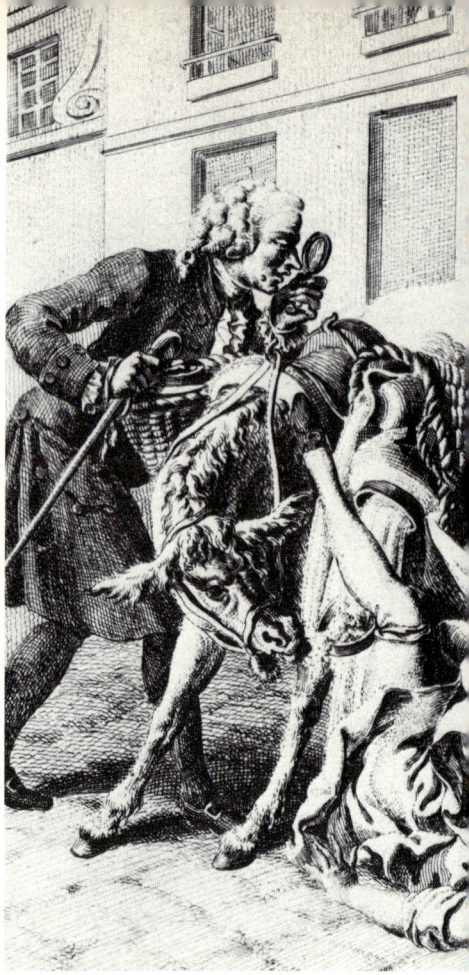

University of Vienna, and wrote his doctoral thesis on the influence of the planets on human health. He was 40 years of age when he stumbled on the discovery that was to make him famous—and infamous. A wealthy English lady who was passing through Vienna was suffering from stomach cramps, and she called on a Jesuit acquaintance of Mesmer's, to ask if he could lend her some magnets. She was convinced that magnets relieved her stomach pains. When Mesmer heard of this he was intrigued, for it seemed to complement his own theory that there was some kind of vital fluid in the body that flowed like the tides, producing health or sickness. If these tides existed, might it not be possible to influence their movements by magnets?

Mesmer tried using magnets on his own patients—and they seemed to work. Shortly afterward, while Mesmer was bleeding a patient—the standard cure for most ailments in those days— he observed that the bleeding increased when he came closer, and decreased when he moved away. This must mean, he thought, that he himself was a kind of magnet. Mesmer coined the term "animal magnetism" to describe his strange power, and he demonstrated its value when curing a nobleman who was suffering from spasms. For six days Mesmer had moved his powerful magnets over the patient's body to no effect. Then, on the sixth day, as the patient choked with asthma, Mesmer took hold of his foot. The spasm abated.

It looked as though Mesmer had gotten the measure of the patient's vital fluids at last. News of his cure spread all over

As the fame of Mesmer's work spread across Europe, so did the derision of people who could not or would not try to understand what the doctor was doing. The cartoonists had a field day.

Above left: "The Magnetism: Mesmer," a cartoon of about 1784.

Above: "The effects of animal magnetism." The girl is overcome by animals responding to incredible, invisible magnetism.

Vienna, and made him one of the most celebrated doctors in Austria. He began to experiment with "magnetized water"—vats of water filled with iron filings into which metal rods were fixed. Patients grasped the rods—or one patient held onto a rod while other sufferers held his other hand. Music was played during the treatment, and eventually the patients went into a trance or had convulsions. They were cured by the dozen.

Then came a temporary setback. Mesmer failed to cure a blind girl—understandably so inasmuch as her blindness was due to a detached retina. A scandal arose, however, and he had to leave Vienna. He moved to Paris, and immediately achieved even greater success. His healing sessions began to look like orgies. The patients—men and women together—were lightly clad to help the animal magnetism flow more easily from one patient to the next. As they massaged one another or pressed their thighs together, according to Mesmer's prescribed method, many of them were convinced they could feel the health-giving effect.

The instrument of Mesmer's downfall was the same as that of Paracelsus: envious fellow doctors who denounced him as a charlatan. As with Paracelsus too, Mesmer's arbitrary and autocratic behavior as much as his natural talents was the cause. When a commission of doctor's declared that his cures were due merely to suggestion rather than to magnetism, Mesmer left France in disgrace. He retired to a villa near Constance in southwestern Germany where he spent his remaining days in peace. The doctors were right that Mesmer

Above: Jacques Casanova, the adventurer, was apparently possessed of occult talents. His name has become a synonym for seducer.

cured by suggestion, of course. What they failed to realize was that Mesmer's cures proved that the power of suggestion is a greater force than anyone had suspected. If the subconscious mind can be convinced by suggestion, it can bring about extraordinary cures. This point was underlined a few years later when one of Mesmer's disciples, the Marquis of Puysegur, was trying to "magnetize" a shepherd boy by stroking his head and, to his astonishment, induced a deep trancelike sleep. He had stumbled on hypnotism. Even today, after almost two centuries, we know little more about the underlying mechanism of hypnotism than did Puysegur. Once more we confront the strange paradox: that a man can be completely self-deceived about the nature of his powers and nevertheless be a genuine magician.

Nowhere is this more apparent than in the case of the man whose name has become synonymous with seduction: Jacques Casanova, the adventurer and confidence trickster who flourished in the second half of the 18th century. Not only was Casanova an accomplished faith healer (he cured an ailing Venetian senator by means of suggestion), but he was also remarkably successful at fortune telling by means of cards and other oracles. Indeed, the accuracy of his predictions sometimes alarmed Casanova himself. For instance, he told one girl that she would go to Paris and become the king's mistress—and that is exactly what happened. Casanova believed that he somehow conjured up real spirits when he was muttering his bogus incantations. What seems more likely is that he possessed the same occult faculty as Paracelsus or Faust to some degree.

Casanova met, and immediately disliked, another charlatan who acquired a reputation as a great magician: the man who called himself the "Count of Saint-Germain." When Saint-Germain arrived in Vienna in the mid-1740s he seemed to be about 30 years old—a man of powerful and dominant personality, with the typical magician's streak of boastfulness and desire to astonish. In Vienna he was befriended by members of the nobility, and was brought to Paris by the Marshal de Belle-Isle. By 1758 he had become a close friend of Louis XV and his mistress Madame de Pompadour.

Part of Saint-Germain's attraction was his reputation as a man of mystery. No one seemed to have any idea of where or when he was born. But his knowledge of history seemed to be enormous, and occasionally he said things that suggested he knew far more about certain events in the remote past than any mere student possibly could know. In short, he implied that he had actually witnessed them in person. He would learnedly discourse on the priesthood of Egypt in a way that suggested he had studied in ancient Thebes or Heliopolis. Another puzzle was that he was never seen to eat, although it is now known that he had a special diet. He explained that he lived on some elixir of which only he knew the formula. He was a student of alchemy, and claimed to have discovered the secret of the Philosopher's Stone. What is certain is that he had learned a great deal about metallurgy and chemistry.

Saint-Germain continues to fascinate students of occultism. Many of them believe he is alive today—possibly in Tibet. The unromantic truth is that he died in his mid-70s in 1784, suffering from rheumatism and morbid depression. Accounts of people who met him indicate that, far from being a man of mystery and an enigma, he struck many intelligent people as a fool, charlatan, boaster, and swindler.

If Saint-Germain seems to have been fundamentally a confidence man, the same cannot be said of his famous contemporary Count Alessandro di Cagliostro. That he was a fraud there can be little doubt, but that he also possessed highly developed occult faculties is fairly certain. His enemies said that Cagliostro's real name was Guiseppe Balsamo, and that he had been a confidence trickster in his native Italy. As a schoolboy he was exuberant and ungovernable, and ran away from seminary school several times. In his teens he became a wanderer, like many talented and penniless young men, and lived by his wits. But he was also an avid student of alchemy, astrology, and ritual magic, and he soon had a wide, if not very coherent, knowledge of occultism.

Above: the Count of Saint-Germain, who admitted this name was false, was and remains one of history's figures of mystery. All accounts agree that he was a charming and knowledgeable man, but no one ever knew where he came from before he arrived in Vienna and from there made his way to the French court.

Left: an illustration from Saint-Germain's manuscript *La Tres Sainte Trinosophie* (The Most Holy Threefold Wisdom). It shows a mystic initiation. The woman is Isis. The man to be initiated is naked—as he came into the world and as he will now be born again. Stripped of all clothing, rank, and power, he may bring to the temple nothing that he owns, but only that which he himself is. The objects on the table are three of the Tarot card suits, symbols of water, fire, and air.

Above: the Count Alessandro di Cagliostro, who was born of Italian peasant parentage. He was quick and clever and early appreciated that man from far places enjoyed great prestige, and that most people will believe any story told with assurance.

Below: Cagliostro's beautiful wife, who assisted him in frauds. Born Lorenza, she became known to Paris society as Seraphinia Felichiani Comtesse de Cagliostro.

At the age of 26 in 1769 Cagliostro fell in love with Lorenza, the beautiful 14-year-old daughter of a coppersmith. They married, and for many years she was his partner in adventure and fraud, her beauty being one of their greatest assets. When Casanova met them in the south of France the year after their marriage as they were returning from a pilgrimage to Santiago de Compostella in Spain, they appeared to be people of means, traveling in style and distributing alms to the poor. In Paris, the couple came under the protection of a nobleman, who then seduced Lorenza and tried to make her leave her husband. Cagliostro had her thrown into jail, but later reunited with her and took her to England.

In London he joined the Freemasons. Soon, however, he founded his own masonic order, infusing its ceremonies with occult rituals purportedly based on ancient Egyptian practices that Cagliostro claimed he had discovered in an Egyptian manuscript on a bookstall. Cagliostro was undoubtedly convinced that his Egyptian masonry was the product of divine inspiration. It was certainly the turning point in his fortunes. From London he journeyed to Venice, Berlin, Nuremberg, and Leipzig. In each city, he visited the masonic lodge, made speeches on his Egyptian rite, and initiated members. His argument seems to have been that the Egyptian rite was as different from, and as superior to, established freemasonry as New Testament Christianity is from Old Testament Judaism. He was feted and admired, and became a rich man.

Cagliostro came to Strasbourg in 1780, and soon became the most talked about man in town. Although he was wealthy, he lived modestly in a room above a tobacco shop. His cures became legendary. He was often able to heal the sick simply by the laying on of hands. On one occasion he successfully delivered a baby after midwives had given up the mother for dead.

It was in Strasbourg that he met the man who was to bring about his downfall: Cardinal de Rohan. He was a churchman who longed for royal favor, but who unfortunately was disliked by Queen Marie Antoinette. Cagliostro deeply impressed Rohan, who spoke of his luminous and hypnotic eyes with almost religious fervor.

The cardinal's downfall occurred in 1785 in the famous Affair of the Diamond Necklace. A pretty swindler who called herself the Countess de la Motte Valois became Rohan's mistress, and persuaded him that the queen wanted him to secretly buy a diamond necklace worth $300,000. In fact, the queen knew nothing of it, and the money raised by the cardinal went straight into the countess's pocket. When the jewelers finally approached the queen for a long overdue installment on the money, the whole affair came to light. The countess was tried and publicly flogged. Rohan and Cagliostro were also tried and, although they were acquitted, the scandal damaged both of them irreparably. In addition, the months that Cagliostro spent in jail before trial broke his nerve—and his luck.

Cagliostro went to London after leaving prison. There he accurately predicted the nature and date of the French Revolution and of the fall of the Bastille. Then he traveled around Europe, often hounded by the police. Finally, he made the

Below: an English cartoon shows Cagliostro at a masonic lodge in London, where he came after his release from the Bastille in 1786. An English brother mason performed a satirical sketch of "a visiting quack." Cagliostro, just to the left of the table, took offense and walked out. The cartoonist has Cagliostro saying as he shows his displeasure, "Per Dio Santo! Son Scoperto!" ("Dear God, I am found out!")

extraordinary error of going to Rome to propagate his Egyptian freemasonry under the nose of the Pope. He was arrested and thrown into the papal prison in the Castel Sant'Angelo, and was later transferred to the even worse prison of San Leo. Eight years after his arrest in 1787, French soldiers captured San Leo prison and searched for Cagliostro, intending to treat him as a revolutionary hero. In fact, he had been dead for several years—though exactly when and how he died is still unknown.

Of all the great charlatan-magicians, Cagliostro is the most tragic. One of his enemies said that he possessed "a demonic power that paralyzes the will." But in retrospect he seems less a demon than a fallen angel.

5

Magic at Work

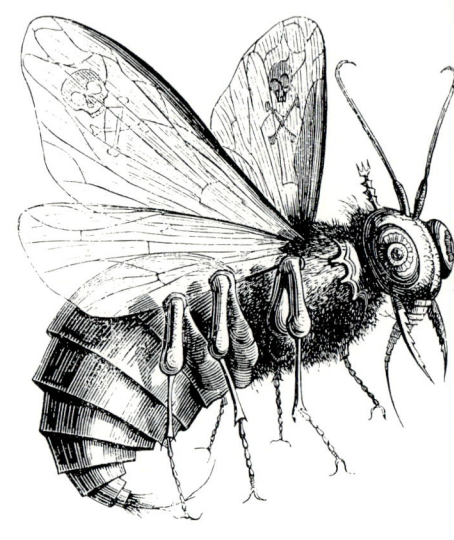

It was 11:30 at night on December 31, 1913, and the room in Paris was filled with the smell of incense. The room was lit by a flame that burned on an altar. Laid out beside this were a chain, a scourge, a dagger, a jar of oil, a loaf of bread, and a flask of wine. The dark robed man who stood before the altar was Aleister Crowley, an English practitioner of magic who liked to refer to himself as the Beast 666 from Revelations. The naked man beside him was his disciple Victor Neuberg. Crowley began to intone:

> Hail! Asi! Hail, Hoor-Apep! Let
> The Silence speech beget...

As he chanted, Crowley rang a bell twice.

Secrets of ritual magic—specific magical ceremonies intended to accomplish specific purposes—have been carefully preserved down the centuries to the present. Above: when called by a magician using ritual magic, Beelzebub—traditionally considered one of the five most powerful demons—appears in the shape of a great fly. Perhaps this is because his name can be translated as "lord of the flies." MacGregor Mathers said that only one small mistake by any magician in summoning up Beelzebub can mean instant death.

Right: a magician invoking an angel before his magic altar, with demons clustering around the edge of the mystic circle that preserves him from harm.

"The shape of a naked boy seemed to form in the air"

As he chanted the words of the ritual, he seized the scourge and whipped Neuberg's bare buttocks. Then he took the dagger and scratched a cross on Neuberg's chest above the heart, and bound the chain about Neuberg's forehead:

The scourge, the dagger, and the chain
Cleanse body, breast, and brain!

This strange ritual continued until the clock sounded midnight—New Year's Day of 1914. Then the priest and his neophyte began to chant in Latin. Suddenly the shape of a naked boy seemed to form in the air in front of them. He was surrounded by thousands of golden wands, which glowed with a clear light. Around each wand two live serpents seemed to be writhing. This was the caduceus, the wand traditionally associated with Mercury, the messenger of the Gods. It indicated that Crowley had succeeded in invoking Mercury—the Roman equivalent of the older Greek god Hermes, traditional founder of magic arts.

To the skeptic, the whole thing sounds absurd, and the vision seems to be some kind of hallucination induced with the help of the incense and the orgiastic flogging. We cannot say if this is so with any certainty. What we can say is that the ceremony Crowley was performing was not some wild invention of his inflamed imagination. It was a traditional magic ceremony of a kind that had been performed thousands of times in the temples of the ancient world. It was no surprise to Crowley that he saw Mercury and his caduceus. He expected to see Mercury, just as a chemist expects to see blue litmus paper turn red when he dips it in acid.

But how is it possible for a modern Westerner to take magic seriously? Is it not a primitive superstition—or, at best, an early form of crude science? No magician would agree. According to Crowley and most other practicing magicians, magic is quite simply the science of "causing changes to occur in conformity with will." This view was put forward by the French magician Eliphas Lévi, of whom Crowley believed himself to be a reincarnation. According to Lévi, magic is based on human will power which is a force "as real as steam or the galvanic current." In short, both Lévi and Crowley believed that magic is the directed use of the power that we have labelled thought pressure. Steam is lighter than air, yet it can drive an engine. Electricity is invisible, yet it can light a whole city. The will is intangible and invisible, yet magicians believe that, if properly directed, it can change the world.

We might expect ritual magic to be something that changes from age to age according to the temperament of individual magicians and the cultures to which they belong. To a minor extent this is true. Yet perhaps the most surprising thing about magic is that the way people have regarded it and the manner in which it has been used have altered little in thousands of years. Anyone who reads about the magic of the ancient Chaldeans or Chinese, or about the modern gypsies or dervishes, soon discovers that certain basic ideas and methods occur again and again. If magic is purely wishful thinking and nonsense, it has managed to be remarkably consistent wishful thinking and nonsense.

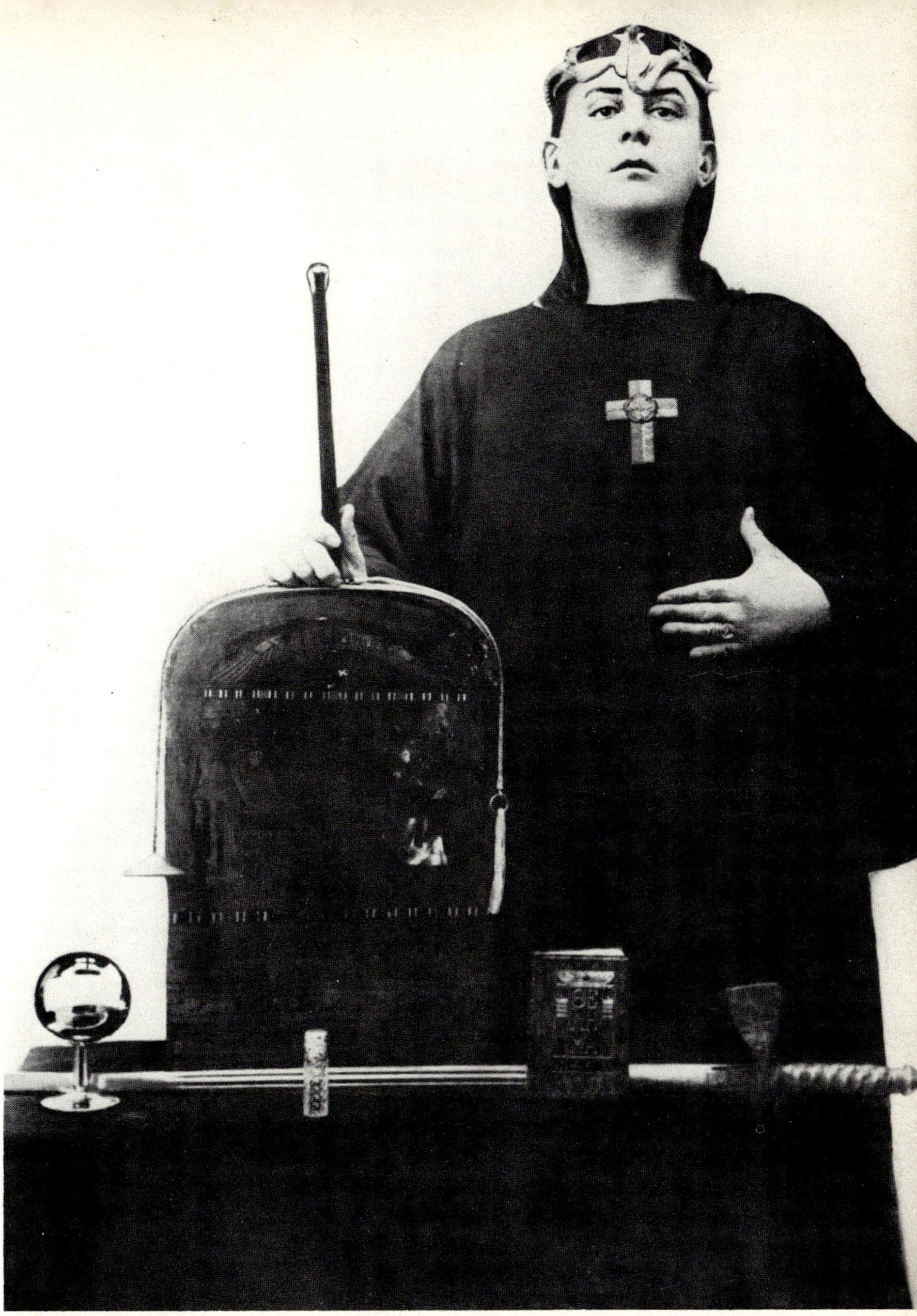

Above: Victor Neuberg, who took part with Aleister Crowley in a series of magical exercises in January, 1914, that have come to be known as the Paris Working. Right: Crowley in 1911 at his altar in special dress and with the equipment for his rituals. Below: a caricatured self-portrait by Crowley. He dramatized himself as the Great Beast, and made his motto "Do What Thou Wilt."

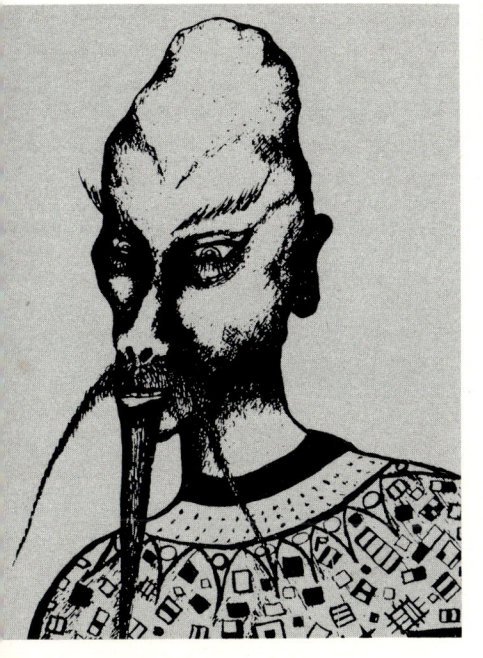

The god Hermes Trismegistus whom Crowley invoked was identical with Thoth, an important god of the ancient Egyptians. Magicians of ancient Alexandria in Egypt declared that Thoth was not a god, but a king who had reigned for more than 3000 years and had written various books on religion and magic. This king was known in Greek as Hermes Trismegistus, Thrice-Greatest Hermes. According to legend, he was buried in the great pyramid of Giza, and when his body was uncovered he was found to be holding an emerald tablet that contained an inscription beginning: "As above, so below." This has two meanings, one religious and one magical. Its religious meaning is that God is identical with the soul—a belief that is one of the central tenets of Hinduism. The magical meaning is that a man is a small model of the universe. Man is the *microcosm* (from Greek words meaning little world), and the universe is the *macrocosm* (great world). Man and the universe are connected by thousands of fine threads—a doctrine later elaborated by Paracelsus. You might say that man is an organ of the universe, just as the heart is an organ of the body. That is why students of magic believe that astrology, which claims that celestial bodies influence human affairs, can predict future events.

Like the Cabala, the many works attributed to Hermes Trismegistus—which in fact were probably written in Alexandria between 300 B.C. and A.D. 300—were a source of inspiration to many great thinkers of the Middle Ages and after. They were studied not only by mystics such as Albertus Magnus, the 13th-century Christian bishop who taught St. Thomas

Below: Hermes Trismegistus appears in this 15th-century mosaic pavement in central Italy. Hermes Trismegistus is said by some to be the Egyptian god Thoth in the form of an earthly king. As this king, Hermes Trismegistus reigned in peace for 3226 years.

Aquinas, but also by Agrippa and Paracelsus. We have already argued that the success of most magicians is due to their possession of strange powers. The question we must now ask is this: Can certain rituals, such as those enacted by Crowley, confer magical powers? For evidence let us look at the careers of three of the most celebrated occultists of the last four centuries.

Dr. John Dee, the most highly regarded magician of Shakespeare's time, is almost unique among magicians in that he possessed practically no occult powers. Perhaps this is why he managed to avoid the usual magician's destiny of spectacular success and tragic downfall.

He was born in 1527, the son of a minor official in the court of King Henry VIII. From childhood on he was an avid reader, and when he went to Cambridge University at the age of 15, he allowed himself only four hours' sleep a night. After Cambridge he went to the University of Louvain in Belgium, where Agrippa had also studied. When Dee read Agrippa's *Occult Philosophy*, he knew that he had stumbled on his life's work— the pursuit of magical knowledge. At the age of 23 he gave a series of free lectures on geometry in Rheims, France, and was so popular that he was offered a professorship. But he preferred to return to England to pursue his occult studies.

When Elizabeth I came to the throne in 1558, she asked Dee to cast a suitable date for her coronation. Dee did so, and from this time on he enjoyed royal protection. Even so, as one suspected of magical practices, he still had to behave with extreme caution. Moreover, Queen Elizabeth was notoriously stingy: her patronage did nothing to improve Dee's finances, and he remained poor all his life. Dee married a lady-in-waiting who bore him eight children. He lived quietly and studied astrology, crystal gazing, and alchemy.

The aim of crystal gazing is to induce a semitrancelike state in which the subconscious mind projects future events as images in the crystal. Dee was too much of an intellectual to be good at this. He realized that what he needed was a working partner with natural occult faculties, especially in scrying. In 1582 he met Edward Kelley, a young Irishman who claimed to have second sight. Kelley was undoubtedly a crook—he had had both his ears cut off for forgery—but it seems equally certain that he did possess second sight, and that he was also a medium. Dee's wife took an immediate dislike to the Irishman, but when Kelley went into a trance and began to get in touch with spirits, Dee was so delighted that he overruled his wife's objections.

How did Dee and Kelley go about summoning the spirits? One famous print shows them in a graveyard practicing necromancy. From what we know of the pious Dee, however, it seems unlikely that he went in for this sort of thing. We can learn more from his *Spiritual Diaries*. It is clear that he went into training before endeavoring to summon the spirits. He abstained for three days from sexual intercourse, overeating, and the consumption of alcohol, and he took care to shave his beard and cut his nails. Then began a two-week period of magical invocations in Latin and Hebrew beginning at dawn

Below: a statuette of the Egyptian god Thoth from the Ptolemaic period, about 323 to 30 B.C. He was worshiped as a moon-god and inventor of hieroglyphics. He was a magician who had known "these formulas which commanded all the forces of nature and subdued the very gods themselves."

Appollonius of Tyana

Mohammed

Portraits from the frontispiece of a book about John Dee, royal magician to Queen Elizabeth I. Published 50 years after his death, it was a disparaging book based on Dee's personal diaries. It succeeded in damaging his reputation.

Edward Kelley

Roger Bacon

Paracelsus

John Dee

and continuing until noon, then beginning again at sunset and continuing until midnight. Kelley, meanwhile, gazed intently into the crystal ball. At the end of 14 days, Kelley would begin to see angels and demons in the crystal. Later, these spirits would walk about the room. Dee, however, does not seem to have seen the spirits, but he recorded lengthy dialogues he had with them.

One's instant response to this is the conviction that Kelley made Dee believe that nonexistent spirits had manifested themselves. The trouble with this view is that the conversations, which came via the mouth of Kelley, were often so crammed with abstruse magical lore that it is almost inconceivable that the illiterate Irishman could have made them up as he went along. Dee, of course, was familiar with the lore, and certain of the demons quoted chunks of Agrippa's *Occult Philosophy*. This makes it possible that Dee transmitted them telepathically to Kelley. The likeliest explanation, however, is that Kelley was a natural medium.

Count Adalbert Laski, a servant of Henry III of France, was so impressed by these seances of Dee and Kelley that he invited them to visit the king of Germany. Dee and his family, and Kelley and his wife spent four years traveling around Europe as guests of various kings and noblemen, and their performances were sensationally successful.

Kelley was a difficult man, given to sudden tantrums and to fits of boredom and depression; but in spite of their ups and downs, he and Dee continued to work together for many years. They finally separated while they were still on their travels in Europe. Kelley achieved some success on his own as an alchemist and scryer, but eventually he died in prison. Dee returned to England in 1589 and lived for another 19 years, hoping in vain that the spirits would lead him to a crock of gold. Today his reputation among occultists is secure, for he was the first magician on record to make use of spirit communication. He was 200 years before his time; but in spite of his lack of worldly success, he remains one of the great names in the history of magic.

In 1801 there appeared in London a work called *The Magus, or Celestial Intelligencer* by Francis Barrett. It was supposed to be "a complete system of occult philosophy." Nowadays it is not highly regarded by students and adepts of the magic arts, because many of the rituals it details are garbled and inaccurate. Nevertheless, it was an important work for it was almost the first attempt at a serious description of magical practices since Agrippa's *Occult Philosophy* nearly three centuries earlier. After Agrippa's time, fear of persecution had driven the magicians underground for 200 years.

The Age of Reason, as thinkers and writers of mid-18th-century Europe called their period, had made magic superfluous—or at least unfashionable. But the tide soon turned again. For the popular imagination, at least, reason was not enough. All over western Europe novels such as Horace Walpole's *The Castle of Otranto* began to appear, in which high adventure and crimes of passion were mixed with supernatural events. Of course, most readers did not really believe

A Prophecy From the Grave

Guy Fawkes was one of the conspirators in the Gunpowder Plot of November 5, 1605 to blow up the English Houses of Parliament. He has since grown into a folktale figure for English children, and the anniversary of the unsuccessful political plot is now a day for fun with fireworks and bonfires. But few know that Guy Fawkes and the scholar-magician John Dee, astrologer to Queen Elizabeth I, are linked in a curious tale.

The story says that Fawkes came upon Dee and his assistant Edward Kelley in a graveyard as they were carrying a body away. They were taking it to a chamber where they were going to raise it from the dead in order to ask questions of it. Fawkes offered to pay for the opportunity of questioning the corpse himself, hoping to find out about the fate of the conspiracy in which he was engaged. Dee angrily refused payment, but agreed to allow him to put his question.

When the half-decayed body rose eerily, Fawkes asked, "Will the end be successful?"

The corpse, lit only by a glimmering blue light, replied, "The end will be death."

And for Guy Fawkes it was. He was caught and executed as a traitor after the plot failed.

Above: detail from a portrait of John Dee painted in 1594. Dee managed to avoid persecution as a witch by his connection with the court—it has even been suggested that he may have acted as a spy for the queen's well-developed intelligence network—but his magic never brought him riches, and he died in poverty.

Left: Edward Kelley, John Dee's disreputable assistant, shown raising a ghost with an assistant of his own. The ghost they called up was said to have buried a large amount of money in life and, reportedly, "satisfied their wicked desires and inquiries."

in the supernatural trappings of such stories—but their enormous popularity shows that ghosts, magic, and the paranormal continued to fascinate. At the end of *The Magus*, Barrett printed an advertisement asking for students to help him found a "magic circle," and an active group was established at Cambridge.

Nine years after publication of *The Magus*, there was born in Paris a remarkable man who, more than any other, was responsible for the great magical revival that swept across Europe in the 19th century: Alphonse-Louis Constant, better known as Eliphas Lévi. The son of a poor shoemaker, Lévi was a dreamy, sickly, highly intelligent and imaginative child with powerful religious inclinations. At the age of 12 in 1822, he decided he was destined for the Church. He had a craving to belong to some spiritual order, some great organization, that would enable him to devote his life to the truths of the spirit. His teacher at the seminary of Saint Nicholas du Chardonnet was Abbot Frere-Colonna, a remarkable idealist who believed that man was slowly ascending toward God, and that a great age of the Holy Spirit was at hand. The abbot had studied Mesmer's doctrines, and believed that they were inspired by the Devil. He devoted some time to denouncing them in class, but succeeded only in awakening young Lévi's interest in such forbidden matters. When the abbot was dismissed through the intrigues of jealous colleagues, Lévi's disillusion with the Church began.

Lévi still hungered for a faith, however. He became a subdeacon, and one of his chief tasks was teaching catechism to the young girls. One day a poor woman begged him to prepare her daughter for first communion, and Lévi's initial feelings of protectiveness developed into a wild infatuation for the girl. Nothing came of it, but the experience convinced him that he was not intended for the priesthood. When he turned away from his vocation, his mother committed suicide.

After 14 years in a seminary, Lévi found the world a hard place to adjust to. He still wanted to be a believer, and dreamed of Frere-Colonna's spiritual rebirth of mankind. So, although he began to write for radical newspapers—and spent time in prison on sedition charges as a result—his search for a faith continued. He discovered the writings of Swedenborg, and then the Cabala with its doctrine that man can overcome original sin and rise toward the godhead. Honoré de Balzac's mystical novel *Louis Lambert* was also a vital influence. Lévi studied that strange fortune-telling deck of cards known as the Tarot, and linked its 22 cards of the Major Arcana with the 22 paths of the Cabala. Lévi came to certain important conclusions about magic. The first was that the will is a far greater power than we realize, and that magic is learning how to use this power. The second was that all space is permeated with a medium that Lévi called astral light, which can take the impression of thoughts and feelings, and is the medium through which thoughts are conveyed in telepathy. Third, he believed deeply in the microcosm-macrocosm doctrine enshrined in Hermes Trismegistus's inscription, "As above, so below."

Lévi was in his 40s when his *Dogma and Ritual of High Magic*

Left: this drawing by Lévi was the frontispiece of his second volume of *Dogma and Ritual*. It is a symbol connected with the Witches' Sabbath (or sabbat). In Lévi's version the torch of knowledge lies between the horns of a goat's head that expresses sin; the caduceus represents eternal life and the breasts humanity; and the two arms—one male and one female —stand for the occult sciences.

Right: Eliphas Lévi in 1862, six years after his first magical treatise, *Dogma and Ritual of High Magic*, was published. It is said that he introduced no very original ideas, but that he was the first to see a connection between the Tarot and the Cabala.

was published in 1856, and it established a reputation that was consolidated four years later by his *History of Magic*. In the first book he describes one of the most curious incidents of his life. On a visit to London, he records, he was asked to try to raise the spirit of the ancient Greek magician Apollonius of Tyana. After a month of preparation and fasting, Lévi spent 12 hours in ritual incantations. At last, the shade of Apollonius appeared in a gray shroud, and telepathically answered questions Lévi put to it about the future of two of his acquaintances. It prophesied the death of both. Lévi's description of the invocation has considerable dramatic quality:

"I kindled two fires with the requisite prepared substances, and began reading the invocations of the 'Ritual' in a voice at first low, but rising by degrees. The smoke spread, the flame caused the objects on which it fell to waver, then it went out, the smoke still floating white and slow about the marble altar. I seemed to feel a quaking of the earth, my ears tingled, my

heart beat quickly. I heaped more twigs and perfumes on the chafing dishes, and as the flames again burst up, I beheld distinctly, before the altar, the figure of a man of more than normal size, which dissolved and vanished away. I re-commenced the evocations, and placed myself within a circle which I had drawn previously between the tripod and the altar. Thereupon the mirror which was behind the altar seemed to brighten in its depth, and a wan form was outlined therein, which increased and seemed to approach by degrees. Three times, and with closed eyes, I invoked Apollonius. When I again looked forth there was a man in front of me, wrapped from head to foot in a species of shroud, which seemed more gray than white. He was lean, melancholy, and beardless, and did not altogether correspond to my preconceived notion of Apollonius. I experienced an abnormally cold sensation, and when I endeavored to question the phantom I could not articulate a syllable. I therefore placed my hand upon the sign of the pentagram, and pointed the sword at the figure, commanding it mentally to obey and not alarm me, in virtue of the said sign. The form thereupon became vague, and suddenly disappeared. I directed it to return, and presently felt, as it were, a breath close by me; something touched my hand which was holding the sword, and the arm became immediately benumbed as far as the elbow. I divined that the sword displeased the spirit, and I therefore placed it point downward, close by me, within the circle. The human figure reappeared immediately, but I experienced such an intense weakness in all my limbs, and a swooning sensation came so quickly over me, that I made two steps to sit down, whereupon I fell into profound lethargy, accompanied by dreams, of which I had only a confused recollection when I came to myself. For several subsequent days, the arm remained benumbed and painful."

In spite of these setbacks, Lévi persisted and, according to his own account, was able to consult the spirit on two more occasions on some fine points of cabalism.

Lévi was a widely respected magician for the remainder of his life, and attracted many disciples. That he had occult powers—or that his disciples were convinced he had—is certain. A disciple to whom Lévi had given a prayer to recite before he fell asleep found that the words of the prayer were glowing in the dark, and that Lévi's spirit was standing by his bed. It seems likely that Lévi possessed the power of projecting his astral body.

His books strike the modern reader as wildly imaginative and confused, but they exerted an immense influence on a whole generation of students of the occult. His death in 1875 was mourned by hundreds of occultists in France, Germany, and England, who regarded him as the great master.

In 1831, when Lévi was still studying for the priesthood, there was born in Russia a woman who was to exert an even greater influence than he on 19th-century occultism: Elena Hahn, later Petrovna, but known as Madame Blavatsky. Born into an aristocratic family, she married at 16, left her husband soon after, and began to travel around the world. She was an

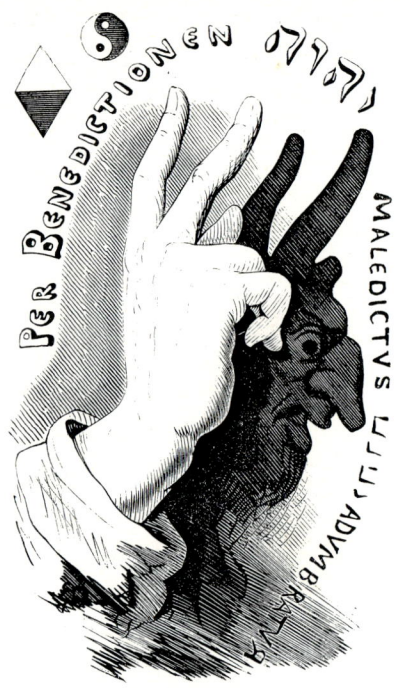

Above: the accursed blessing, as drawn by Lévi. The fingers held in the position for a Christian benediction become a demon in the shadow they throw. This is a symbol of good and evil as two inseparable sides of one coin.

Below: Lévi's symbol of the magic head from the Zohar (the Book of Splendor of the Cabala). He equates it with the face of God saying, "The forehead of God and His eyes form a triangle in the sky, and their reflection forms a triangle in the eyes."

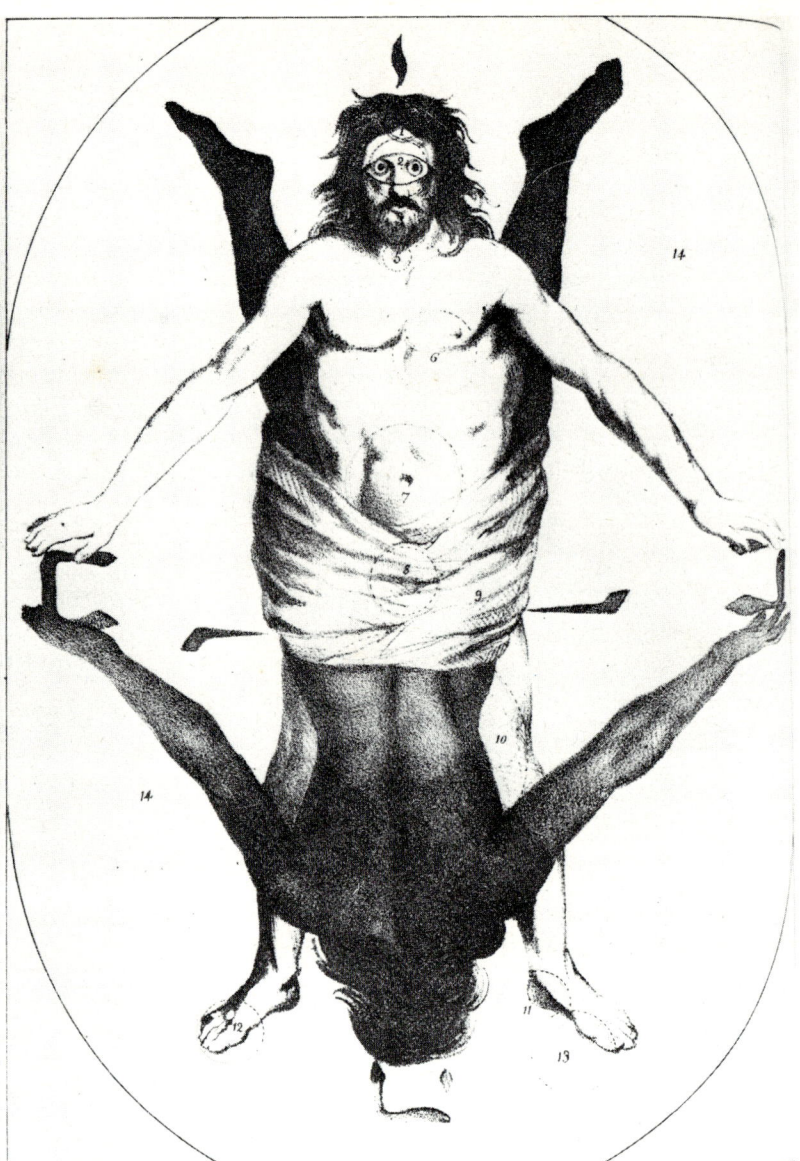

Above: Lévi calls this drawing "the great cabalistic symbol of Zohar." Like many symbolic expressions of the Cabala, the two figures form a six-pointed star as a representation of the mystical number six. Lévi said the Zohar was one of the masterpieces of occultism.

explosive, charming, delightful personality. For a while she worked as a bareback rider in a circus, and dabbled in many odd interests. She had undoubted mediumistic powers, and throughout her life odd manifestations were apt to occur in her presence: inexplicable rappings, ringing of bells, and movements of objects. In fact, it seems that she had the power of raising poltergeists. After living carelessly until she was just past 40, and then wondering how to make a living, she decided to turn her occult abilities to account and become a medium.

On going to the United States she met Colonel Olcott, a lawyer and journalist who became her lifelong admirer and tireless publicist. She told Olcott that she was in touch with a certain spiritual Brotherhood of Luxor, presumably priests of ancient Egypt, and he believed her—as he believed everything else she told him. Together they formed the Theosophical Society, a movement for the study of ancient wisdom. For three years it flourished in America. In 1879, as interest seemed to wane, they decided to move to India, which Madame Blavatsky regarded as the fountainhead of spiritual wisdom.

In Bombay, Theosophy was an immediate success. The charismatic personality of Madame Blavatsky fascinated the Hindus even more than it had fascinated the Americans. She claimed that the Secret Masters in Tibet, a group of spiritual initiates, had imparted their wisdom to her. When disciples asked her questions about these matters, paper notes fell from the air. The notes contained detailed replies to the questions and were signed "Koot Hoomi." These notes later became famous as the Mahatma Letters. Koot Hoomi, a semidivine Master, was even seen by some devotees one moonlight night.

In 1884 the bombshell came. A housekeeper with whom Madame Blavatsky had quarreled told a Western journalist that most of the magical effects were merely tricks. The Mahatma Letters were simply dropped through a crack in the ceiling of the room in which the disciples had gathered, and the seven-foot-tall Koot Hoomi was actually a model carried around on someone's shoulders. Examination of a cabinet in which many manifestations had occurred revealed a secret panel. The Society for Psychical Research, which had been investigating her powers, issued a skeptical report.

It might seem that the Blavatsky reputation was irretrievable. Not a bit of it. Madame Blavatsky set sail for London—and soon the Theosophical Society was flourishing again, although it never achieved anything like its earlier success. Once again, accounts of Madame Blavatsky's magical powers began to circulate among occultists. The poet W. B. Yeats, a serious and long-term student of the occult—reported that when he visited Madame Blavatsky, her cuckoo clock made hooting noises at him. A. P. Sinnett, who later became her faithful disciple, complained when he visited her that he had attempted to raise spirits at seances, but could not even get rapping sounds. "Oh, raps are the easiest thing to get," she replied— and raps immediately sounded from all parts of the room.

When Madame Blavatsky died in 1891, six years after the fiasco that drove her out of India, she left behind a host of disciples who firmly believed in the existence of Koot Hoomi and the Tibetan Masters. She also left behind two huge books, *Isis Unveiled* and *The Secret Doctrine*, in which she explains that the earth is destined to evolve through seven "root races," of which we are the fifth. Much of these enormous, bewildering books is taken up with descriptions of the root races.

In retrospect, it seems fairly certain that Madame Blavatsky was a genuine medium of unusual powers. It is more certain that, when her somewhat erratic powers were feeble, she helped them out with trickery—a temptation to which dozens of bona fide mediums and magicians have succumbed. She was in short both a charlatan and a genuine magician, and her hypnotically powerful personality made her one of the most remarkable women of the 19th century.

Above: Madame Blavatsky, the Russian-born woman who had an enormous influence on the great 19th-century occult revival. Below: Colonel H. S. Olcott, who supported and promoted all the work of Madame Blavatsky.

6

The Great Magical Revival

One day in 1885 a middle-aged clergyman named Woodford was passing an idle hour at a secondhand bookstall on Farringdon Street in London. Among the dusty volumes he came upon a bound, handwritten manuscript that was obviously in cipher. Woodford was a student of the occult, and he recognized certain symbols of the Cabala in the text. He bought the manuscript but, after several unsuccessful attempts to decode it, put it aside. Two years later, in the summer of 1887, he sent the manuscript to a friend, Dr. William Wynn Westcott, a coroner who was interested in occultism and freemasonry. Westcott was familiar

Above: Aleister Crowley in special robes for a magical ceremony in the Golden Dawn in 1899, the year after he joined the group.

Right: this insignia was worn by members of the Golden Dawn who had advanced to a higher magical level within the Order. The Golden Dawn drew on the sources of ancient wisdom preserved by the Rosicrucians, as the symbolic rose indicates. Much of the other symbolism comes from the Cabala.

"The Isis-Urana Temple of the Golden Dawn"

with the first major work on ciphers, the *Steganographia* by the 15th-century alchemist Abbot Johann Trithemius, and it did not take him long to conclude that the mysterious pages were actually written in Trithemius's code. When deciphered they proved to be five magical rituals for introducing newcomers into a secret society, together with notes on various cabalistic matters.

Concealed among the pages Wescott found a letter in German, which stated that anyone interested in these rituals should contact a certain Fräulein Sprengel at an address in Stuttgart. Westcott lost no time in writing to her. Fräulein Sprengel replied, divulging that she was a member of a German magical order. A correspondence about magic ensued, and eventually Fräulein Sprengel gave Westcott permission to found an English branch of the order, and to use the rituals to initiate members. Accordingly, in 1888, Wescott founded a society called The Isis-Urania Temple of the Golden Dawn. (Its pretentious title perhaps reflects the influence of Madame Blavatsky, who had arrived in London from India a few months previously.) Two other students of the occult were co-founders: William Woodman, a retired doctor who had studied the Cabala in Hebrew, and Samuel Liddell Mathers, an eccentric scholar of aristocratic leanings. Before long the Golden Dawn had branches in Edinburgh, Weston-super-Mare, and Bradford, and an enthusiastic following of displaced intellectuals and cranks. Its members included the beautiful actress Florence Farr, the poet W. B. Yeats, and the young and as yet unknown Aleister Crowley.

This, at any rate, is the story of the founding of the Golden Dawn as put about by Westcott and Mathers. In recent years Ellic Howe, the historian of magic, has looked into the matter closely, and has concluded that Fräulein Sprengel never existed. The cipher manuscript was probably genuine, but it came from a collection of occultist Fred Hockley, who died in 1885, and not from a bookstall in Farringdon Street. Westcott, probably with the connivance of Mathers, forged various letters in German purporting to come from Fräulein Sprengel. His aim evidently was to give the society a certain authority rooted in ancient practices. Mathers was later to denounce the Sprengel letters as forgeries, although he must have known about them from the beginning. Westcott seems to have been a Jekyll and Hyde character. Indeed, his split personality was so marked that he wrote in two completely different styles of handwriting. As for Mathers, who was to change his name to MacGregor Mathers and pose as a Scottish aristocrat, he was one of these curious figures who seem to occur so often in the history of magic—a kind of confidence trickster whose aim was not so much to swindle as to gain respect, admiration, and power.

Does all this mean, then, that the Order of the Golden Dawn was nothing more than a combination of chicanery and wishful thinking? By no means. Its members did, beyond question, pursue serious and genuine studies of the magical arts. At this point, then, we must have a closer look at the whole subject of magic and those who practice it.

First of all, we have to admit that common sense insists that

Above: Dr. W. R. Woodman in masonic dress. Woodman became a Golden Dawn Chief through Mathers who was a fellow occultist freemason. Older than the other two, he died before the Golden Dawn had become fully developed.

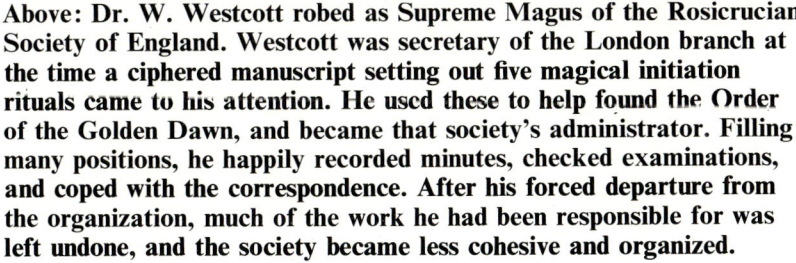

Above: Dr. W. Westcott robed as Supreme Magus of the Rosicrucian Society of England. Westcott was secretary of the London branch at the time a ciphered manuscript setting out five magical initiation rituals came to his attention. He used these to help found the Order of the Golden Dawn, and became that society's administrator. Filling many positions, he happily recorded minutes, checked examinations, and coped with the correspondence. After his forced departure from the organization, much of the work he had been responsible for was left undone, and the society became less cohesive and organized.

Right: one of the rare photographs of Samuel Liddell "MacGregor" Mathers. By all accounts, Mathers was the most eccentric of the Golden Dawn founders. Born in England, he took up the habit of wearing full Scots Highland dress after he went to Paris, and called himself Count MacGregor of Glenstrae. He had an imperious temperament, and the history of the Order is full of his quarrels. Here he holds the Lotus Wand in a Rite of Isis performed in Paris.

Two of the most famous members of the Order of the Golden Dawn.

Above: W. B. Yeats, one of the greatest poets of the 20th century, was active one way and another for more than 20 years in the Order. He was initiated in 1890, and was thereafter known by the magical name Daemon est Deus Inversus. This means "the Devil is the reverse side of God." This portrait of Yeats was painted in 1900 by his artist father.

Right: the actress Florence Farr. She was a beautiful woman with a considerable talent for magical ceremonies, and became the head of the London Temple after the resignation of Dr. Westcott.

magic is bound to be nonsense. How could some semireligious ceremony have the slightest influence on the real world? Clergymen in church may pray for rain, or prosperity, or victory in battle, but they do not expect their prayers to produce a definite effect; they merely hope that God will pay attention. So why should some magic ceremony, not even addressed to God, have the power to influence actual events?

This is, I repeat, the commonsense view, the so-called scientific approach. But every day, thousands of events occur that science refuses to recognize because they appear to flout scientific laws. Dowsing, telepathy, precognition of future events, and spectres of the living are only a few examples. And what of those strange, heightened states of consciousness such as the one that John G. Bennett experienced while at Gurdjieff's Institute? Perhaps we cannot really blame scientists for declining to pay too much attention to these things. The aim of science is to describe the universe in terms of natural laws, especially laws that forge unbreakable links between cause and effect— between an occurrence and the forces that make it happen. It is the apparent absence of such a link in magical events that makes scientists skeptical of them. The occultist responds to such skepticism by claiming that scientists refuse, or are unable, to spread their net of inquiry wide enough to encompass strange events. What is beyond dispute is that such events do occur.

When we try to take account of occult events, and to devise some kind of theory that helps to account for them, we discover an interesting thing. Such a theory has already existed for thousands of years. It does not matter whether we call it magic, occultism, shamanism, the Hermetic tradition as based on the works of Hermes Trismegistus. It all amounts to the same thing. Its basic assertion is that there is a far more intimate connection between man and nature than we are inclined to believe. The world is full of unseen forces, and of laws of whose nature we have no inkling. Perhaps there is some strange medium that stretches throughout space—such as Eliphas Lévi's astral light—that transmits these forces as the air transmits sound waves.

How do we make contact with such forces? The answer seems to be that you have to want to with an intense inner compulsion. In his autobiography, the painter Oscar Kokoschka tells of how his mother, who was having tea with his aunt one day in Prague, Czechoslovakia, suddenly leaped to her feet and announced that she must rush home because her youngest son was bleeding. The aunt tried to persuade her that her idea was nonsense, but his mother hurried home—and found that her son had cut his leg with a hatchet while trying to chop down a tree. He would certainly have bled to death if she had arrived any later. This story—and hundred of others like it equally well attested—indicates that strange powers come into operation where our deepest desires or needs are involved. As we go through our everyday lives, we do not need to exercise much will power; but occasionally, something stirs us to some really deep effort. It is this kind of effort that is likely to produce magical effects. The 20th-century poet Robert Graves has remarked that many young men use a form of unconscious

The Ritual Magic of the Golden Dawn

The Order of the Golden Dawn was established in London in 1887. It was a secret society whose members, among them famous people, were serious and dedicated. They wanted to establish magic rituals that would open pathways into the world beyond the normal senses. Aleister Crowley, who had been expelled from the Golden Dawn, formed his own order in 1907. Crowley used amended versions of Golden Dawn rituals. It was Crowley's public performance of the Rites of Eleusis in a London auditorium in 1909 that brought him widespread notoriety.

The Rites of Eleusis were a series of seven rituals aimed at invoking the ancient gods. In the ceremonies the will power of the magician was the motivating power, but his will was focused and reinforced by elaborate ritual magic. Crowley presided, Leila Waddell played the violin, and the set rituals were strictly observed. To invoke Saturn, for example, members of the Order recited appropriate prayers around an altar inscribed with symbols dedicated to Saturn. On one occasion the public was shocked when, during the invocation of Saturn, Leila Waddell sat astride Crowley on the altar!

Above: Aleister Crowley when he was 30. This was about the time that he was traveling with his wife in Egypt, and encountered Aiwass, one of the Secret Chiefs, through her as a medium. Aiwass dictated to him the Book of the Law, which became the basis of most of his later teachings.

Right: Crowley about 10 years later. Wearing the headdress of Horus, he is making the sign of Pan, which indicates creative energy.

"sorcery" to seduce young women. This is another word for thought pressure.

We could say, then, that organizations such as the Hermetic Order of the Golden Dawn set out to experiment with will power, and to explore the possibilities of reaching deep subconscious levels of the will. Perhaps their magic was a hit-and-miss affair that worked only occasionally; but at least they were trying to learn about the possiblities of the true will.

The magic practiced by the members of the Golden Dawn was based on a number of simple principles. To begin with, they believed that certain basic symbols or ideas have a deep meaning for all human beings. On one occasion, Mathers handed Florence Farr a piece of cardboard with a geometrical symbol on it, and told her to close her eyes and place it against her forehead. She immediately saw in her mind's eye a cliff top above the sea, with gulls shrieking. Mathers had shown her the water symbol from the Cabala. There is a close connection between such symbols and the theory of archetypes of the psychologist Carl Jung, who believed that certain symbols are able to strike a chord in the unconscious mind of every human being.

The Golden Dawn taught its students to try to train their imagination, which is the trigger of the will, and gain control over it. One of their exercises was to control likes and dislikes until they could like something they normally hated, and hate something they usually liked. Another exercise was to attempt to see the world through other people's eyes rather than their own—in other words, to completely change their normal point

Left: a self-portrait by Crowley as the Beast 666, the Antichrist of the Apocalypse. His mother had called him this because of his wildness as a child. The device on his skull is the Horus forelock, symbol of solar-phallic power.

Right: the Stele of Revealing, exhibit number 666 in the Boulak Museum, Cairo. It concerns Ankh-f-n-Khonsu, an ancient Egyptian priest. Crowley, who saw and studied the stele in Cairo, believed he had been Ankh-f-n-Khonsu in one of his previous incarnations.

of view. Many modern psychologists would agree that such exercises are valuable and healthy. They are, in fact, similar to exercises practiced in yoga and other meditation disciplines.

The Golden Dawn also made a genuine attempt to draw together all that was best in the ancient magical traditions: Hermeticism, Cabalism, Enochian magic (based on the Apocryphal *Book of Enoch*, which tells of the fall of the Angels and their magic practices), and such magic textbooks as *The Key of Solomon, The Magic of Abrahemelin the Mage*, and the *Grimoire of Pope Honorius*.

On the face of it, the Golden Dawn should have been a wholly beneficial and healthy influence. Unfortunately, too many of its leading figures were driven by the craving that has been the downfall of so many magicians: the will to power, not only over themselves but also over everyone else. Gerald Yorke, a friend of Aleister Crowley, concluded that the story of the Golden Dawn showed that "the majority of those who attempt to tread the occult path of power become the victims of their creative imagination, inflate their egos, and fall." There was a great deal of infighting for the leadership of the Golden Dawn. Dr. Westcott saw himself as the leader, but MacGregor Mathers felt the position should rightly be his. Mathers claimed to be in direct touch with Secret Chiefs, semidivine spirits, who dictated new rituals to him through his wife as a medium. Then there was A. E. Waite, a learned American historian of magic. His interests, however, were more mystical than magical, and he was not a very inspiring person. Finally, there was Aleister Crowley, a remarkable and demonic magician whose career brought ruin to many others as well as himself.

Above: a sketch Crowley made of a devouring demon. His effect on the people who came into contact with him was like this demon: few escaped from his inner circle with their reason unimpaired.

Crowley was the son of a wealthy and puritanical brewer. He was born in Leamington near Stratford-upon-Avon in 1875. His birthplace gave him opportunity to remark with typical bombast and arrogance: "It is a strange coincidence that one small county [Leamington and Stratford are in Warwickshire] should have given England her two greatest poets—for one must not forget Shakespeare." It sounds like a joke, but in fact Crowley was convinced that he was a great poet. However, though his verse shows considerable talent, he lacked the discipline and sense of language to be even a good poet.

Crowley was a spoiled child who developed an intense dislike of the Plymouth Brethren, the strict religious sect to which his father belonged. He was also obsessed by sex. His first of numerous seductions occurred with a young servant when he was 14 years old. At university he wrote a great deal of poetry, which he published at his own expense. He also developed an incurable desire that lasted all his life to shock respectable people. In his late teens he discovered Mathers' translation of a book called *The Kabbalah Unveiled*, as well as a work by A. E. Waite on ceremonial magic. He quickly established contact with the Golden Dawn.

By the time Crowley entered the Golden Dawn in 1898, the struggle for its control had already been going on for some time. In 1891 Mathers had returned from France to announce that he had met three of the Secret Chiefs in Paris, and had had various magical secrets imparted to him. Dr. Woodman died that year

Above: Rose Kelly, first wife of Crowley. It was through her that the flamboyant occultist made contact with Aiwass, although until then she had shown no occult gift.

Right: Leila Waddell played the violin in Crowley's public Rites of Eleusis, which attracted considerable mocking publicity. As one of Crowley's magical assistants, she has the Mark of the Beast between her breasts.

Left: Crowley with Maria Theresa Ferrarri de Miramar, the second woman he married in 1929. This was during the long bleak period when he was struggling to fight off his addiction to heroin. Rose, the first wife whom he had long since abandoned with their child, had died hopelessly insane.

Villa — and Family — in part!

Right: Crowley and Leah Hirsig, at the Abbey of Thelema, the Sicilian villa in which Crowley tried to establish a new community of his disciples. Leah, whom he usually called the Ape of Thoth, held the office of Scarlet Woman, the Beast's special sexual partner. Their baby Poupée, here in Leah's arms, died shortly afterward.

and for the next six years there was a certain amount of tension within the movement. Dr. Westcott resigned from the Order— apparently having been told by his superiors on the London Council that magic was not a suitable occupation for a respectable public official. Mathers spent a great deal of time in Paris working on magical manuscripts at the Bibliothèque Nationale, so the struggle for leadership of the movement continued.

In August 1899 Crowley rented a house in Boleskine, Scotland on the shores of Loch Ness, conferred on himself the title "Laird of Boleskine," donned a kilt, and proceeded to practice the magic of Abrahamelin the Mage—a system which, he claimed, he had learned about in the writings of John Dee.

In December 1899, convinced that it was time he moved up to

a higher grade in the Golden Dawn, Crowley went to London to demand initiation. This was refused through the efforts of Yeats and various other senior members, who regarded him as an overgrown juvenile delinquent. Crowley therefore went to Paris and persuaded Mathers to perform the necessary rituals. He also took the opportunity to stir up trouble, convincing Mathers that he had a revolt on his hands. Mathers sent him back to London with instructions to break into the Golden Dawn headquarters, and to put new locks on all the doors. Yeats, Florence Farr, and the other London initiates were enraged.

The legal wrangle that ensued in 1901 broke up the original Golden Dawn 13 years after it had been founded. One group of members, under the leadership of A. E. Waite, managed to continue for another four years, still calling themselves the Golden Dawn. Another group, including Yeats, Florence Farr, and the novelist Arthur Machen, was led until 1905 by Dr. R. W. Felkin, who then founded a magical society called the Stella Matutina, or Morning Star. Finally, in the 1920s, a talented young medium and occultist who called herself Dion Fortune founded the Society of the Inner Light, based on Golden Dawn rituals obtained from Mrs. Mathers—Mathers himself having died in the influenza epidemic of 1918.

The same year of the legal problems the Golden Dawn had received another blow in the form of a sudden spate of unwelcome publicity. It happened when a couple of confidence tricksters who called themselves Mr. and Mrs. Horos were accused of raping a 16-year-old girl. Mrs. Horos had learned that it was supposed to have been Fräulein Sprengel who had given the Golden Dawn its charter. She went to Paris and introduced herself to Mathers as Fräulein Sprengel. Oddly enough, Mathers was taken in—which could argue that he was not at that time aware that Fräulein Sprengel had been invented by Westcott. Mathers soon became suspicious of the couple, whereupon Mrs. Horos and her husband stole some of the rituals of the Golden Dawn and fled to London. There they launched into a career of confidence trickery based on a mixture of spurious occultism, extortion, and sex. When charged with their crimes they claimed to be leaders of the Golden Dawn. As a consequence, many of the most intimate secrets of the order were made public and sensationalized by the press. The publicity, combined with the power struggles within it, sealed the fate of the Golden Dawn.

Crowley had decided to get away before the Horos scandal broke. Late in 1900 he had gone to Mexico, where he studied the Cabala, practiced yoga, and—according to his own account—finally became a true magician. When he returned to Paris in 1902 he tried to persuade Mathers to take up yoga. Mathers declined, and their relation became several degrees colder. Eventually it turned into hatred, with Mathers and Crowley pronouncing magical curses on one another. Crowley claimed that his curses were actually responsible for the death of Mathers.

Back in England, Crowley married Rose Kelly, and they traveled to Ceylon and Egypt. They called themselves the

Above: Crowley in Arab dress. His main contribution to the development of magic has been his welding of the Eastern and Western traditions into a single system of thought and ritual. Below: Crowley taking a pose as the Chinese god of laughter.

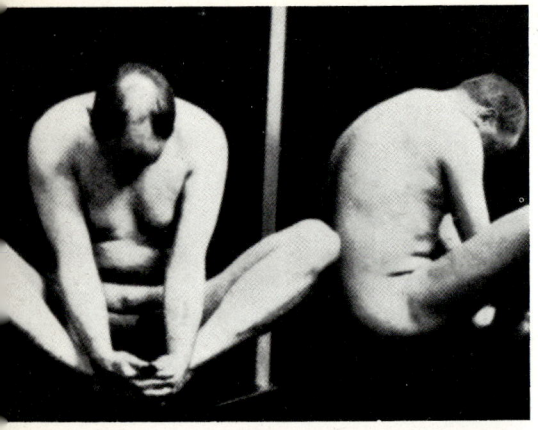

Left: a sequence of pictures of about 1912 in which Crowley demonstrates the yoga technique of breath control known as pranayama. He does the exercises in various of the traditional yoga positions. Yoga breath control —which includes measured inhalation and exhalation as well as breathing with alternate nostrils —is an important part of yoga. It was partly Crowley's great enthusiasm for yoga that cooled his relationship with Mathers.

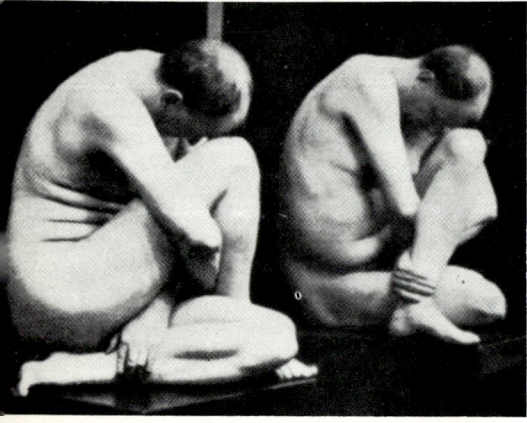

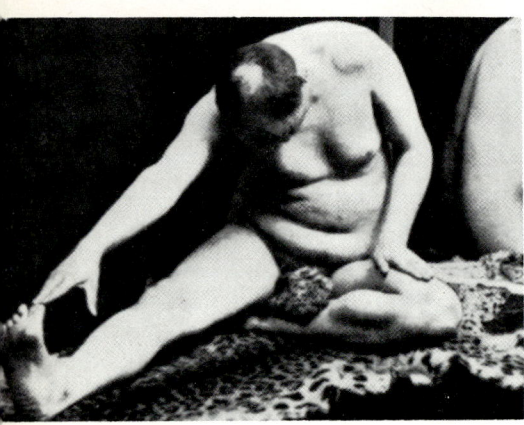

Prince and Princess Chioa Khan. In Cairo, Crowley performed various rituals with the intention of invoking the Egyptian god Horus. On April 8, 1904, he received instructions from his wife, who had taken to uttering strange messages while in a trance-like state, to go into a room he had furnished as a temple. Suddenly he heard a disembodied voice ordering him to write. What Crowley wrote was an odd document called *The Book of the Law*, which became the cornerstone of his later teaching. He claimed that it was dictated by Aiwass, one of the Secret Chiefs. Its basic teaching was expressed in the phrase: "Do what you will."

In 1905 Crowley went to the Himalayas to attempt the climb of Kanchenjunga, third highest mountain in the world. During the climb he quarreled with the rest of the team and, when they were buried in an avalanche, made no attempt to help them. Several were killed. He deserted his wife and baby in India where the baby died of typhoid. Rose later became an alcoholic, and died insane. In a magazine called *The Equinox* Crowley began to publish the secret rituals of the Golden Dawn. Mathers took him to court for this, but lost his case.

In 1912 Crowley received a communication from another magical organization, the Order of the Temple of the Orient, reproaching him for publishing its secrets. Puzzled by the accusation, Crowley went to see Theodor Reuss, one of the O.T.O.'s leaders. It appeared that the secret in question was something called sex magic. It arose from the system of yoga known as Tantra, which attempts to use the power of sexual energy to fuel the drive toward higher consciousness. The O.T.O. had, it seems, developed its own form of Tantric techniques. Crowley was fascinated, and promptly availed himself of Reuss's permission to set up an English branch of the O.T.O. Magical ritual performed by Crowley often involved sex magic —with his disciple Victor Neuberg it was an act of sodomy. Sex magic remained one of Crowley's central enthusiasms for the rest of his life—though addiction to heroin and cocaine lessened his sex drive in later years.

In the United States during World War I Crowley had an endless series of mistresses, each of whom he liked to call the "Scarlet Woman." He undoubtedly had an exceptional sexual appetite, but it must also be said that he genuinely believed that sex magic heightened his self-awareness, and enabled him to tap increasingly profound levels of consciousness. At all events, during this period Crowley steadily developed a kind of hypnotic power that it is as difficult to account for as it is to describe. William Seabrook, an American writer on the occult, witnessed the use of this power one day when he and Crowley were walking on Fifth Avenue in New York City. Crowley began to follow a complete stranger who was walking along the sidewalk. Crowley followed a few yards behind, keeping in perfect step with him. Suddenly, Crowley allowed his knees to buckle, and dropped momentarily to the ground. At exactly the same moment, the man he was following collapsed in precisely the same manner.

By the early 1920s Crowley, who was suffering from asthma, was almost permanently in debt. A legacy of $12,000 enabled him to move to a small farmhouse in Cefalu, Italy. He called it the Abbey of Thelema, which means "Do what you will," began to practice magic, and invited disciples to join him. He provided apparently limitless quantities of drugs for anyone who wished to use them, and attractive women devotees were expected to help Crowley practice his sex magic. Even with the legacy, however, the money problem remained pressing. Crowley wrote a novel called *Diary of a Drug Fiend* and started his *Confessions*, which he called his hagiography (the biography of a saint). He announced that the earth had now passed beyond Christianity and had entered the new epoch of Crowleyanity. But when one of his disciples died after sacrificing a cat and drinking its blood, the resulting newspaper scandal drove Crowley out of Sicily.

The British press denounced him as "the wickedest man in the world" and, although he loved the publicity, he soon discovered that his notoriety made publishers shy away from his books. He deserted his disciples, one of whom committed suicide, and married again. His second wife, like the first, became insane. Hoping to make money, he sued the English sculptress Nina Hamnett for calling him a black magician. But when witnesses described Crowley's magic, the judge stopped the case, declaring he had never heard such "dreadful, horrible, blasphemous, and abominable stuff."

By the outbreak of World War II Crowley had added alcoholism to his drug addiction even though his daily intake of heroin at that time would have killed a dozen ordinary men. Every now and again he found rich disciples to support him until, inevitably, they lost patience with him. He retired to a rooming house near Hastings in southern England, and died there in December 1947 at the age of 72. John Symonds, a writer who had met him in his last years, later wrote his biography—a hilarious but often disturbing book. Other friends, notably Richard Cammell and Israel Regardie, wrote more sober and admiring accounts of his career. But it was not until the magical revival that began in the mid-1960s that Crowley's reputation began to rise again. Nowadays more than a dozen of his books are in print, and a new generation ardently practices the magic rituals described in them. The Beast has finally achieved the fame he craved. Nonetheless, and fortunately, the great age of Crowleyanity seems as far away as ever.

Above: Crowley as an old man at the English seaside boarding house where he died in December 1947.

7

Three Modern Magicians

On January 1, 1917, the temperature in the Russian city of Petrograd—now Leningrad—was sub-zero. From a bridge over the frozen Neva River a few spectators watched a group of policemen who stood around a hole in the ice. A diver emerged, grasping the end of a rope that disappeared into the dark water beneath him. When he was out, the policemen heaved on the rope. A body broke the surface and slid onto the ice. The corpse was a bearded man in his late 40s; his face was battered and swollen. He had been bound with ropes, but before dying he had managed to free one hand, which was raised to his chest as if making the sign

Rasputin, the enigmatic Russian monk who aroused violent hatred and equally passionate devotion.

Above: a hostile cartoon showing Rasputin with the czar captured in his hand—a bitter reference to Rasputin's influence at court.

Right: the young Rasputin as he was when his hypnotic power was first recognized in Russia.

"Rasputin really was a miracle-worker and a man of strange powers"

of the cross. He was wearing only one boot; the other was in the hands of a police inspector who stood nearby. It was this boot, found by a boy, that had led police to the spot.

The police inspector turned to one of his men: "Go and phone Makarov. Tell him we've found Rasputin. I'd say he's been shot."

Grigori Rasputin, who had been murdered three days before, was one of the most notorious figures in Petrograd. Now that he was dead, he would become a legend all over the world—a symbol of evil, cunning, and lust. If ever you see a magazine story titled "Rasputin, the Mad Monk," you can be sure it will be full of lurid details of how Rasputin spent his days in drunken carousing, his nights in sexual debauchery; how he deceived the czar and czarina into thinking he was a miracle worker; how he was the evil genius who brought about the Russian Revolution and the downfall of the Romanov dynasty. It is all untrue. Yet it makes such a good story that there is little chance that Rasputin will ever receive justice. The truth about him is that he really was a miracle worker and a man of strange powers. He was certainly no saint—very few magicians are—and tales of his heavy drinking and sexual prowess are undoubtedly based on fact. But he was no diabolical schemer.

Rasputin was born in the village of Pokrovskoe in 1870. His father was a fairly well-to-do peasant. As a young man, Rasputin had a reputation for wildness until he visited a monastery and spent four months there in prayer and meditation. For the remainder of his life, he was obsessed by religion. He married at 19 and became a prosperous carter. Then the call came again; he left his family and took to the road as a kind of wandering monk. When eventually he returned, he was a changed man, exuding an extraordinarily powerful magnetism. The young people of his village were fascinated by him. He converted one room in his house into a church, and it was always full. The local priest became envious of his following, however, and Rasputin was forced to leave home again.

Rasputin had always possessed the gift of second sight. One day during his childhood this gift had revealed to him the identity of a peasant who had stolen a horse and hidden it in a barn. Now, on his second round of travels, he also began to develop extraordinary healing powers. He would kneel by the beds of the sick and pray; then he would lay his hands on them, and cure many of them. When he came to what is now Leningrad, probably late in 1903, he already had a reputation as a wonder worker. Soon he was accepted in aristocratic society in spite of his rough peasant manners.

It was in in 1907 that he suddenly became the power behind the throne. Three years before, Czarina Alexandra had given birth to a longed-for heir to the throne, Prince Alexei. But it was soon apparent that Alexei had inherited hemophilia, a disease that prevents the blood from clotting, and from which a victim may bleed to death even with a small cut. At the age of three, the prince fell and bruised himself so severely that an internal hemorrhage developed. He lay in a fever for days, and doctors despaired of his life. Then the czarina recalled the man of god she had met two years earlier, and sent for Rasputin. As soon as he came in he said calmly: "Do not worry the child. He will be all

Above: the daily gathering of his women disciples in Rasputin's dining room. The women stayed there all day, talking about him among themselves when he was not there, drinking in his words when he was, and glowing with rapture at any sign of special favor.
Left: Rasputin recovering from the first attempt on his life.

right." He laid his hand on the boy's forehead, sat down on the edge of the bed, and began to talk to him in a quiet voice. Then he knelt and prayed. In a few minutes the boy was in a deep and peaceful sleep, and the crisis was over.

Henceforward the czarina felt a powerful emotional dependence on Rasputin—a dependence nourished by the thinly veiled hostility with which Alexandra, a German, was treated at court. Rasputin's homely strength brought her a feeling of security. The czar also began to confide in Rasputin, who became a man of influence at court. Nicholas II was a poor ruler, not so much cruel as weak, and too indecisive to stem the rising tide of social discontent. His opponents began to believe that Rasputin was responsible for some of the czar's reactionary policies, and a host of powerful enemies began to gather. On several occasions

Right: a caricature of the rumored orgies at the court, in the style of an icon, or holy picture. The nude figure dancing with Rasputin greatly resembles the czarina.

the czar had to give way to the pressure and order Rasputin to leave the city. On one such occasion, the young prince fell and hurt himself again. For several days he tossed in agony, until he seemed too weak to survive. The czarina dispatched a telegram to Rasputin, and he telegraphed back: "The illness is not as dangerous as it seems." From the moment it was received, the prince began to recover.

World War I brought political revolution and military catastrophe to Russia. Its outbreak was marked by a strange coincidence: Rasputin was stabbed by a madwoman at precisely the same moment as the Archduke Franz Ferdinand was shot at Sarajevo. Rasputin hated war, and might have been able to dissuade the czar from leading Russia into the conflict. But he

113

was in bed recovering from his stab wound when the moment of decision came.

Rasputin's end was planned by conspirators in the last days of 1916. He was lured to a cellar by Prince Felix Yussupov, a man he trusted. After feeding him poisoned cakes, Yussupov shot him in the back; then Rasputin was beaten with an iron bar. Such was his immense vitality that he was still alive when the murderers dropped him through the hole in the ice into the Neva. Among his papers was found a strange testament addressed to the czar. It stated that he had a strong feeling he would die by violence before January 1, 1917, and that if he were killed by peasants, the czar would reign for many years to come; but, if he were killed by aristocrats—as he was—then "none of your children or relations will remain alive for more than two years." He was right. The czar and his family were all murdered in July 1918 an amazing example, among many, of Rasputin's gift of precognition.

Rasputin—in fact as well as in legend—was one of the most remarkable men in Russia. Also remarkable was his compatriot and near contemporary Georgei Gurdjieff, who greatly influenced 20th-century occultism. Gurdjieff differs from most other men of strange powers in one important respect: he was not primarily a mage or wonder worker, but a philosopher obsessed by the problems of human futility. Why are human beings so weak? Why is human consciousness so narrow? Why do we spend our lives in a state of dullness resembling sleep? Above all, by what practical methods can we break through to the great "source of power, meaning, and purpose" buried deep within ourselves? It was to questions like these that Gurdjieff addressed his life and work.

Gurdjieff was born in Armenia in 1873. His parents were Greek but he was Russian by nationality. From an early age he was intrigued by magic. One of the young men in his village could predict the future with astonishing accuracy after sitting between two lighted candles and going into a trance. At about this time Gurdjieff also witnessed a demonstration of the power of suggestion. He saw a boy who belonged to one of the many obscure local religious sects trapped in the middle of a magic circle drawn on the ground by some children of the village. He was psychologically incapable of stepping beyond the perimeter of the circle.

While still in his teens, Gurdjieff set out on what became 20 years of travel in Asia, Africa, and Europe in search of the secret wisdom that, he was convinced, was somewhere to be found. He learned the techniques of yoga and other forms of meditation in Tibetan monasteries and in Arab mosques; he studied hypnosis; he spent months with dervishes and with fakirs. In 1912, he returned to Russia, ready to teach some of the mysteries he had learned. Among the close circle of people who joined his group in Moscow was Peter Ouspensky, a young occultist and philosopher who was to become his most distinguished student.

On the outbreak of the Russian Revolution in 1917, Gurdjieff left Moscow for his family home, then in the Caucasus. There he founded his Institute for the Harmonious Development of Man, and was soon joined by Ouspensky and others of his disciples.

Above: the Russian mystic G. I. Gurdjieff with three pets. Gurdjieff shared with Rasputin the ability to attract many people who became his devoted disciples.

Right: Peter Ouspensky, one of Gurdjieff's most important students. Ouspensky eventually decided that he could not work with Gurdjieff personally, but continued to teach Gurdjieff's ideas. He always acknowledged that Gurdjieff's theories were the basis of his own philosophy.

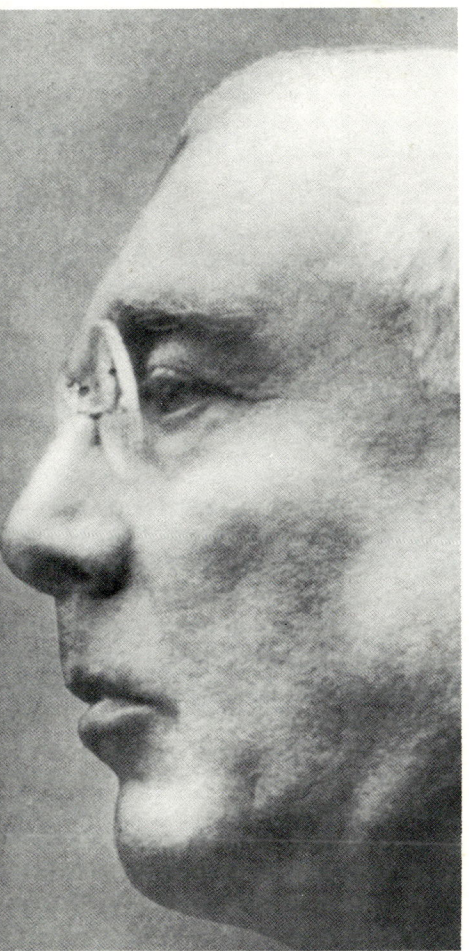

However, political conditions became too harsh in the Caucasus and, after attempting to settle in Istanbul and in Germany, Gurdjieff reestablished the Institute at the Prieuré near Paris in 1922.

Gurdjieff's system of teaching was based on the idea that, under normal circumstances, man is asleep, and that he is enslaved by a robot that controls not only his automatic functions but also much of his intellectual and emotional life. Gurdjieff's aim was to teach man how to outflank the robot by taking control of the vital reserves that exist in all of us, but that most people can tap only in times of crisis. We can all remember occasions in our lives when, faced with exceptionally difficult and perhaps dangerous situations, we have been forced—if only briefly—to excel ourselves physically or mentally. At the moment of success we feel marvelously alive. We are aware of a feeling of freedom—and rightly so, for the greatest freedom consists in our capacity to control and direct our own most deep-seated powers. We say, with quite literal truth, "I didn't know I had it in me!"

Gurdjieff's method was to force his pupils constantly to extend their mental and physical limits. They lived almost monastic lives at the Prieuré, working from dawn to dusk and performing exercises designed to bring the mind, emotions, and body into harmony and under control. The aim was to achieve a state that Gurdjieff called "self-remembering"—a state in which a person is not only intensely aware of his surroundings but also aware of himself observing and participating in them: a marriage of total inner and outer awareness. If you want to test how difficult this is, try a simple exercise. Close your eyes and direct your attention inward until you are aware only of your inner self. Now open your eyes and direct your attention toward the outside world. Now try to direct your attention to both at once—your inner self and the outside world. You will find that you can only do it for a few seconds at a time; then you "forget," and become aware only of either your inner self or the outside world. In certain moments of great excitement or intensity, however, you realize that you can maintain a state of self-remembering for much longer.

Undoubtedly, Gurdjieff's mastery of these disciplines gave him remarkable Psi powers—the way he could revitalize an exhausted follower by some inexplicable transmission of energy is only one example. He was also able to establish telepathic links with his followers. Ouspensky has recalled how, when they were in Finland, he began to hear Gurdjieff's voice inside his chest, and was able to carry on conversations with Gurdjieff who was in another part of the house. At the Prieuré Gurdjieff's pupils would give displays of telepathy for visitors, transmitting the names or shapes of various hidden objects from the audience to the stage. Gurdjieff obviously had profound psychic gifts. One day he told his pupils that a newcomer, who was out of the room, was susceptible to a certain chord of music. When the person came in he struck the chord on the piano, and she immediately underwent a kind of hysterical fit.

There are many stories of Gurdjieff's fund-raising skills that demonstrate not only his special psychological insight but also his sense of humor. Before one of his parties to raise money in

New York, Gurdjieff asked Fritz Peters to teach him all the most obscene four letter words he knew. When a large number of respectable and rich New Yorkers arrived, Gurdjieff began to talk to them about his ideas, gradually introducing more and more talk of sex. Finally his conversation consisted almost entirely of four letter words. His guests relaxed, and then began to flirt with one another. Eventually, all inhibitions gone, they proceeded to behave with total abandon. Suddenly Gurdjieff stood up in the center of the room, thunderously demanded their attention, and then pointed out that he had revealed to them something about themselves that they had never suspected. Surely, he asked, that was worth a large contribution to his institute? At the end of the evening, he was some thousands of dollars richer.

During his lifetime Gurdjieff did not publish any books on the techniques of his teaching, and his pupils were bound to secrecy on the subject. Since his death in Paris in 1949, however, many of his works have been published, and there has been a flood of memoirs by disciples and admirers. Gurdjieff was in almost every respect the antithesis of Aleister Crowley. Whereas Crowley craved publicity, Gurdjieff shunned it. Crowley was forgotten for two decades after his death; Gurdjieff, on the contrary, has become steadily better known, and his influence continues to grow. One of the main reasons for this is that there was so little of the charlatan about him. He is no cult figure with hordes of gullible disciples. What he has to teach makes an appeal to the intelligence, and can be fully understood only by those who are prepared to make a serious effort.

Nevertheless, Gurdjieff undoubtedly understood all the tricks of thought pressure. One of the most typical stories of him is told by the writer and traveler Rom Landau. One day, Landau was sitting in a restaurant with an attractive lady novelist. She was facing away from Gurdjieff, who was sitting on the other side of the restaurant. Suddenly she turned as if she had been struck, and her eyes met Gurdjieff's. Then, blushing, she turned away. Later she admitted to Landau that Gurdjieff had somehow "struck her through her sexual center," inducing a powerful sexual response as if with an intimate caress.

Like Rasputin, Gurdjieff was no saint in his personal relations with women. Unlike Rasputin, however, he knew how to direct and control his extraordinary powers. His disciples regard him as one of the greatest men of the 20th century, and it is not necessary to be a disciple of Gurdjieff's to think that they may be right.

No account of 20th-century occultism would be complete without a word about one of its most remarkable women magicians: Violet Mary Firth, who called herself Dion Fortune. She represents a type of psychic that we have not yet discussed—that is, one who has been sensitive to psychic phenomena from earliest childhood. Another well known psychic, Phoebe Payne, has described how as a child she always saw pretty "auras" surrounding flowers, and was surprised to discover later that they were invisible to most people. Dion Fortune's early insights were less definite than that, but she found herself abnormally sensitive to the atmosphere of places, and able to sense people's hidden thoughts and feelings. Her parents were followers of Christian

Above: Gurdjieff shortly before his death in 1949, when he was 77 years old. His work is still continued by many of his students. Right: Gurdjieff's funeral. For a week after his death his body lay in state while his followers kept a day and night vigil.

Science, and her upbringing in this faith made her aware that there are spiritual forces which operate on a completely different level from the physical forces around us. From the beginning she "walked in two worlds," and later she proved to be a good medium.

At the age of 20 in 1911 she became a teacher in a private school. The principal was a highly domineering woman—a power-hungry bully who had studied the occult in India. After several fierce arguments with the principal, Dion Fortune decided to quit her job. A colleague advised her to leave without telling the principal, saying that if she did not, she would never get away. Against this advice she told her superior. The principal said she was welcome to leave if she first admitted that she was incompetent and had no self-confidence. Dion Fortune indignantly denied the charges. The principal then fixed her with her eyes and repeated the statement hundreds of times for four hours.

Eventually some deep instinct warned Dion Fortune to pretend to give way, and to beg her principal's pardon. The older woman then relented and let her go. But the damage was done: Dion Fortune was a physical and mental wreck for the next three years. After more than a year of the illness, she later wrote, "my body was like an electric battery that has been completely discharged." A psychologist's diagnosis would probably be that the principal had used a kind of hypnotic power to deflate her self-esteem, to make her feel helpless and accident-prone. The effect was to drain her vital reserves, as Gurdjieff would have put it, so that the slightest effort exhausted her. She came to the conclusion

Dion Fortune, who was born Violet Mary Firth. Her magical career appears to have developed as a result of psychic attacks made against her by enemies. She established the Fraternity of the Inner Light, one of the successors to the Golden Dawn.

that the woman had damaged her with a "psychic attack," causing her astral body to leak vital energy. She plunged deep into the study of occultism as an antidote. Perhaps the most interesting part of her account of this experience is her statement that the principal had used not merely hypnotism but also telepathic suggestion—in other words, thought pressure.

In 1920 she met the widow of MacGregor Mathers, who was running a remnant of the original Golden Dawn. Mrs. Mathers at first liked the attractive younger woman, and even agreed when Dion Fortune proposed forming a group of occultists more open to the general public—an idea directly opposed to the secrecy of the original Order. However, after Dion Fortune had written a number of books and articles on occultism, Mrs. Mathers began to feel threatened by the energy and talent of the newcomer. It seems probable that Mrs. Mathers hoped to turn the Golden Dawn into a source of income. In any case, Mrs. Mathers ordered her to stop publicizing the secrets of the Order. According to Dion Fortune, when she ignored the other woman's wishes, Mrs. Mathers launched a black-magic attack on her. The opening salvo seems to have been a plague of black cats: dozens of them invaded Dion Fortune's house, and two of her friends were bothered by the odor of cats in their respective offices several miles away. Then one morning Dion Fortune saw a giant cat walking down the stairs toward her. As she stared, terrified, it vanished—and she realized that someone was using a kind of telepathic hypnotism on her. An hour later, the street outside her home was filled with dozens of howling black cats.

Dion Fortune's major struggle occurred when she made an astral journey. Her description of this is interesting because it gives us some insight into what magicians actually do when they visit the astral plane. A number of her followers formed a circle around her as she lay down and went into a light trance. "In the language of psychology," she wrote, "it is autohypnosis by means of a symbol." (Bear in mind that the Golden Dawn believed certain symbols are universal archetypes from the racial unconscious. Each of these symbols has a precise meaning, and will therefore elicit a particular response.) "The trained initiate, therefore, does not wander on the astral plane like an uneasy ghost, but comes and goes by well-known corridors." In other words, it is essentially a voyage into inner space, which the occultist believes to have a geography as precise as the world we live in, and to be common territory, like the world outside us, in which separate individuals may sometimes meet.

As soon as she had entered this inner space, Dion Fortune became aware of Mrs. Mathers in her magical robes, barring her path. Mrs. Mathers was of a higher grade in magic than Dion Fortune and, therefore, theoretically, stronger. "There ensued a battle of wills in which I experienced the sensation of being whirled through the air and falling from a great height, and found myself back in my body." When she emerged from her trance, her followers were in disarray: she had somersaulted across the room, bowling them over, and was lying in a corner. Realizing that if she were to continue as a magician she had to return to the fight, she ordered the group to reform the circle. After invoking the Secret Chiefs, she went into a trance. "This time, there was a short sharp struggle, and I was through. I had the Vision of the Inner Chiefs and returned. The fight was over. I have never had any trouble since." That night when she undressed to go to bed, Dion Fortune found that her back was scratched—as if clawed by a huge cat.

Of course this story could be pure invention. Yet, in one important respect, that is not the question at issue. We have no way of determining whether the story is objectively true—whether Dion Fortune actually journeyed the corridors of the astral plane. The question is whether the account has its own kind of integrity, and whether the experience was different in kind from an ordinary nightmare. Dion Fortune, like other magicians, certainly took the concept of the magical attack very seriously. She described in one of her books how one of her followers, Netta Fornario, was killed by an "astral attack." Miss Fornario had gone to the Holy Isle of Iona in western Scotland to practice astral travel. One day she seemed panic stricken and told her landlady that she was being attacked telepathically—her silver jewelery had all turned black overnight. The next day her body was found some miles away, dressed only in a magical robe. The soles of her feet were lacerated as if she had run over sharp stones. She had died of a heart attack, and Dion Fortune was convinced that Mrs. Mathers was responsible.

Unfortunately, there is no biography of Dion Fortune, so it is impossible to summarize her life in the 1930s. However, much of her time was spent writing, and her *Psychic Self Defense* and *The Mystical Quabalah* are regarded as classics by occultists.

In 1945 Dion Fortune, using another name, visited a Jungian psychologist. She told him she was convinced that she was approaching a crisis in her life, and wished to undergo analysis. The psychologist's wife was immediately struck by Dion Fortune, even though she only saw her walking through her husband's waiting room. She asked later who it was, and when the doctor asked why she wanted to know, she replied: "I couldn't help noticing that she was just a burned-out shell." One day the doctor and his patient began to discuss the Cabala, and the doctor said that the best book on the subject was Dion Fortune's—whereupon his patient admitted her identity.

At Christmas she arranged to visit the doctor early in the New Year. As he saw her to the door, he had a strong intuition that she would not keep the appointment. Some days later, when he banked a check she had sent him, it was returned marked "drawer deceased." What had seemed to be a general malaise had suddenly flared up into acute leukemia. The doctor, who told me this story and asked that his name be withheld, believed that she had foreseen her crisis and possible death. But she had never told him the details. It seems possible that she had again been involved in some magical battle. But it may have been purely physical causes that undermined her health. Although slim in youth, she became very fat in later life like many mediums do. It has been suggested that such obesity may be due to a peculiar hormone imbalance in mediums. Obesity can certainly damage the health. However, it may be that Dion Fortune had never fully recovered from the original psychic attack by her school principal 34 years earlier.

The Woman Cursed With Cats

Dion Fortune, whose real name was Violet Firth, was just beginning to make a name for herself in occult circles when she met the widow of MacGregor Mathers. Mrs. Mathers was trying to revive the Order of the Golden Dawn, which her husband had helped found.

To begin with Mrs. Mathers was interested in the younger woman, and befriended her. But they disagreed about methods, and their budding friendship turned to bitter rivalry. According to Dion Fortune, Mrs. Mathers began to work spells against her. This took the form of an invasion of cats. The whole house smelled of them. They lounged around doorsteps and windowsills. There seemed no way to get rid of them.

One day Dion Fortune was stunned to see coming down the staircase toward her a giant tabby cat, twice the size of a tiger. It was silent, ominous, absolutely solid, and tangible. Then it vanished. It had been a thought form, projected by someone who possessed immense psychic powers.

Heart pounding, Dion Fortune stared at the place where the huge cat had been, and she knew. The psychic war was on.

They Live Among Us

In Paris in the year 1960 there appeared on the bookstalls a volume with the euphonious title *Le Matin de Magiciens* (The Morning of Magicians) by Louis Pauwels and Jacques Bergier. It is a curious hodgepodge of a book, as the authors themselves recognized, for they wrote in the first chapter: "Skip chapters if you want to; begin where you like, and read in any direction; this book is a multiple-use tool, like the knives campers use . . ." To everyone's astonishment the book became a best seller, running through edition after edition in France. Serious critics were irritated and baffled by its success; they pointed out that the book

Scientists attempting to pinpoint psychic powers are using more and more automation in their tests, pitting ESP against a battery of the most sophisticated machines.

Above: determining which card to select during a test of ESP.

Right: in a test of precognition, the girl tries to influence which of the bulbs will flash next.

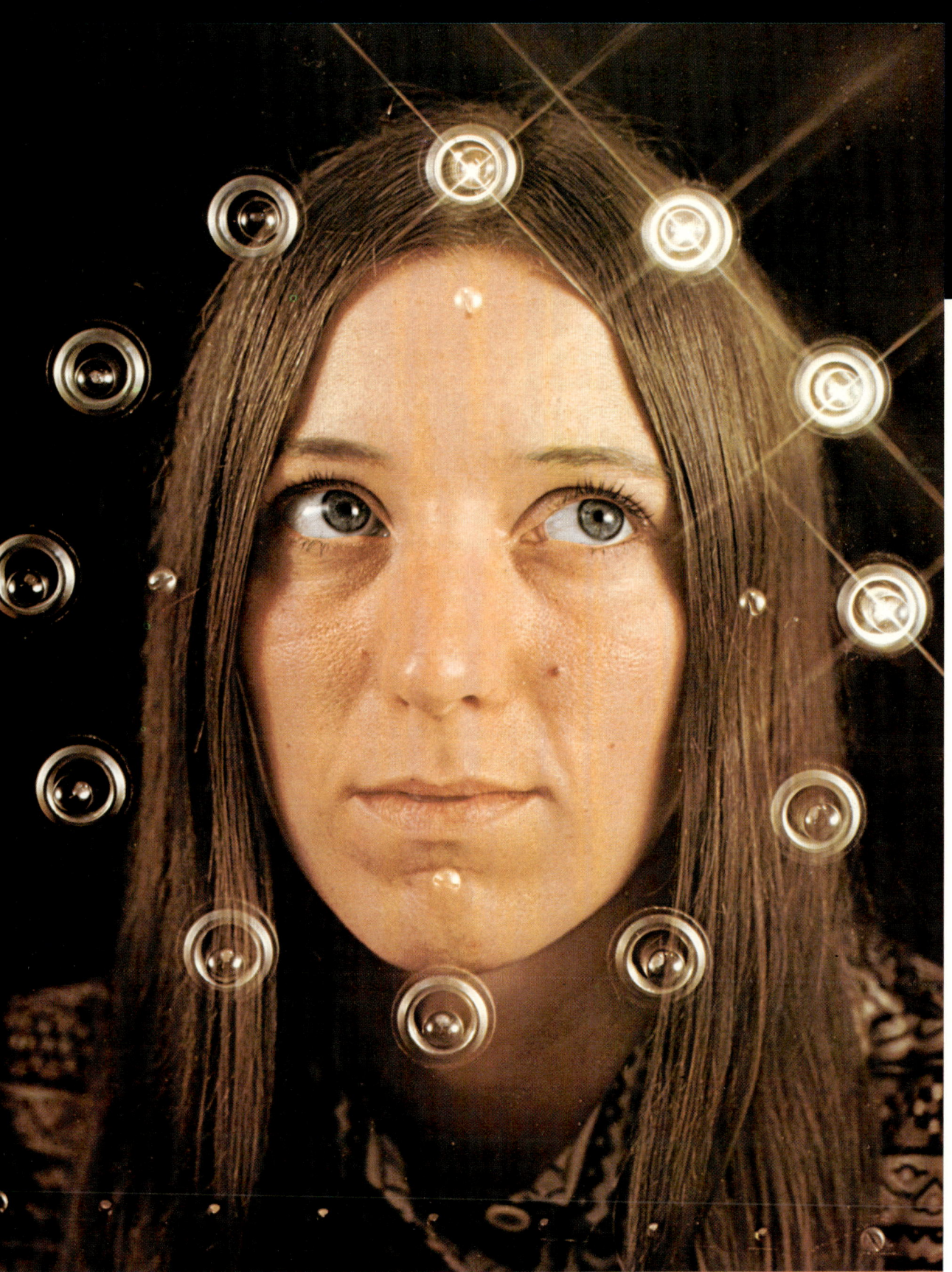

"The most widespread occult revival in history"

was merely a series of wild speculations on magic, alchemy, telepathy, prophecy, strange cults, the Great Pyramid, Hitler's astrologers, the Cabala, flying saucers, and a thousand other topics. This mass of eccentricity was held together by one simple theme: the world is a stranger and richer place than science is willing to recognize.

It was a message that apparently had wide appeal in France, especially to the young. They were less interested in the book's argument about the narrowness of science than in the imaginative appeal of its magical wonders. Other writers saw that there was money to be made out of the occult. Books on astrology, reincarnation, and visitors from outer space rolled off the presses, and there was no sign of any loss of interest. The craze spread to other countries, notably Germany, England, and the United States. In 1968 a German book called *Remembrance of the Future* made a fortune and a name for its author, Erich von Daniken. Translated into English as *Chariots of the Gods?* it sold more copies than any other book except the Bible. Daniken's thesis was that the earth was visited thousands of years ago by spacemen who left signs of their presence in many ancient cultures. Stanley Kubrick's film *2001, A Space Odyssey,* was based on the same idea. It became a kind of cult classic, and its admirers went to see it again and again, just as they might attend a religious ceremony. The great occult boom had arrived.

Curiously enough, a powerful resurgence of interest in the occult has occurred toward the end of every century for the past 400 years. Is this pure chance—or is there, as some people believe, a hidden law that governs such apparently cyclic occult revivals? The question is impossible to answer, but it is clear that we are now in the middle of the most widespread occult revival in history. One of its most significant and encouraging features is that it has captured the interest of a large number of scientists. All over the world universities and other institutions have established laboratories of parapsychology—the scientific investigation of extrasensory perception, clairvoyance, psychokinesis, and other psychic phenomena.

One of the earliest and most famous of these institutes was set up by the biologist Dr. J. B. Rhine at Duke University, North Carolina in the 1920s. Rhine wanted to investigate the belief of gamblers that they can influence the fall of the dice by will power. Eighteen exhaustive series of tests were organized over eight years, and the results mathematically analyzed. There could be no doubt whatever that the results showed an influence on the dice well above what could be expected from mere chance. Perhaps the most interesting finding, however, was that people tested for the first time often showed a high score above chance, but by the third trial, the results usually leveled off to what would be expected from chance. In other words, people got the best results when they were fresh and interested. As they got bored their powers diminished.

In the Netherlands a similar Institute of Parapsychology was set up at the University of Utrecht, with Professor Willem H. C. Tenhaeff in charge. Tenhaeff has devoted much time to testing the powers of the psychic Gerard Croiset.

Left: J. B. Rhine. In 1927, when he and his wife Louisa were both young biologists, they started the Parapsychology Laboratory at Duke University in North Carolina. It has become the best-known center for serious research into the nature of psychic phenomena.

Right: W. H. C. Tenhaeff, the Dutch parapsychologist. About the age of Rhine, Tenhaeff has spent much of his time studying the psychological characteristics of psychic sensitives, in particular the Dutchman Gerard Croiset.

Below: the German professor Hans Bender watching an ESP test as part of an experiment. His area of particular interest has been study of poltergeist phenomena.

Above: Gerard Croiset explaining a police case in which he had helped to Professor Bender.
One of the experiments in which Croiset has participated is the "chair test." In this Croiset predicts the characteristics and some previous experiences of the person whom he foretells will occupy a certain chair in a lecture hall at a future date. These tests have shown impressive abilities of precognition by Croiset.

Croiset was born in 1909. He was unfortunate in being an unhealthy child, and in having to spend much of his childhood in foster homes. But from an early age he somehow knew about things that were happening in other places. Once when a teacher returned to school after a day's absence, Croiset was able to tell him that he had spent the day in a distant place with a girl who wore a red rose in her dress, and whom he would shortly marry. The teacher was amazed. He had, in fact, taken the day off to see his fiancée, who had worn a red rose.

When he was 25 years old Croiset visited the house of an acquaintance, and picked up a stick lying on a table. Immediately his mind became crowded with images of an automobile accident, and of a body lying on the roadside in a grassy place. The owner of the stick was astonished: it was an accurate description of an incident that frequently occupied his own mind. He told Croiset that he must be clairvoyant. Croiset now began to develop his faculty, and had clear visions of the future—of the Nazi invasion of the Netherlands, and of the loss of the Dutch East Indies to the Japanese, for example.

In recent years Croiset has become internationally known as a psychometrist—a person with the gift of reading the past associations of objects by holding them in his hand. The authenticity of this faculty in Croiset cannot be doubted, for he has been employed on numerous occasions by the Dutch police—and often with remarkable success. In 1949, for instance, Croiset was asked to help in a case of a sex crime. The police had suspects, but were by no means certain which, if any, was guilty. Croiset was handed two wrapped objects. Without opening the first he declared correctly that it was a tobacco box. He described the house from which it came and the two middle-aged brothers who lived in the house. He went on to give detailed descriptions of the characters of each of the brothers, and he identified them as the rapists. The second package contained a sack. Croiset immediately saw a cow in connection with it and, in fact, it was used as a cow blanket. He described how the two brothers had taken the girl, a mentally retarded child, to a cowshed with hay on the floor, and raped her. After that, the girl had been put into the sack, and the brothers had discussed what to do with her. One wanted to bury her alive, the other to drown her. The brothers quarreled over this, and the girl was allowed to live.

The two men, who had been among the suspects, were tried separately and convicted. Croiset again correctly foretold that one of them would commit suicide within a week or two of conviction. He was also able to tell the police that the brothers had committed other crimes—among them the rape of a Jewish girl in hiding from the Nazis during the war. He was even able to show them the house where this crime had taken place.

Another Dutchman has become even more famous than Gerard Croiset as a psychometrist who occasionally aids the police. He is Pieter van der Hurk, better known as Peter Hurkos. He also has scored some remarkable hits. In 1958 he was asked by the police of Miami, Florida to sit in the cab of a murdered cab driver and give them his impressions of the killer. As he sat there, Hurkos described the murder of the driver in detail. Then he described the killer as tall and thin, with a tattoo on his right arm and a rolling walk like a sailor. His name, Hurkos said, was Smitty, and he had also been responsible for another murder in Miami—that of a man shot to death in his apartment. The police were stunned. There had been such a murder recently but, as far as they knew, it had no connection with the killing of the cab driver. They searched their files and came up with a photograph of an ex-sailor named Charles Smith. Shortly afterward a waitress interviewed by the police recognized the man in the photograph as a drunk sailor who had boasted to her of killing two men. A wanted alert went out for Smith, who was arrested in New Orleans and sent back to Miami. He confessed to the murder of the cab driver and was sentenced to life imprisonment.

Unlike Croiset, Hurkos was not born clairvoyant. He acquired his extraordinary gift in the Netherlands during World War II as the result of an accident. Knocked uncon-

The Long-distance Psychic Detective

Gerard Croiset Junior, son of the world-famous Dutch psychic who has helped police solve many baffling cases, inherited his father's strange powers. He demonstrated this when he assisted in the case of two missing girls in South Carolina—and he did it from thousands of miles away. It all started when one of the girls' desperate mother, having heard about the Croisets' miraculous ability to locate missing persons, wrote to them in Holland with a plea for help. Croiset Junior replied.

What had happened was that two teenage girls had gone for a walk on Folly Beach near Charleston, South Carolina. They were never seen again. In his reply to the mother, Croiset drew a map of Folly Beach—which he had never seen—including such details as a bus stop and a parked bulldozer. He also wrote a page-and-a-half of comments. The accuracy of the map convinced skeptical police to take him seriously.

In the letter Croiset said: "The girls will be there [on the beach]; they will be together." The police found the girls where Croiset indicated. And they were together—buried in shallow graves in the sand. They had been murdered.

When movie actress Sharon Tate—pregnant with her first child—and four friends were brutally murdered in her home, the world was appalled at the frightening, mindless savagery of the killers.

Left: police cover the bodies of the victims, found scattered in and around the luxurious house.

Below: psychic Peter Hurkos was called in to help reconstruct the crime. Here he studies the room where Sharon Tate died.

scious after a fall from a ladder, he woke up in the hospital with a fractured skull. As he recovered he found to his amazement that he could read people's thoughts, and seemed to know the future. Once when a nurse took his pulse, he told her to be careful or she might lose a suitacase belonging to a friend. The nurse had, in fact, just arrived at the hospital by train, and had left a friend's suitcase behind in the dining car. Hurkos told another patient that he ought to be ashamed of himself for selling the gold watch his father had left him when he died. This, too, was true.

His new faculty almost cost Hurkos his life. A patient who had been discharged from the hospital came to shake his hand—and, in that moment of contact, Hurkos knew that the man

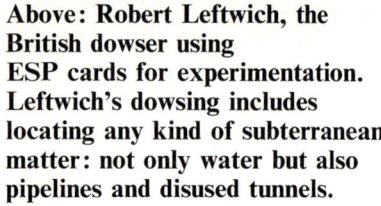

**Above: Robert Leftwich, the
British dowser using
ESP cards for experimentation.
Leftwich's dowsing includes
locating any kind of subterranean
matter: not only water but also
pipelines and disused tunnels.**

would shortly be murdered in the street. The victim was involved in resistance against the Nazis. When gossip about Hurkos' prediction reached the Dutch underground movement, it was assumed that Hurkos was a German counterespionage agent and a member was sent to kill him. It took Hurkos some fast talking to convince his would-be assassin that he was not in the pay of the Nazis.

When Hurkos came out of the hospital he found that he was unable to do normal work. He no longer possessed the power of concentration required for everyday tasks. This is significant. It may well be that psychic powers are inherent in all of us, but that we unconsciously suppress them—not because they are of little help to us in everyday circumstances, but because they would actually impede our survival in the modern world. Croiset had become bankrupt as a grocer before he began to use his clairvoyant powers. Likewise, it was only after someone suggested that Hurkos exploit his extraordinary gift on the stage that he made enough money to support himself.

It is also interesting that Croiset was frequently sick as a child, and that Hurkos' gifts emerged only after an accident. This is not to suggest that strange powers are necessarily accompanied by sickness but only that sickness may be one of the factors which releases psychic sensitivity. On the other hand, many healthy people have deliberately cultivated their psychic powers because they needed them. The tiger hunter Jim Corbett, whose *Man Eaters of Kumaon* has become a modern classic, recounts how his life was saved again and again by his "jungle sensitiveness"—his sudden intuitive knowledge that a man-eater was lying in wait for him.

Another psychic whom I myself have met is the British dowser Robert Leftwich. Leftwich was described in a magazine article as a man of tremendous energy. The article had discussed his dowsing abilities, which he had successfully demonstrated on television, and also his power to project his astral body. Leftwich had also explained how he had used his psychic powers as a child at school. When the class was instructed to learn a long poem by heart, Leftwich would memorize only a few lines. The teacher customarily looked around the class and chose someone to recite each successive passage of the poem. When the passage that he had learned was coming up, Leftwich would will the teacher to ask him to recite. He claimed that the trick had always worked.

Above: Leftwich with his divining rod. It dips down over the spot where the specific element he is looking for is buried. According to Leftwich, it is perfectly possible to go dowsing in the rain. Water in the air does not detract from water underground.

Right: dowsing through another person. Leftwich, blindfolded, can sense when the woman has crossed the underground water.

I was anxious to meet a man who seemed to combine psychic abilities with enormous zest and vitality. I visited him at his home in Sussex, and later he came to my home in Cornwall. His dowsing abilities are undoubtedly remarkable. He demonstrated the dowsing in the house. I hid a coin under a carpet while he was out of the room. He came in with his divining rod and walked around. The rod bent downward violently as he stood over the coin. He explained that for him dowsing is a matter of tuning in the mind to the specific object. If he had been looking for some other object—a playing card or a matchbox—the rod would have ignored the coin, and dipped over the card or matches. He further explained that the rod could also be made to react over everything except what he was looking for. To demonstrate he walked around the room again, and this time the rod twisted violently in his hands until he stood above the coin; then it became still.

We also did thought transference tests with playing cards. I chose a card from the deck while Leftwich stood on the other side of the room, and tried to transmit its identity to him. His score was exceptionally high. But he is convinced that his powers do not depend just on telepathy, so we tried another test. I shuffled a deck of cards and threw the cards face down on the table. At a certain point he said, "Stop. That's the ace of clubs." He was right. He scored four out of seven on this test.

Leftwich also demonstrated a form of telepathic dowsing. He stood with his back to my wife, and asked her to walk away from him across the garden. We knew where underground waterpipes were located, but he did not. At a certain point, however, he called "Stop!" She had just crossed an underground waterpipe, and he had located it by using her mind as a transmitter.

The usual explanation of dowsing is that the mind tunes in to some form of electric field. This was the explanation put forward by the philosopher Professor C. E. M. Joad in one of the British Broadcasting Corporation's *Brains Trust* broadcasts of 1946. But, after suggesting that water emits some form of electrical radiation that can be detected by the dowser, Joad went on to admit that he had no idea of the explanation of map dowsing. The map dowser holds a pendulum over a map, and the pendulum begins to swing or vibrate when it is held over the substance he is looking for—water, oil, minerals, or even gold. Joad described how he had witnessed map dowsing in action. A large-scale map, from which all rivers and streams had been carefully removed, was laid out on a table. The map dowser went over it with a pendulum, on the end of which was a small bobbin that could spin. The bobbin spun every time the pendulum was suspended over a place where the dowser detected water. At the end of the session, the dowser had located every river, stream, and pond in the area.

Obviously Joad's theory about radiation cannot explain this. Then how can it be explained? Once again, we are driven to return to the hypothesis that the secret lies in our own minds, but not necessarily in the subconscious mind—the Freudian "basement" that is supposed to contain all our most primitive animal impulses. Leftwich, like many other occultists, believes

Above: there are practical applications of dowsing. Here for instance Leftwich is dowsing over a map. Using this method, he is able to locate underground hazards, such as abandoned tunnels, or sources of water in isolated areas that are difficult to reach. This enables development plans to be made with considerably greater knowledge of the site than would be possible from a survey done by the conventional methods.

Right: the resident site engineer demonstrates a sophisticated set of divining rods that a large building contracting firm has considered a worthwhile investment. The small strings contain samples of different materials, such as copper, lead, cast iron, plastic. The user holds the appropriate string in his fingers, and the rods react if they pass over the material. Apparently anyone can use the rods, although some people get a reaction more easily than others. The builders use the rods mainly to locate underground pipes, high-tension voltage lines, and other obstructions on the sites.

that the answer may lie in a part of the mind which could be called the "superconscious." If the mind can have a subconscious basement, might it not also possess a superconscious "attic"?

It was nearly a century ago that respectable scientists such as Sir William Crookes and Sir Oliver Lodge began to take an interest in the paranormal. At that time it looked as if the answers to the questions raised might rest reassuringly within the concepts of life after death, and of a universe of benevolent spirits doing their best to give help and guidance to the living on earth. But since that time every decade has revealed new mysteries, and the problem of finding a single explanation becomes increasingly difficult.

Let us take a look at some of the experiences of Dr. Andija Puharich, a researcher whom Aldous Huxley described as "one of the most brilliant minds on parapsychology." In 1952 Dr. Puharich investigated the case of Harry Stone, a young Dutch sculptor. In deep trance states Stone spoke ancient Egyptian and wrote hieroglyphics—neither of which he had the slightest knowledge of in his normal state. The messages purported to come from one Ra Ho Tep, an Egyptian of the Fourth Dynasty about 2700 B.C.

In 1963 Puharich heard about José Arigó, a Brazilian healer called the "surgeon of the rusty knife." In April of that year he went to Arigó's town to watch the wonder worker in action. The surgeon proved to be a barrel-chested peasant who thought himself possessed by the spirit of a dead German doctor. Puharich watched Arigó deal with 200 patients in four hours, performing many operations without anesthetic and at great speed. Arigó removed a tumor from Puharich's own arm in a few seconds. Puharich felt nothing, and the flesh healed in four days without disinfectant or antibiotics. In 1971 Arigó was killed in a car accident. Puharich received the news by telephone, but was unable to confirm it from any of the news agencies. Later that day he discovered that Arigó had been killed that morning, as his caller had said. But when Puharich looked for the phone number of the caller, which he had written on a notepad, it had vanished. Moreover, his secretary who had been with him throughout the day could not recollect him taking the phone call.

This anecdote is recounted in Puharich's most baffling book, *Uri, a Journal of the Mystery of Uri Geller*. Puharich was drawn to Geller by accounts of his feats of mind reading, spoon bending, and his curious power over watches. At his first meeting with Geller, Puharich witnessed some remarkable feats. Geller told a woman to hold a ring in her hand, and placed his left hand over her clenched fist for 30 seconds. At the end of that time the ring was found to be broken into two pieces. Geller also demonstrated his powers of telepathy by performing a reading of the future. He wrote three numbers on a pad and placed it face down on the table. Then he asked Puharich to think of three numbers. Puharich selected the numbers 4, 3 and 2. Uri then turned over the pad—on which was written the figures 4, 3, 2. Geller explained that his experiment did not involve precognition, because he had transmitted the numbers to Puharich. In still other demonstrations of his strange powers, Geller changed the time on Puharich's watch as Puharich held it in his own hand, and raised the temperature of a metal thermometer by eight degrees without touching it.

If this were all it would be remarkable enough. But Puharich goes on to make such a startling claim that one's first response is to doubt his sincerity. Briefly he says that Geller is a kind of savior or messiah, controlled by beings from outer space that are hovering a few million miles away in a spaceship called *Spectra*. These beings had apparently visited earth on a number of previous occasions, and had also selected the patriarch Abraham and the Pharaoh Imhotep as avatars, or incarnations of a divine being.

Given the present worldwide interest in the occult, one might expect Puharich's book to have created a sensation and become a best seller. Instead, it was received with a mixture of indifference and hostility. This is not to say that most critics thought Puharich was a liar. Many of them obviously felt that Puharich was sincere but mistaken. Geller has told me that everything in Puharich's book is factually accurate, but that he himself does not necessarily accept the notion that he is a messiah. This raises some fascinating questions, not merely about Geller and Puharich but also about the whole subject of the occult. The fact that a person possesses certain powers proves nothing about the source of those powers. Impressive documentary evidence seems to prove beyond all doubt that the Victorian medium Daniel Dunglass Home was able to wash his face in red hot coals without getting singed, and could cause heavy tables to float through the air. But this does not prove, as he claimed, that his powers came from spirits rather than from his own subconscious mind. Joan of Arc declared that she had been ordered to save France by St. Michael and St. Catherine, and the Church that has sanctified her apparently accepts her claim. But did her voices have any greater reality than those of the beings that visited Geller? In the long history of messianic religious movements, dozens of messiahs have astounded their followers by apparently genuine miracles, such as levitating, healing the sick, and conferring immunity against weapons.

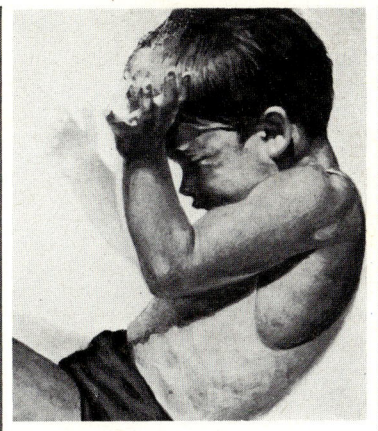

A Great Bowl Hanging in the Sky

One day in December 1949, when the boy that would grow up to be the psychic Uri Geller was only three years old, he wandered across the street from the apartment in which he lived with his mother in Tel Aviv, Israel. He crawled through the fence into the magnificent garden of a big house, and wandered in the unaccustomed splendor until the beauty and peace lulled him to sleep.

When he woke he noticed with fascination that a great silent bowl was settling down from the sky. Suddenly between the small boy and the bowl was the shadow of an enormous figure with no arms or legs. A blinding ray came from the place where the face should be. This ray struck the child so forcibly that he toppled over and went into another deep sleep. When he woke the second time, he was cold, it was dusk, and the bowl was gone. He remembered the dazzling light; but instead of being afraid, he felt quiet and peaceful. Uri scampered home and told his mother about his experience. She spanked him for running away, and for making up such stories.

Is it possible, however, that Uri Geller owes his psychic power to the mysterious ray shot he told his mother about?

But as their promises about the end of the world have proven untrue, we must conclude that most of them were self-deceivers, however authentic their strange powers. Similarly, Puharich's claims regarding Geller's gifts may be true—but this does not prove that Geller is a messiah or that the spaceship *Spectra* exists.

This still leaves us with the basic question: What is the source of energy or power behind these events—and behind so many psychic phenomena? There seem to be two possibilities: what we have called the superconscious, or spirits or celestial intelligences. The problem with the idea of a superconscious is that, while it is easy enough to understand its role in map dowsing or precognition, it is altogether more difficult to under-

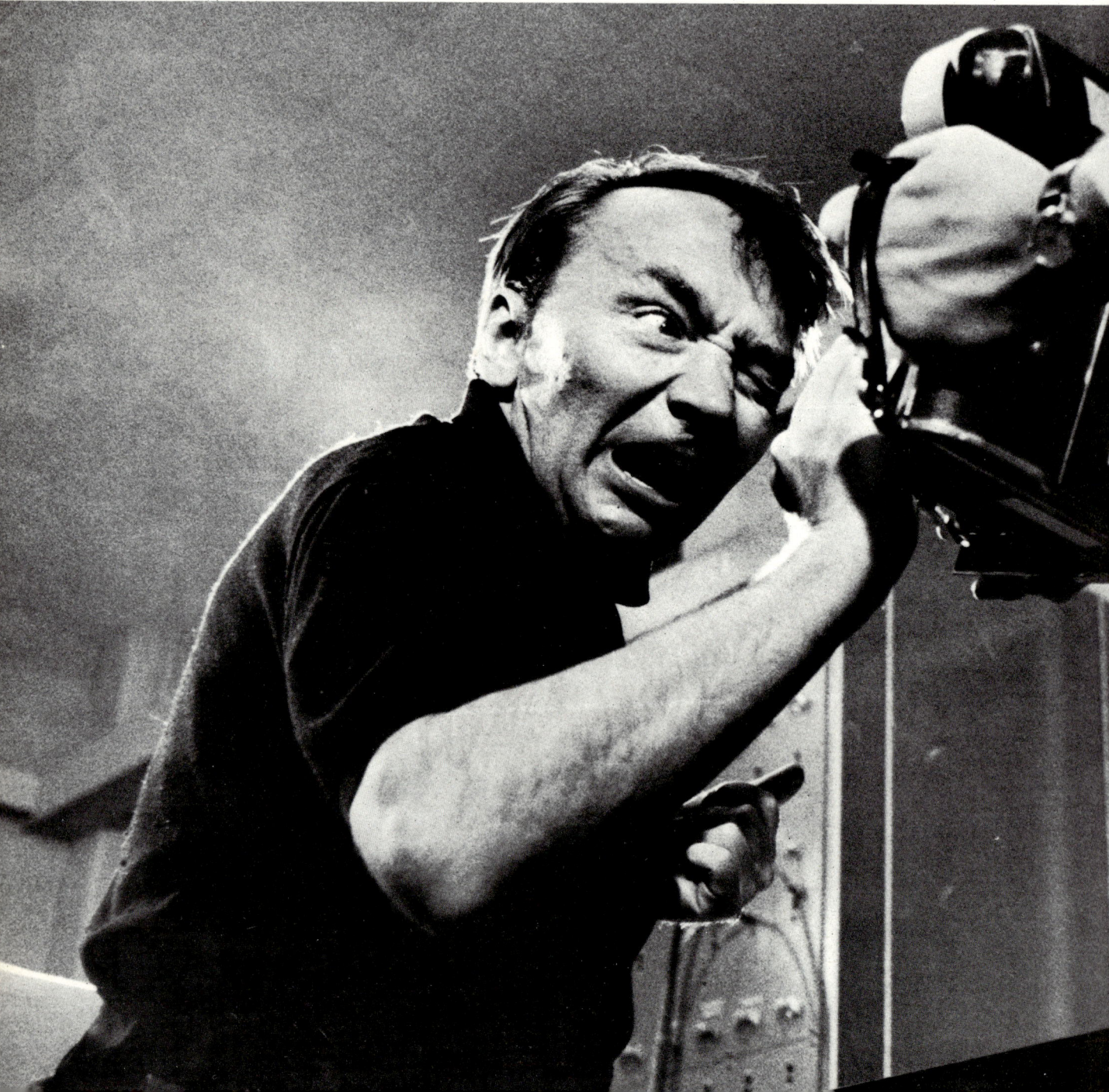

Below: with an enormous explosion of energy Ted Serios yells "Now!" and his assistant flicks the shutter. But instead of Serios' face, the picture shows a foggy image of what he says is going on in his head—images projected directly from his mind onto film.

stand why it should conceive flying saucers and beings from outer space. Is it possible that the superconscious possesses a sense of humor? Many students of the paranormal would say that this is, indeed, a possibility, to the extent that the activities of the superconscious may be completely freakish and unexplainable.

Consider the curious case of the Abbot Vachère of Mirebeau in France. In 1913 the abbot was regarded as a kindly and conscientious member of the church, well liked by the Pope himself, but without any remarkable talent. He was in his sixtieth year when the first of a series of strange and rather embarrassing events began and drops of reddish moisture began to ooze from the hands and feet of the figure of Jesus in a

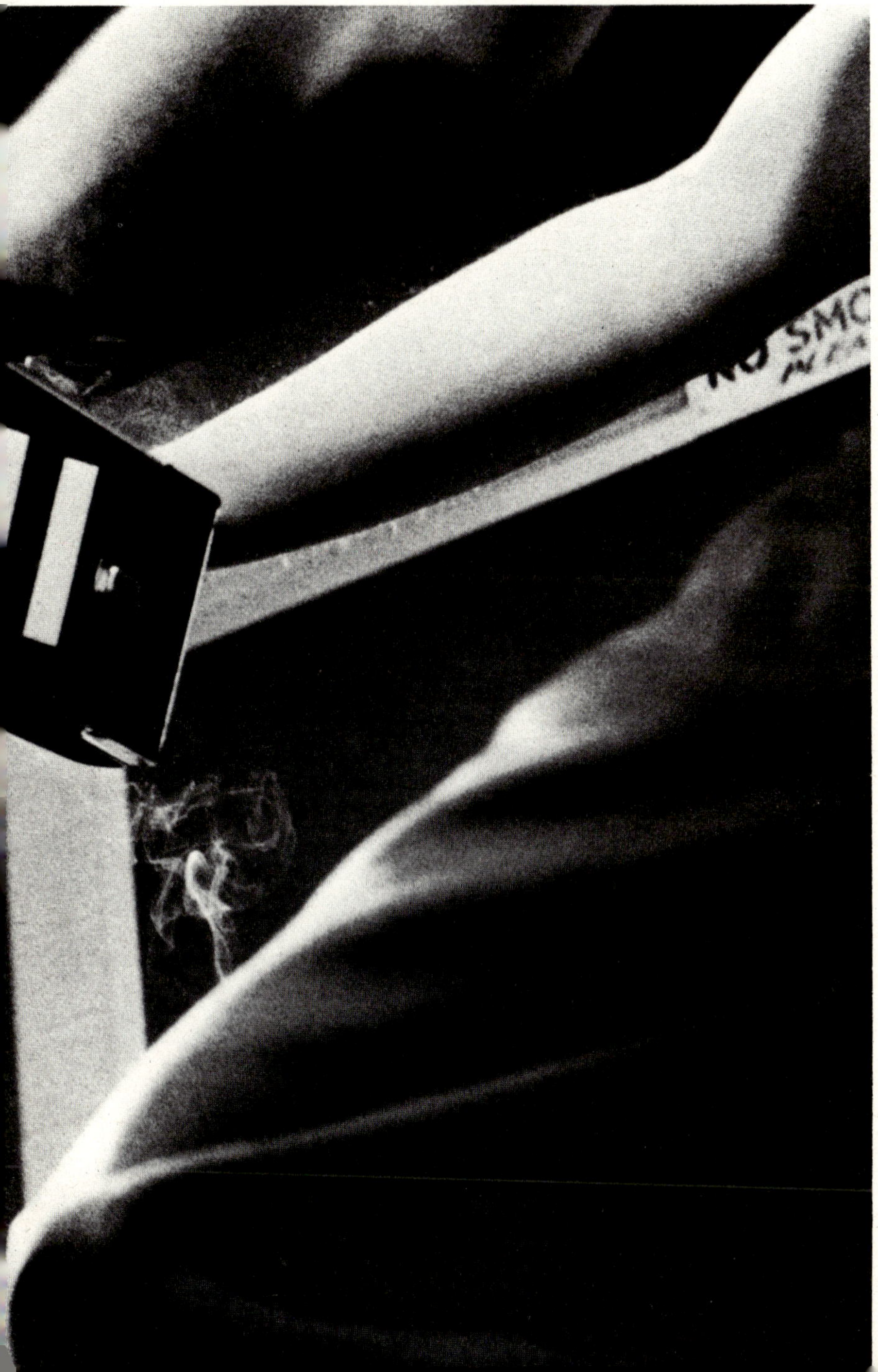

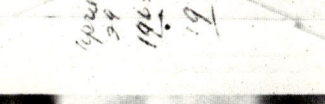

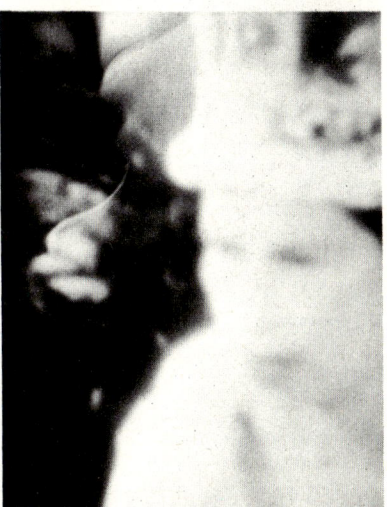

Above: two of the clearer thought-photographs obtained by Serios during tests conducted by the psychiatrist Dr. Eisenbud. The top one is of Queen Elizabeth II, the lower one of cars with what Eisenbud identifies as Serios' eye mysteriously superimposed.

painting that hung in Vachère's private chapel. Vachère reported the matter to his Bishop who asked to see the picture. It was dispatched to the Bishop, but failed to bleed. When it was returned to its chapel, however, the bleeding started again.

Later, a gang of workmen were building Stations of the Cross near the abbot's home, and Vachère pinned up an ordinary color print of Jesus in their hut. This also began to bleed. The bishop investigated, decided that Vachère was a fraud, and excommunicated the abbot. The bewildered and unhappy Vachère visited his friends at Aix-la-Chapelle; with him in the house, a statue and a picture belonging to his hostess began to bleed.

Many people felt that the bleeding indicated that Abbot Vachère was a saint—or, at least, that he had been selected by God for some special destiny. The Church had no reason to think so, and refused to investigate the phenomena which, however, continued to occur until the abbot died in 1921.

The evidence leaves little doubt that the phenomena were genuine. On the other hand, the Church probably showed common sense in refusing to accept them as evidence of sanctity. Possibly the bleeding statues and pictures were a trick perpetrated by the abbot's superconscious. In any event, like the fakirs' wonders, the phenomena were spiritually worthless.

In a demonstration of his work for a German television team filming in Denver, Serios began by drawing a sketch of his idea of a primitive man (right). Then, using a cylinder that he calls a gismo, and which was prepared by the film makers to be sure no devices were added, he produced a series of pictures. At first they were totally black, but finally one came up with a crouching man (above left). Later the team noticed the coincidental resemblance of what Serios had photographed to an exhibit of a primitive group in the Field Museum of Natural History located in Chicago.

This story illustrates the fact that most human beings, churchmen as well as scientists, find supernatural phenomena embarrassing and prefer to ignore them. Such phenomena fail to conform to the laws of nature as we know them. Consequently they tend to be regarded as irrelevant freaks rather than as interesting pieces of some as yet unsolved universal jigsaw puzzle.

A similar attitude was shown toward a series of experiments made by Dr. Jule Eisenbud, a psychiatrist and member of the faculty of the University of Colorado Medical School. In 1963 Eisenbud published an article arguing that it is impossible to devise a truly repeatable experiment in the field of paranormal phenomena. A correspondent disagreed and sent him a magazine clipping about a man called Ted Serios. According to the article, Serios could take photographs by means of the mind alone. He would take a polaroid camera in his hands, stare hard into the lens, and somehow produce photographs of recognizable places, of faces or people, or of objects such as cars and buses.

Eisenbud's interest was aroused and he arranged a demonstration. Serios proved to be a bellhop of alcoholic tendencies, who also claimed to have the power of projecting his astral body. But the second claim was unconnected with the ability he demonstrated to Eisenbud. He stared down a small paper tube, which he called his "gismo," toward the camera lens. After a number of failures he succeeded in producing two blurry pictures of a water tower and a hotel. In considerable excitement, Eisenbud immediately got in touch with various scientists and told them what had happened. To his astonishment, they showed only polite interest, and had no wish to see a demonstration. Eisenbud was encountering the reaction we have mentioned above—the embarrassment effect produced by freakish and apparently inexplicable events.

Eisenbud refused to be deterred, however. He continued to test Serios, and some of the resulting "thought photographs" were spectacular. Naturally Eisenbud's first suspicion—like that of everybody else who tested Serios—had been that the trick lay in the gismo. Serios insisted that the tube of paper merely helped him to concentrate, and close examination of the gismo revealed nothing suspicious. Eisenbud concluded that Serios's powers were genuine, even if they made no sense in terms of any scientific law.

Charles Reynolds and David Eisendrath, two reporters who had watched Serios at work, were convinced he was a fake. They constructed a small device that could be hidden inside the gismo, with a lens at one end and a piece of unexposed film at the other. When this was pointed at the camera, the result was a picture not unlike those that Serios had produced. The account of their invention was printed in *Popular Photography* in 1967, and it gave all the skeptics fresh ammunition. Since then, their article has been cited by people who believe that Serios is a fake, as evidence that he performed his thought photography by sleight of hand. In March, 1974 *Time* magazine ran an article on the occult revival, and included a brief account of Serios and the *Popular Photography* article. *Time* concluded: "Many of

Serios's followers were shattered. Again, the millennium was deferred."

Now it is certainly possible that Serios is a fraud. But Reynolds and Eisendrath have done nothing to prove the contention. They merely demonstrated that they themselves could construct a gismo fitted with a lens and film. Dr. Eisenbud vainly pointed out that he and other experimenters had examined Serios's gismo for such fraud, and had found none.

My aim here is not to defend Serios—although thought photography is no less extraordinary than paintings that bleed or spoons that bend—but to point out that orthodox science is still a long way from taking a balanced and truly scientific attitude toward paranormal phenomena. There exists a deeply ingrained emotional prejudice that is just as likely to obscure the truth as are the wishful thinking of gullible parapsychologists and the dishonesty of fraudulent psychics.

Finally, if we discard the idea of the superconscious, is it remotely possible that some of these strange forces come from outside man? Might there be other intelligences—either spirits of the dead or creatures from other worlds—that are controlling or influencing the destiny of this planet?

The idea of life outside earth has received support from a number of scientists, but it must be admitted that the evidence is far from convincing. Some scientists have suggested that certain radio signals received from outer space may have been sent by intelligent beings. We also have the curious accounts of people who claim to have been in communication with creatures from flying saucers.

William Paley, a late 18th-century British theologian, used his watch as an argument for the existence of God. He argued that when we open the back and see the works, it is impossible not to recognize that it has been created by an intelligent mind. Therefore when we contemplate the universe, which is far more complex than a watch, how is it possible not to believe that it was created by an intelligent being? The followers of the scientist Charles Darwin were contemptuous of this argument. They insisted that the complexity of the universe—like the complexity of a snow crystal—is due to the operation of natural laws. This argument is not very convincing either, for the complexity of the universe in infinitely greater than that of a snow crystal. Next time you take a walk in the countryside, look at every living thing—trees, flowers, insects, birds, rivers, clouds. Then ask yourself whether you can imagine that they could have been produced by purely mechanical laws.

Intelligences from outer space or the human superconscious mind? Either explanation is possible, and it may be that there is truth in both. But for the human race at this point in history, the most fruitful line of inquiry undoubtedly lies within ourselves. The secret of the powers of shamans, of magicians, of psychics and clairvoyants probably lies in some unexplored part of our inner space. When man invents a spacecraft that will carry him to his own inner moons and planets, he will have discovered the secret that every magician has sought—a secret more fascinating than the Philosopher's Stone or the Elixir of Life.

La Reconnaissance Infinie (The Infinite Search), a 1933 work by the Belgian surrealist artist René Magritte. The painting seems to call up many of the questions we have about the inexplicability of the universe—and about our place in its mysterious scheme.

Picture Credits

2 The Metropolitan Museum of Art, Catherine D. Wentworth Fund, 1950

4 Harry Price Library, University of London

7-9(C) © Yale Joel 1974

9(B) Colin Wilson

10-1 © Yale Joel 1974

12 from J. G. Bennett, *Witness: The Story of a Search*, Hodder and Stoughton Limited, London, 1962

13 from J. G. Bennett, *Gurdjieff: Making a New World*, Turnstone Books, London, 1973

14-5 A. Eisenstaedt *Life* © Time Inc. 1975

17 Leif Geiges, Staufen, Germany

18(L) Victoria & Albert Museum, London/Photo Eileen Tweedy © Aldus Books

18(R) Don Snyder *Life* © Time Inc. 1975

20-1 Brian Lewis/Linden Artists © Aldus Books

22 photos Dmitri Kasterine © Aldus Books

23 from Rolf Alexander, M.D., *The Power of the Mind*, T. Werner Laurie, Ltd., London, 1956

24 Herbert A. Parkyn, *Suggestive Therapeutics and Hypnotism*, Chicago, 1900

25 Victoria & Albert Museum, London/Photo Eileen Tweedy © Aldus Books

26 Nicolaes Witsen, *Noord en Oost Tartarye*, 1705

27 The Mansell Collection

28 The Metropolitan Museum of Art, Catherine D. Wentworth Fund, 1950

29 reproduced by Gracious Permission of Her Majesty The Queen

30(L) The Mansell Collection

30(R) Victoria & Albert Museum, London/Photo Eileen Tweedy © Aldus Books

31 George du Maurier, *Trilby*, London, 1895

32-3 reproduced by permission of the British Library Board

32(B) Süddeutscher Verlag-Bilderdienst, München

33(B) Ullstein GmbH-Bilderdienst, West Berlin

34(T) reproduced by permission of the British Library Board

34-5(B), 36(T) British Library/Photos R. B. Fleming © Aldus Books

36(B) photo Donald Cooper for the Royal Shakespeare Company

37 The Mansell Collection

38-41 reproduced by permission of the British Library Board

42 Harry Price Library, University of London

43 Raghubir Singh/The John Hillelson Agency

44-5 from André Sollier and Zsolt Györbiró, *Japanese Archery: Zen in Action*, John Weatherhill, Inc., Tokyo

46(B) *The Gospel of Sri Ramakrishna*, translated by Swami Nikhilananda, Sri Ramakrishna Math, Mylapore, Madras, 1957

47(T) Victoria & Albert Museum. British Crown Copyright

47(B) from *How You Can Talk With God*, Self-Realization Fellowship, Los Angeles, 1973

48-9(T) Harry Price Library, University of London

49(B) Elda Hartley/Colorific!

50(TL) Jacob Boehme, *Die Weidergebuhrt*, 1682

50(TR) Jacob Boehme, *Theosophia Revelata*, 1715

50(B) reproduced by permission of the British Library Board

52-3 Bruno Elettori © Aldus Books

54(T) William White, *Emanuel Swedenborg*, London, 1867

54(B) trans. and ed. Alfred Acton, *The Mechanical Inventions of Emanuel Swedenborg*, Swedenborg Scientific Association, Philadelphia, 1939

55 Michael Holford Library photo

57(T) The National Gallery of Scotland/Photo Tom Scott © Aldus Books

57(B) Vincent van Gogh: *The Starry Night* (1889). Oil on canvas 29 × 36¼ inches. Collection, The Museum of Modern Art, New York. Acquired through the Lillie P. Bliss Bequest.

58 Bibliothèque Nationale, Paris

59 Mary Evans Picture Library

62 Victoria & Albert Museum, London/Photo Eileen Tweedy © Aldus Books

63 Ann Dunn © Aldus Books

64 Henry Cornelius Agrippa, *De Occultia Philosophia*, 1633

66-7 Gianetto Coppola © Aldus Books

68 Henry Cornelius Agrippa, *De Occultia Philosophia*, 1633

69 photo Eileen Tweedy © Aldus Books

70(L) Paracelsus: *Prognosticatio*, 1536

70(R) Musée du Louvre, Paris/Photo Giraudon

71 Paracelsus: *Der Grosse Wundartzney*, 1562

72-3 Bibliothèque Nationale, Paris

74 MacQuitty International Collection

75(L) Bibliothèque de Troyes/Photo © Aldus Books

75(R) *Radio Times* Hulton Picture Library

76(T) Musée de Versailles/Photo © Aldus Books

76(B) *Memoire pour Le Comte de Cagliostro*, Paris 1786

77 British Museum/Photo R. B. Fleming © Aldus Books

79 *The Astrologer of the Nineteenth Century*, London, 1825

81(TL) Jean Overton Fuller, *The Magical Dilemma of Victor Neuburg*, W. H. Allen & Co., Ltd., London, 1965

81(TR)(B) ed. John Symonds and Kenneth Grant, *The Confessions of Aleister Crowley*, Jonathan Cape Ltd., London, and Farrar, Straus & Giroux, Inc., New York

82 Siena Cathedral/Scala

83 Michael Holford Library photo

84 reproduced by permission of the Trustees of the British Museum

85 The Mansell Collection

86 *The Astrologer of the Nineteenth Century*, London, 1825

87 Ashmolean Museum, Oxford

88 Eliphas Lévi, *Dogme et Rituel de la Haute Magie, Vol. I*, Paris 1861

89 Christopher McIntosh, *Eliphas Lévi and the French Occult Revival*, Rider & Co., London, 1972

90(TL) Eliphas Lévi, *Dogme et Rituel de la Haute Magie, Vol. I.* Paris 1861

90(TR)(B) Eliphas Lévi, *Histoire de la Magie*, Paris, 1860

91(T) The Mansell Collection

91(B) *Radio Times* Hulton Picture Library

92 ed. John Symonds and Kenneth Grant, *The Confessions of Aleister Crowley*, Jonathan Cape Ltd., London, and Farrar, Straus & Giroux, Inc., New York

93 Frater Volo Intellegere

95(T) Francis King: *Ritual Magic in England*, Neville Spearman Ltd., London, 1970

95(B) ed. John Symonds and Kenneth Grant, *The Confessions of Aleister Crowley*, Jonathan Cape Ltd., London, and Farrar, Straus & Giroux, Inc., New York

96(L) National Gallery of Ireland

96(R) The Mansell Collection

98-9 Gianetto Coppola © Aldus Books

100-4 ed. John Symonds and Kenneth Grant, *The Confessions of Aleister Crowley*, Jonathan Cape Ltd., London, and Farrar, Straus & Giroux, Inc., New York

105(T) *Radio Times* Hulton Picture Library

105(B)-7 ed. John Symonds and Kenneth Grant, *The Confessions of Aleister Crowley*, Jonathan Cape Ltd., London, and Farrar, Straus & Giroux, Inc., New York

108 René Fulop-Muller, *Rasputin, the Holy Devil*, G. P. Putnam's Sons, 1928

109 The Mansell Collection

111(T) *Radio Times* Hulton Picture Library

111(B) The Mansell Collection

112 *Radio Times* Hulton Picture Library

113 René Fulop-Muller, *Rasputin, the Holy Devil*, G. P. Putnam's Sons, 1928

115(T) from J. G. Bennett, *Witness: The Story of a Search*, Hodder and Stoughton Limited, London, 1962

115(B) Rom Landau, *God is My Adventure*, Faber & Faber Ltd., London, 1939

116 Margaret Anderson

117 from J. G. Bennett, *Witness: The Story of a Search*, Hodder and Stoughton Limited, London, 1962

118 Helios Book Service

120-1 Bruno Elettori © Aldus Books

122-3 Henry Groskinsky © Time Inc. 1975

125-6 Leif Geiges, Staufen, Germany

127 photo Henk Brusse

128(L) Rex Features Ltd.

128(TR) Associated Press

129 Julian Wasser *Life* © Time Inc. 1975

130-3 photos Dmitri Kasterine © Aldus Books

134 © Yale Joel 1974

136-7 Bruno Elettori © Aldus Books

138 Jerry Brimacombe © Time Inc. 1975

139(R), 140(L) Psycho-Physical Research Foundation

141(T) Field Museum of Natural History, Chicago

141(B) Psycho-Physical Research Foundation

143 R. Magritte, *La Reconnaissance Infinie*, 1933 © by A.D.A.G.P., Paris, 1974

Spirits and
Spirit Worlds

Spirits and Spirit Worlds

by Roy Stemman

Aldus Books · Jupiter Books

Series Coordinator: John Mason
Design Director: Günter Radtke
Picture Editor: Peter Cook
Editor: Eleanor Van Zandt
Copy Editor: Mitzi Bales
Research: Frances Vargo
General Consultant: Beppie Harrison

SBN 490 00333 8

© 1975 Aldus Books Limited London

First published in the United Kingdom
in 1975 by Aldus Books Limited
17 Conway Street, London W1P 6BS

Distributed by Jupiter Books
167 Hermitage Road, London N4 1LZ

Printed and bound in Italy by
Amilcare Pizzi S.p.A.
Cinisello Balsamo (Milano)

**Frontispiece: psychic painting by Ethel Le Rossignol.
Above: Victorian photograph of a spirit materializing.**

EDITORIAL CONSULTANTS:

COLIN WILSON
DR. CHRISTOPHER EVANS

After we die, what? This question has been tantalizing mankind since we first began to wonder. Although science firmly claims that death is the end, religion and popular legend still maintain that the spirit goes on—and some even believe that it is possible for the living to make contact with the dead. In the middle of the last century, this conviction seemed suddenly bolstered by new evidence: in a small cottage in New York, a message given in raps was said to come from a dead man. This event opened the floodgates. All over America and Europe the spirits hastened to communicate. Mediums flourished—and so did fraud. Belief and disbelief came together in elaborate tests and ingenious equipment and, at the end, the question still remained. Do the spirits speak? Here is the evidence we have so far.

1

The Hydesville Rappings

John Fox was determined to discover the cause of the strange noises that had kept his family awake for several nights. He rattled a window in the tiny cottage, expecting to find the sashes loose. As if in reply, an echoing rattle sounded in the room.

"Do as I do," said his seven-year-old daughter Kate, as she clapped her hands playfully. The same number of raps was heard as if tapped out by invisible hands.

"No, do just as I do. Count one, two, three, four," chimed in Margaret aged 10. When exactly four raps were heard, Margaret was too frightened to go on with the game the children had started.

THE BIRTHPLACE OF
MODERN SPIRITUALISM
UPON THIS SITE STOOD THE HYDESVILLE COTTAGE
THE HOME OF THE
FOX SISTERS
THROUGH WHOSE MEDIUMSHIP COMMUNICATION
WITH THE SPIRIT WORLD WAS ESTABLISHED
MARCH 31, 1848
THERE IS NO DEATH
THERE ARE NO DEAD
PLACED HERE BY M.E. CADWALLADER
DEC. 5, 1927

"The unseen presence in the cottage"

The mysterious rappings in the little house in Hydesville, New York in 1848 not only disrupted the Fox family, but also heralded the birth of Spiritualism. The years following the experience of the Fox family with the rappings saw the beginning and growth of this controversial new movement—called a religion by some—as people on both sides of the Atlantic tried to make contact with departed spirits.

The Fox family devised a simple method of communicating with the unseen presence in the cottage. They asked it questions that could be answered simply "yes" (one rap) or "no" (two raps). Using this code, the presence identified itself as the spirit of a murdered peddler whose body had been buried beneath the cottage. News of the rappings spread rapidly in the small town, and soon the Foxes invited their neighbors into the house to hear conversations with the dead peddler's spirit. When John Fox suggested digging in the cellar to search for the peddler's body, there were plenty of volunteers. However, the dig had to be abandoned when water was struck.

A few months later, however, digging in the cellar was resumed. At a depth of five feet the diggers found a plank, and below the plank, buried in charcoal and quicklime, fragments of hair and bones believed to be part of a human skeleton.

The rest of the skeleton was found 56 years later according to a story in the *Boston Journal* of November 23, 1904. The paper reported that part of a rough wall a yard from the cellar had fallen down. During excavations to repair it, workmen unearthed an almost complete human skeleton. There was a peddler's tin box near the bones. This discovery led to the theory that the murderer—if there was one—first buried the body in the cellar of the house and then, fearing discovery, dug it up and buried it between the two walls.

Spiritualists believe the peddler caused the rappings in order to bring his murderer to justice. If so, the attempt was a failure. The Foxes made his name out as Charles B. Rosma, but such a person was never traced. A maid, Lucretia Pulver, who four years before had worked for tenants of the house in which the Foxes lived, came forward at the time of the rapping sensation. She told of a peddler's visit to the house when it was rented by her employers, a Mr. and Mrs. Bell. The peddler stayed the night, said Miss Pulver, and she was sent home to her parents. On her return, she was told that the peddler had left.

Even before the Foxes moved in the cottage had had an uncanny reputation, and the previous tenant had left because of the mysterious noises. But there was nothing new about such rappings. History and legend are full of stories of similar disturbances. The Fox family made history by being the first to establish a dialogue with the noises. March 31, 1848, the day on which the first communication occurred, is now regarded as the birth date of Spiritualism.

However, the ground had been prepared for the Spiritualist movement. The most illustrious of its forerunners was Emanuel Swedenborg. This Swedish philosopher and scientist, born in 1688, was a man of wide-ranging abilities. He was an authority on metallurgy, an astronomer, a zoologist, anatomist, physicist, financier, and a profound biblical scholar. In middle age, he

Above: a drawing of the dramatic moment in the Fox house when the girls, Kate and Margaret, first playfully challenged the strange rattling and rapping noises to repeat their own patterns of raps. To the family's surprise, the exact patterns were repeated.

Above: the parents of the girls, John Fox and his wife Margaret. Right: a 1930s postcard of the original Fox cottage in which the mysterious rappings were first heard. The cottage has since burned down, and an exact replica stands as a replacement.

SPIRITUALISM ORIGINATED MARCH 31 1848 IN THIS HOUSE, NEWARK, N.Y.

developed psychic powers, often in the form of visions.

Swedenborg began to write seriously about the spiritual world in 1744. In dreams during sleep and in visions during wakefulness he wandered in the next world where he was instructed, so he claimed, by the spirits of kings, popes, saints, and biblical personages. His accounts aroused considerable interest in the afterlife, and introduced a new concept of its nature. The established Christian belief was that on a person's death, his soul went to Heaven or Hell—or, as Catholics believe, to Purgatory. In any case, the soul's afterlife was believed to be totally different from its earthly life, and totally separated from this world. By contrast, Swedenborg described afterlife as being very similar to this life, and his talks with the dead indicated—to those who believed him—that communication between the two worlds was possible.

About 75 years after his death, Swedenborg's own spirit featured in the mystical experience of another man who was also prone to visions. Andrew Jackson Davis, known as the Poughkeepsie Seer, was an 18-year-old apprentice shoemaker. One day in 1844 he went into a state of semitrance and wandered from his home in Poughkeepsie, New York. The next morning he found himself 40 miles away in the mountains where, he later claimed, he met the spirits of Swedenborg and of the 2nd-century Greek physician Claudius Galen. During that encounter he experienced a state of mental illumination. Although Davis had had no education, he began teaching and writing on the body's supernormal powers. These he referred to as human magnetism and electricity. In 1845 he began to dictate while in trance an impressive work entitled *The Principles of Nature, Her Divine Revelations, and a Voice to Mankind*. In the book, which took 15 months to produce and which was taken down by a minister, Davis made this prediction:

"It is a truth that spirits commune with one another while one is in the body and the other in the higher spheres—and this, too, when the person in the body is unconscious of the influx, and hence cannot be convinced of the fact; and this truth will ere long present itself in the form of a living demonstration. And the world will hail with delight the ushering in of that era when the interiors of men will be opened, and the spiritual communion will be established. . . ."

In his notes dated March 31, 1848, are the following words: "About daylight this morning a warm breathing passed over my face and I heard a voice, tender and strong, saying: 'Brother, the good work has begun—behold a living demonstration is born.' I was left wondering what could be meant by such a message." It soon became clear what the voice may have meant, for it was on that very day that the Fox family for the first time established a form of communication with the unseen. The remarkable coincidence of Davis' revelation and the Hydesville rappings helped establish his reputation as the prophet of Spiritualism.

The presence in the Hydesville cottage soon began to manifest

Above: Andrew Jackson Davis, another forerunner of Spiritualism. At 17 he discovered he could diagnose disease while in a trance. At 18 he saw Swedenborg and a 2nd-century Greek doctor in a vision. (The College of Psychic Studies) Below: a seance in 1871 when spirit communication became a vogue in fashionable society.

itself in various other ways besides rappings. Gurgling sounds as from the throat, a death struggle, the heavy dragging of a body across the room are all reported to have been heard, night after night. The Foxes, unable to stand it any longer, finally left the house to live with other members of the family. But, according to Nandor Fodor's *Encyclopaedia of Psychic Science,* "the raps continued in the house even after they had left."

The noises also seem to have followed the Fox family. Kate went to her brother David's house in Auburn, and Margaret to her older sister Leah's in Rochester. The raps broke out in both houses, but were particularly violent in Leah's home. One of the tenants became the center of psychic attention in the form of poltergeist activity. Objects were thrown at him, but without ever causing him any injury. Recalling these events, Leah Fox later wrote in her book *The Missing Link* that the family appeared to be the victims of an intelligent but spiteful manifestation. They became convinced that no earthly power could relieve them.

"While on our knees pins would be stuck into different parts of our persons. Mother's cap would be removed from her head, her comb jerked out of her hair, and every conceivable thing done to annoy us." Once a loud noise came from high up on the roof, Leah reported. "It sounded like the frequent discharge of heavy artillery. It was stated to us the next day that the sounds were

Above: the replica of the Fox family's house in Hydesville, New York. It was built during the 1950s by John Drummond, who is shown in this picture.

THE BIRTHPLACE AND SHRINE OF MODERN SPIRITUALISM

ERECTED BY THE MOST GENEROUS CONTRIBUTIONS OF SPIRITUALISTS AND THEIR FRIENDS THE WORLD OVER, IN HONOR OF EVERY GIFTED SPIRITUAL MEDIUM FROM THE TIME OF THE FOX SISTERS IN 1848 TO OUR SPIRITUAL MEDIUMS OF THE PRESENT AND FUTURE.

THIS CORNER-STONE WAS PURCHASED AND LAID BY THE MINISTRY OF SPIRITUAL AND DIVINE SCIENCE AND FRIENDS, ON JULY 4TH 1955.

Right: the cornerstone of a shrine to Spiritualism started in 1955 and left uncompleted. The stone is located at the rear of the replica Fox cottage.

heard a mile away. We feared that the roof would fall in upon us."

They decided, again, to try to communicate with the invisible noisy force that was causing such havoc. They would recite the alphabet and the raps would respond at a certain letter. In this way a message was slowly spelled out. The first message Leah and her household received was: "Dear friends, you must proclaim this truth in the world. This is the dawning of a new era; you must not try to conceal it any longer. When you do your duty God will protect you and good spirits will watch over you."

From that moment on, as the Foxes received more communications, the spirits became more orderly. The family held seances during which a table rocked, objects moved, a guitar seemingly played itself, and sitters felt the touch of invisible hands.

The first meeting of a small band of people calling themselves Spiritualists was held on November 14, 1849, in the Corinthian Hall, Rochester. Public reaction to the demonstrations given by the Fox sisters at this meeting was mixed, and some of it was hostile. A group of citizens formed a committee to investigate the Spiritualists' claims. When this committee did not dismiss the phenomena as fraud, indignant skeptics appointed another committee. Its members, too, found no evidence of fraud. They reported that when the Fox sisters were standing on pillows "with a handkerchief tied around the bottom of their dresses, tight to the ankles, we all heard rapping on the wall and floor distinctly."

Many people still found the claims of the sisters outrageous, and some responded to them with violence. On one occasion, the sisters narrowly escaped being lynched. Attention was soon partly diverted from them as others began to demonstrate similar powers. Throughout the country, various people found they could produce raps and table tappings in their own homes.

In the growing enthusiasm for the new belief, the Fox sisters found themselves in demand. Although she had not been involved in the original rappings at the Hydesville home, the eldest sister Leah became the first professional medium. She gave private seances from November 28, 1849, and within six months her younger sisters had followed her example. Then the sisters set out on a propaganda tour that took them to Albany, Troy, and New York City. In Troy their lives were threatened, but they continued because, they said, the strange raps had asked them to "proclaim this truth to the world."

In New York in 1850 the influential newspaperman Horace Greeley, editor of the *New York Tribune,* was their first sitter. Fearing for their safety, he advised them to charge an extremely high admission fee to deter potential trouble makers. Four years later in 1854 America's first Spiritualist organization, the Society for the Diffusion of Spiritual Knowledge, was founded in New York by a wealthy merchant. It sponsored free public sittings given by Kate who received $1200 a year—a very large sum for the time—for her mediumistic services. Greeley, speaking on behalf of a number of sitters, affirmed: "Whatever may be the origin or cause of the 'rappings,' the ladies in whose presence they occur do not make them. We tested this thoroughly and to our entire satisfaction."

This was in contradiction to a theory put forward in 1851 that the Fox sisters had produced the raps by snapping their knee or

Margaret Fox's Confession

Margaret Fox was a little girl of 10 when the first strange rappings were heard in the house she lived in. Her sister Kate was three years younger, and her married sister Leah was considerably older. After the interest and belief in the rappings had led to the establishment of Spiritualism, it was Leah who became the first professional medium. She took command over her sisters.

In later years the relationship between Leah and the other two became strained. It blew up when Margaret was left in poverty and illness by widowhood. In an attempt to hurt the successful Leah—and perhaps to profit from the publicity — Margaret publicly confessed to fraud in 1888.

Her published confession said that the raps had been made at first by bumping or dropping an apple on the floor. Later she and Kate developed such perfect control of their muscles that they could snap the joints of their fingers and toes without detection. Margaret demonstrated her technique of producing raps before an audience at a New York theater.

Was it "all fraud, hypocrisy, and delusion" as Margaret herself said? Thousands of Spiritualists refused to believe it—and the movement grew on.

Above: Kate Fox. On her trip to England, given to her by her grateful patron Charles Livermore, she conducted seances in London for Sir William Crookes, and held joint seances with two of Britain's most famous mediums, D. D. Home and Mrs. Samuel Guppy.

Below: Sir William Crookes in 1884. A physicist, Crookes went into psychic research in 1870 when he announced his intention to make a thorough investigation into Spiritualist phenomena.

toe joints, although the noises were often said to have emanated from walls or doors some distance from the girls. Critics of Spiritualism were given further ammunition from an unexpected source. In April 1851—just three years after the first rappings—an alleged confession of fraud by Margaret Fox was published by one of her relatives. Surprisingly, Margaret's guilty admission had no effect on the progress of Spiritualism. Converts were joining the ranks every day, mediums were springing up everywhere, and the phenomena were becoming more remarkable.

When Margaret married and Leah remarried in the 1850s, they both retired from public mediumship temporarily. Their youngest sister Kate not only continued to be a medium, but also began to produce spirit forms at her seances as well as raps. In 1861 she was engaged to conduct seances exclusively for Charles F. Livermore, a rich New York banker. Livermore wanted to contact his wife Estelle, who had died a year earlier. In her five years as Livermore's private medium, Kate is reported to have given nearly 400 seances, most of them in Livermore's home. Prominent persons were among the sitters. Doors and windows were locked before each sitting commenced, and careful records were kept. It was during this period that Kate began to produce spirit forms, but it was not until the 43rd seance that the spirit was recognized as Estelle. According to the reports, Kate remained conscious as a form slowly materialized. The materialization became more substantial as time went on, but it was never able to speak more than a few words. Communication took place mainly through raps and writing. Estelle and another spirit form, described as Benjamin Franklin, wrote on cards brought by Livermore. To avoid fraud, Kate's hands were held by one of the sitters while the banker's dead wife wrote her messages. The writing on the card was said to be the same as Estelle's when alive. At the 388th sitting Estelle announced that it was her last appearance. Livermore never saw her again.

The banker showed his gratitude to Kate by giving her a trip to England in 1871. By then the English Spiritualist movement was well established. Kate gave seances for a number of eminent men including Sir William Crookes, who later became one of the foremost investigators of Spiritualist phenomena. She also gave joint sittings with two other famous mediums, Mrs. Samuel Guppy and Daniel Dunglas Home.

There was an astonishing story in connection with Mrs. Guppy. It seems that two other mediums, Frank Herne and Charles Williams, were once holding a joint seance with eight sitters. They were in a house near the center of the city, and Mrs. Guppy was at her own home three miles away. One of the sitters jokingly suggested that the spirits try to bring Mrs. Guppy to their seance—a tremendous feat considering how large Mrs. Guppy was. Suddenly there was a heavy bump on the table, and one or two screams. When a match was struck, Mrs. Guppy was there, on top of the table.

Three of the sitters, including the editor of the weekly newspaper *The Spiritualist,* accompanied Mrs. Guppy back home. After questioning those in Mrs. Guppy's household, they were satisfied that the medium had been at home until the time of her sudden appearance in the seance room across town.

The story was understandably treated with scorn by the daily press, but Spiritualists counted it simply as another seance wonder. They recalled that three years earlier D. D. Home—the medium with whom Kate Fox held joint sittings in England—was reported to have defied the laws of gravity three stories above a London street. Home performed this feat on December 13, 1868 in the presence of three witnesses, one of them Lord Adare.

In a trance, Home told the three men not to be afraid and not to leave their places. He then went out into the hallway and into a room next door. The three heard a window being thrown open, and a few moments later Home appeared outside their window standing upright. He opened the window from outside and came in to join his dumbfounded sitters. He laughed at the

Mrs Guppy Drops In

Two London mediums, Frank Herne and Charles Williams, were holding a joint seance with a respectable circle of sitters. The voices of the spirits John King and his daughter Katie were heard, and Katie was asked to bring something to the sitters—which she willingly agreed to do. One sitter perhaps jokingly suggested that Katie produce Mrs. Guppy, a well-known medium of majestic dimensions. Katie chuckled and said she would. John King shouted out, "You can't do it, Katie," but she declared "I will." The sitters were all laughing when there came a loud thump on the table, and a couple of them screamed. Someone lit a match—and there was Mrs. Guppy, her considerable bulk deposited neatly on the seance table. She was in trance and held a pen and an account book.

When Mrs. Guppy was gently awakened, she was somewhat upset. The last she remembered she had been sitting comfortably in her own home—about three miles away—writing up her accounts. Several sitters escorted the medium to her house, where an anxious friend waited. According to the friend, the two had been in Mrs. Guppy's room together when, suddenly, Mrs. Guppy was gone "leaving only a slight haze near the ceiling."

Above: a picture by an English spirit photographer. It includes the medium Mrs. Guppy (on the right) with friends. These pictures, apparently normal photographs in which psychic shapes appeared when developed, became a great fashion among 19th-century photographers.

thought of what a policeman would have done had he seen him "turning round and round along the wall in the air." Then he asked Lord Adare to go and close the window in the next room. When Lord Adare returned, he said that the window had been open only a foot, and he could not imagine how the medium had squeezed through the opening. "Come and see," said Home. According to Lord Adare, this is what happened next:

"I went with him; he told me to open the window as it was before. I did so; he told me to stand a little distance off; he then went through the open space, head first, quite rapidly, his body being nearly horizontal and apparently rigid. He came in again, feet foremost, and we returned to the other room. It was so dark I could not see clearly how he was supported outside. He did not appear to grasp, or rest upon, the balustrade, but rather to be swung out and in. . . . When Home awoke he was much agitated; he said he felt as if he had gone through some peril, and that he had a most horrible desire to throw himself out of the window; he remained in a very nervous condition for some time, then gradually became quiet."

Modern researchers have found minor discrepancies in the reports of the witnesses to this apparently miraculous feat, but the discrepancies are not weighty evidence against the possible genuineness of the act. Almost the only scientific explanation that would fit all the aspects of this case is that Home hypnotized the others into believing they had seen him levitate.

D. D. Home, born in Scotland in 1833, was one of the most outstanding mediums in Spiritualist history. An illegitimate child, he claimed to be the natural son of Alexander, tenth Earl of Home. He was adopted by a childless aunt, Mrs. McNeill Cook, who took him to America. As a youth he lived in Greenville, Connecticut, and Troy, New York. During this period he saw his first vision—that of a childhood friend who had died. Four years later came a second vision in which the exact hour of his mother's death was predicted.

Next, rappings began to occur in Home's presence. This was just two years after the Hydesville rappings. His aunt thought he was possessed and called in Congregationalist, Baptist, and Methodist ministers for exorcism. When the rappings continued, she turned the boy out of the house. From that time on he appears to have lived on the hospitality of those attracted by his unusual psychic gifts. Returning to Europe, Home gave seances for aristocrats and royalty including Napoleon III of France. As far as is known, Home was never detected in fraud.

Among his remarkable feats was the ability to grow taller under spirit guidance. Lord Adare reported one such incident when Home said that the spirit present was strong and tall. Said Lord Adare: "Home grew, I should say, at least six inches. Mr. Jencken, who is a taller man than Home, stood beside him, so there could be no mistake about it. Home's natural height is, I believe, 5 feet 10 inches. I should say he grew to 6 feet 4 inches or 6 feet 6 inches. I placed my hands on his feet, and they were level on the ground. . . . He appeared to grow also in breadth and size all over, but there was no way of testing that."

The Mr. Jencken mentioned in this account married Kate Fox in 1872 during her trip to England at her patron's expense. In the

Below: the medium Daniel Dunglas Home. Although the phenomena he produced were spectacular— he levitated, rooms shook as if by thunder, phantom hands appeared—he was never exposed in any fraudulent activity. He impressed people as diverse as Elizabeth Barrett Browning and Emperor Napoleon III of France.

Above: a satirical caricature of Home entitled "Home Sweet Home," complete with phantom hands dispensing money and gifts to the medium. Although Home steadfastly refused to accept money for his talents, he did live very comfortably on the sometimes lavish hospitality of his rich and famous friends.

Right: Home levitating. He most often rose perpendicularly with his arms above his head, and then would hover for about five minutes. He often asked his sitters not to look at him at the moment he was rising, lest the trance be shattered. One of the sitters did touch his foot as he went past overhead, and said that it "was withdrawn with a palpable shudder. It sprang from touch as a bird would."

next years, bitter personal problems divided the three Fox sisters. Kate and Margaret allied themselves against Leah, who had returned to mediumship, and tried to ruin her career.

On May 27, 1888, Margaret Fox for the second time publicly confessed to fraud in a sensational letter to the *New York Herald*. She denounced Spiritualism and promised a complete exposure. She kept her promise with a series of interviews and lectures. In an appearance at New York's Academy of Music, she produced raps on stage and explained how they were achieved by snapping her toe joints. Two months later, Kate Fox returned to New York and made a similar confession of guilt, joining her sister in the exposure meetings. Possibly Margaret and Kate hoped to make money from their confession, but if so, they were disappointed.

MODERN AMERICAN SPIRITUALISM.

ORESS

BY EMMA HARDINGE.

NEW YORK:
MDCCCLXX.

Above: the title page of Emma Hardinge Britten's 1870 book on American Spiritualism. The disembodied head has the third eye of clairvoyance in its forehead. It looks down on the pyramid, the traditional symbol of the ancient occult wisdom. Below: Emma Hardinge Britten actively promoted Spiritualism.

This may explain why, just over a year later, Margaret Fox completely retracted her confession in an interview reported in the New York press. According to the *Encyclopaedia of Psychic Science*, "she spoke of her great financial difficulties at the time, of an excitement that almost upset her mental equilibrium and blamed the strong psychological influence of persons inimical to Spiritualism for her action."

These confusing confessions and retractions were not to continue much longer. One after the other the Fox sisters died: Leah in 1890, and her two younger sisters while they were still in their fifties—Kate in 1892 and Margaret in 1893. Although the scandal caused by the confessions of Margaret and Kate had shaken Spiritualism, the movement was too well established to be destroyed by it. Spiritualism had become worldwide in the nearly 50 years since the rappings at Hydesville. Many famous people had witnessed psychic phenomena and testified to their authenticity. Even if the Fox sisters had been fraudulent, there were many other remarkable mediums who were not so proved.

Early converts of Spiritualism had lost no time in spreading the good word. Within five years of Hydesville, Spiritualism had leaped the Atlantic. The first Spiritualist church in England was established in Keighley, Yorkshire in 1853. Two years later the *Yorkshire Spiritual Telegraph,* first Spiritualist newspaper in Britain, was published in the same town.

The creation of a Spiritualist movement in Britain is attributed to two visiting American mediums, Mrs. W. R. Hayden and Mrs. Roberts. The latter advertised her gifts in *The Times* of London in 1853, saying: "Spiritual Manifestations and Communications from departed friends, which so much gratifies enlightened minds, exemplified daily."

Britain soon produced its own mediums. One of the earliest and most impressive pioneers in the field was Emma Hardinge Britten, a talented musician. She was converted to Spiritualism in the 1850s while on a professional visit to America.

Emma Hardinge Britten and her mother had sailed to the United States on the steamship *Pacific*. They had become friendly with some of the ship's officers, whom they continued to meet whenever the ship came into port. One of these officers figured in Emma Hardinge Britten's first mediumistic experience. According to her own account, the *Pacific* was due to arrive in New York again in February 1856. Expecting a parcel from England to be brought personally by a ship's officer, she went to the docks, but the overdue ship had not yet arrived. The delay was not considered serious for storms often slowed down winter crossings.

That night, however, just as she and her mother were about to retire, Emma Hardinge Britten felt a chill coupled with an impression of a spirit presence. "A sensation as if water was streaming over me accompanied the icy chilliness I experienced, and a feeling of indescribable terror possessed my whole being," she said. Her mother, who was already interested in Spiritualism, persuaded her to try to communicate with the spirits, and suggested the use of a method that had been told to her by the medium Mrs. Kellogg. On a table the young woman arranged slips of paper bearing the letters of the alphabet. Seemingly controlled by an unseen power, her hand spelled out the words:

"Philip Smith, *Pacific*." Then she felt an ice-cold hand laid on her arm, and the message continued: "My dear Emma, I have come to tell you I am dead. The ship *Pacific* is lost, and all on board have perished; she and her crew will never be heard from more."

Next morning, after an almost sleepless night, Emma Hardinge Britten hurried to the home of Mrs. Kellogg. Despite the power of the message, she still doubted its authenticity. She ran up the two flights of stairs to the medium's apartment, and was astonished to find her coming out of her room with a fixed glazed look in her eyes as if in a trance. In a forced unnatural voice the medium greeted her visitor with chillingly familiar words: "My dear Emma, I have come to tell you I am dead. The ship *Pacific* is lost, and all on board have perished. She and her crew will never be heard from more." In time, the sad news was confirmed: the *Pacific* and its crew were never heard of again.

Emma Hardinge Britten traveled all over the United States, Canada, Australia, New Zealand, and Britain for many years in the cause of Spiritualism. She was a brilliant speaker and tireless organizer. She also founded and for five years edited *Two Worlds*, a Spiritualist publication that is still in existence.

A few years after Emma Hardinge Britten's conversion to Spiritualism in America, something happened to boost Spiritualism in her native England. Thirteen-year-old Robert James Lees of Leicester began to develop great powers as a medium. In the year 1861, soon after the death of Queen Victoria's husband Prince Albert, the Lees family had a seance in their home. While young Lees was in a trance, the spirit of a man claiming to be Prince Albert sent a message to Queen Victoria, expressing a desire to communicate through Lees' mediumship. A newspaper editor who was at the seance published the request, which was brought to Her Majesty's notice. Queen Victoria, who already had an interest in psychic matters, sent two members of her court to a seance in Lees' home. The Queen's representatives gave false names. According to witnesses, the Prince Consort communicated through Lees when the young medium went into his trance. The Prince greeted the visitors as his friends and called them by their correct names.

Also while in a trance, Lees wrote a letter to the Queen. He signed it with a private name used only between the Queen and Prince Albert. The Queen was so impressed that she sent for Lees in order to speak to her dead husband through him. She wanted Lees to remain permanently at court but, it is said, the Prince Consort expressed a preference for another medium. This was John Brown, a servant at Balmoral, the Queen's estate in Scotland. Queen Victoria's long—and, some say, intimate—friendship with the lowly servant of rough character has been the subject of conjecture and controversy for over a century.

Above: Queen Victoria with John Brown, her personal manservant. He reportedly was also a medium who enabled the widowed Queen to communicate with her beloved Albert. The evidence for Brown's mediumship is mixed, but the Queen certainly believed that he had genuine premonitions of the future, and relied on him greatly.

Right: Robert James Lees. According to his daughter Eva Lees, he was only 13 or 14 when he delivered his first spirit message to Queen Victoria from Prince Albert. Miss Lees says the messages went on until the Queen's death. Lees also reportedly helped the police to identify and locate the dreaded London killer, Jack the Ripper. Controversy about the truth of that goes on vigorously even now.

Above: Abraham Lincoln and the young medium Nettie Colburn Maynard, who in trance gave him a lecture about the necessity for emancipation of the slaves.

Above: President Lincoln with a group of emancipated slaves. It remains a subject of argument between historians and Spiritualists as to the extent to which Lincoln was influenced by spirit guidance in his decision to free the slaves. Certainly at the start of the Civil War it had not been his intention to end slavery in the South.

Above: Mary Todd Lincoln in a spirit photograph by W. Mumler. She had arrived for the sitting incognito and veiled in mourning. When the print was taken, the photographer recognized the late President. Mary Lincoln agreed and added, "I am his widow."

Spiritualists argue that Brown's influence over the Queen was due entirely to his mediumship—that she tolerated his rude and outspoken nature because he made it possible for her to speak to her beloved husband.

At the same time that Robert James Lees is said to have been receiving spirit messages from Prince Albert, President Abraham Lincoln was taking an interest in Spiritualism.

If we believe a story told by Colonel Simon F. Kase—a lobbyist for railroad interests who moved freely in the highest government circles—messages from the spirit world changed the course of American history. In his book *The Emancipation Proclamation. How, and By Whom It Was Given to President Lincoln in 1861*, Colonel Kase gives an eye-witness account of the extraordinary events. He says that he first met the President about a railroad project. During subsequent meetings the two men discussed Spiritualism which, given the wide interest in it at the time, seems plausible.

It was some four weeks after his original meeting with Lincoln that, according to Kase, he was in the visitors' gallery of the House of Representatives. An old lady approached him, gave him her card, and said, "Call me when it suits you."

Kase saw his friend Judge Wattels nearby, and asked him who the lady was. The judge identified her as Mrs. Laurie. When Kase asked for more information, he said: "Well, sir, I have been twice to her house; she lives in Georgetown, and she has a daughter, now married to a Mr. Miller. She plays a piano with her eyes closed, and the piano rises up and beats the time on the floor as perfectly as the time is kept upon the instrument, and they call it Spiritualism." Kase said he would like to attend a seance, and Judge Wattels offered to accompany him that evening.

"The arrangement being perfected," Kase wrote, "we went and arrived there about eight o'clock in the evening. Who should we meet there but President Lincoln and his lady. After speaking and passing the courtesies of the day, perhaps ten minutes intervening, I saw a young girl approaching the President with a measured step, with her eyes closed, and walking up to . . . the President, accosted him as follows:

" 'Sir, you have been called to the position that you now occupy for a very great purpose. The world is in universal bondage; it must be physically set free, that it may mentally rise to its proper status. There is a Spiritual Congress supervising the affairs of this nation as well as a Congress at Washington. This Republic is leading the van of Republics throughout the world.' "

The teenage girl was Nettie Colburn Maynard, a medium known to the Laurie seances. The young girl, in trance, lectured the President for an hour on the importance of emancipating the slaves. Her argument was that the Civil War could not end until slavery was abolished because God destined all men to be free. "Her language was truly sublime," Kase reported, "and full of arguments, grand in the extreme, that from the time his proclamation of freedom was issued there would be no reverse to our army. As soon as this young girl came out of the trance she ran off, frightened to think that she had been talking to the President.

"Immediately, Mrs. Miller [daughter of the hostess Mrs. Laurie] commenced playing the piano, and the front side of it commenced to beat the time by rising off the floor and coming down with a heavy thud, beating the time of the tune played. I got up and requested the privilege of sitting on it that I might verify to the world that it moved. 'Yes,' the medium said, 'you, and as many more as see proper may get on it.' "

"Judge Wattels, the two soldiers who accompanied the President, and myself, got on the instrument. The medium commenced to play, the instrument commenced to go with all our weight on it, rising four inches at least. It was too rough riding; we got off whilst the instrument beat the time until the tune was played out."

Kase reported a second visit to Mrs. Laurie's home two evenings later, when the President and his wife were again present. He said that Lincoln was once more addressed by the young medium on the subject of freeing the slaves.

"Thus it was," wrote Kase, "that President Lincoln was convinced as to the course he should pursue; the command coming from that all-seeing Spirit through the instrumentality of the angel world was not to be overlooked. He, like a faithful servant, when convinced of his duty, feared not to do it, and to proclaim freedom by the Emancipation Proclamation to four million slaves. The proclamation was issued on September 22, 1862, to take effect the first day of January, 1863. In the intermediate time the backbone of the rebellion was broken, the Union army had, in diverse places, 26 battles, every one of them except two being a success upon the Union side. Thus, the prediction of the medium was verified."

There is no confirmation from Lincoln that Spiritualism influenced his decision. However, it is startling enough that, within a few years of Spiritualism's obscure beginnings, the President of the United States and the Queen of England were taking a keen interest in the new movement. And if the Spiritualist version of Abraham Lincoln's historic freeing of the slaves is believed, Spiritualism was already influencing a nation's destiny.

President Lincoln and the Dancing Piano

During the presidency of Abraham Lincoln the vogue for the new Spiritualism was at its height among fashionable people. Even the President—a far from fashionable man—was drawn into it. Colonel Simon F. Kase, a lobbyist who had several times met Lincoln to discuss a railroad project with him, tells of encountering the President at a seance in the home of Mrs. Laurie and daughter Mrs. Miller. She was known for making a piano beat time on the floor as she played while in trance.

Kase said of the occasion that Mrs. Miller began to play, and the front of the piano in truth rose off the floor and beat the time of the tune with heavy thuds. Kase asked if he could sit on the instrument so that he could "verify to the world that it moved." The medium composedly answered that he and as many others as wished could sit on the piano. Four men did: Kase, a judge, and two of the soldiers who were accompanying Lincoln. Mrs. Miller again began to play and the piano—heedless of its load—began to rise and thump, lifting at least four inches off the floor. Kase concluded ruefully: "It was too rough riding; we got off while the instrument beat the time until the tune was played out."

Man's Immortal Spirit

The belief that death is the end of the personality is, in the context of human history, a novel one. Almost all people since the beginning of the human race have believed in some form of life after death. Only in recent times, and only in Western countries, have a large number of people maintained that death is oblivion. It may be this disbelief in the afterlife that provoked the growth of Spiritualism in the West. For Spiritualism is unflagging—and at times desperate—in its efforts to prove survival. To ancient Egyptians (or, in fact, to modern devout Christians, for example, the Spiritualist preoccu-

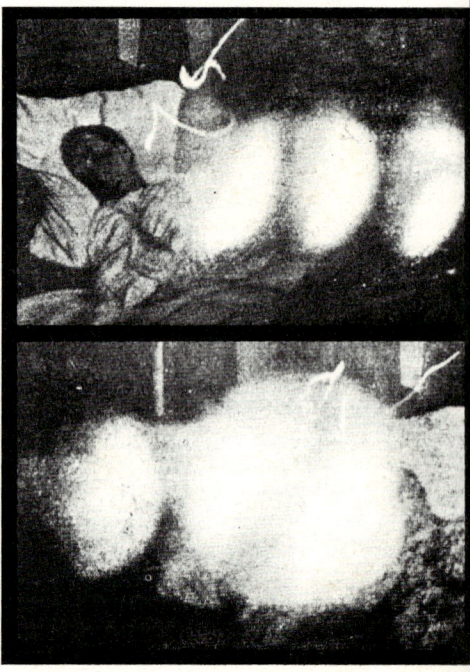

27

"Burying their dead equipped with food and books"

pation with life after death would seem irrelevant. They take an afterlife for granted.

Nonetheless, while taking survival for granted in the sense of believing in it without proof, people have gone to some pains to prepare for it. For believers in the great religions the preparation is spiritual or ethical, such as doing good works. Among ancient peoples it often took a practical form. Some 50,000 years ago Neanderthals were burying their dead equipped with food and tools—reflecting a belief that the afterlife was similar to the earthly life. The tombs of the Etruscans, who flourished in Italy before the Romans, have been found to contain furniture and chariots for the use of departed spirits.

In ancient civilizations the death of a royal personage required elaborate preparations so that his spirit could live in the next world in the style to which he was accustomed on earth. In the 1920s archeologists excavating the royal death pits of Ur, in what is now Iraq, were astonished to find the remains of Queen Shubad surrounded by 68 other people—women of the court and soldiers armed with spears. The evidence indicated that these royal attendants had gone to their deaths voluntarily for the archeological team found no apparent signs of struggle or violence. The bodies were laid out in orderly rows. It is possible that the royal servants of the queen either took poison or narcotics before the pits were covered. This mass sacrifice, which took place 4500 years ago, was based on the belief that the souls of the attendants would continue to serve the queen in death.

About 500 years ago the Inca peoples of South America practiced a similar kind of sacrifice for the benefit of their dead emperor, whom they believed to be a god—though apparently those who were sacrificed were unwilling victims. When the emperor died, his body was mummified and wrapped in beautiful cloth. His preserved remains were carefully attended by retainers, and produced at festivals as an object of veneration. The Incas believed that the emperor's soul had journeyed to another world. Therefore, during the funeral ceremonies for him, his favorite wives and servants, strangled after being intoxicated, were sent with him in death.

Other peoples held similar beliefs but expressed them without human sacrifice. In the tomb of Meketre, an Egyptian nobleman of Thebes, excavators found painted wooden models of the man's servants. It was believed that, in the other world, the dead man would use magic to bring them back to life to serve him again.

More than any other ancient peoples, the Egyptians were concerned with the afterlife. It is mainly through the elaborate preparations they made for the survival of their pharaohs and notables that we have obtained our knowledge of their way of life, craftsmanship, and culture. The great pyramids in which the pharaohs were entombed contained beautiful paintings, furniture, and jewelry intended for the enjoyment of the spirit of the god-kings. A basic part of Egyptian belief was the idea that in order for the spirit, or *ka*, to survive, the body must also survive. That is why the corpse was so carefully mummified and offerings of food were left at intervals in the pharaoh's tomb.

In time Egyptian beliefs about the afterlife became more democratic, and the idea of immortality was extended to include

Below: the Stone Age grave of a mother and child. The broken pottery on each side of the skeletons were storage jars that held the food provided for afterlife.

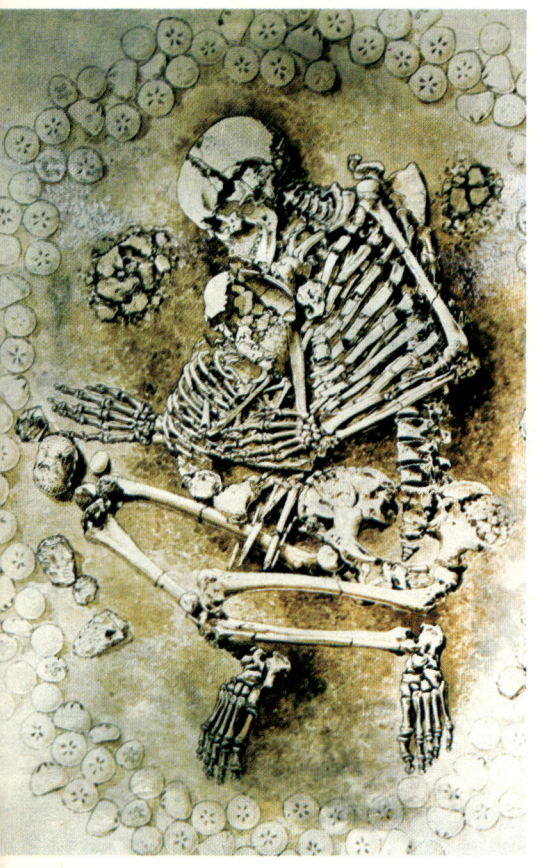

Above: funerary honors for an Inca emperor. The dead man, under a canopy, has life breathed into him through a tube—a tradition still practiced in parts of South America—while his successor watches. Wives and servants of the dead emperor are buried alive to serve him in the next world. Left: a dead Cayapa Indian from Ecuador, laid to rest in a boat and supplied with food for the long journey that his tribe believes begins with his death. Above right: an Egyptian model of a boat carved in about 1400 B.C., placed in a tomb to provide a safe passage to the next world. Below right: another method of providing for the beyond appears in the work of Kaene Qaugei, a Ghanaian craftsman who makes coffins in the shape of birds, crocodiles, cars, and boats. The man who ordered this one, in the shape of a Mercedes, had never owned a car in his life, but was obviously determined to reach the next world grandly.

Right: *Charon Crossing the Styx* by the 16th-century artist Joachim Patinir. The theme of this painting comes from one of the beliefs of the ancient Greeks about afterlife. This view maintained that the souls of the dead went to a gloomy underworld, Hades, where they existed as vague shadows. To get to Hades over the Styx river, souls had to pay the ferryman Charon. The needed coin was thoughtfully placed under the tongues of the dead so they could pay their way.

Left: *The Last Judgment* by the 15th-century painter Jan van Eyck. The Christian belief of the afterlife holds that the good will go to Heaven for their just reward, and the bad will go to Hell for their just punishment. Unhappily for Christian followers, ministers much more often stressed the torments of Hell than the joys of Heaven.

ordinary people as well as rulers. It was believed that every soul had to face judgment, and in order to do so, had to take a long and wearisome pilgrimage to the seat of the god Osiris, ruler of the underworld. There, in the presence of Osiris and 42 judges, the dead person's heart would be weighed on the scales of justice. The soul had to be able to say that in life the person had not been guilty of any one of a long list of sins, including the mistreatment of cattle and the stealing of food from the dead.

Zoroastrianism, the religion of the ancient peoples of Persia, also conceived of the afterlife as involving a journey and a judgment. On the fourth day after death, a person's soul crossed the Bridge of Parting. The middle section of this structure was like a wide sword blade. The sharp bridge stayed flat for a righteous soul so that it could easily walk across. Then it was met on the other side by a beautiful maiden who was a spiritual embodiment of the soul's good deeds while on earth. The righteous ones entered paradise, "the Abode of Song," where luxurious gifts were bestowed upon them. When a wicked man tried to cross the bridge, however, its midsection turned on its edge, causing the evildoer to plunge into a stinking abyss below.

According to the Aztecs, the way in which a person died— not his actions during life—determined the kind of existence he would have in the next world. Those who were sacrificed to the gods in the Aztecs' gory ceremonies would enter the paradise of the sun god, and would be transformed into butterflies or hummingbirds. Women who died in childbirth shared this idyllic afterlife. Others were destined for afterlives of a rather colorless type.

A graphic conception of a luxurious Paradise is contained in the Koran, the sacred book of the Islamic religion. Those chosen by Allah "shall recline on jeweled couches face to face, and there shall wait on them immortal youths with bowls and ewers and a cup of purest wine . . . with fruits of their own choice and flesh of fowls that they relish. And there shall be the dark-eyed houris [pure maidens], chaste as hidden pearls. . . . There they shall hear no idle talk, no sinful speech, but only the greeting, 'Peace! Peace!'" In contrast, the spirits of the wicked are condemned by Allah to hellfire and a diet of boiling water and "decaying filth."

The ancient Greeks held a number of views about the afterlife. One of the most widespread was that the soul of the deceased journeyed to an underworld called Hades, ruled over by the god of that name. This was a gloomy place where the spirits existed as vague shadows, somewhat similar to the Sheol, or "place of departed spirits," of the Jewish faith. The Greeks also had their hell, called Tartaros, and heaven, known as the Elysian fields. In heaven the chosen few enjoyed eternal spring. Great emphasis was put on attaining this reward by the Orphic sect. The Orphics took their name from the singer Orpheus who, according to

Below: this painting of *Dante and His Poem* was done by a 15th-century artist. Dante's *Divine Comedy* shows the afterworld as it was believed to be in the Middle Ages. Virgil leads Dante through the realms of Hell and Purgatory, a mountain of many terraces where souls work out their salvation. Then Dante's adored Beatrice shows him the nine spheres of Paradise, where he is finally granted an instant of mystic union with God.

Right: a young Buddhist monk of Tibet who is different from all others of his age. He is an Incarnate Lama, which means that he is the reincarnation of a head of a monastery and will in turn become the head. He was chosen as an Incarnate by certain signs of revelation shortly after his birth, which closely followed the death of the monastery's chief lama. The Dalai Lama, Tibet's supreme religious leader, is also chosen by this system of reincarnation.

Above: a statue of Buddha in Kamakura, Japan. Buddhism was founded by the Hindu Prince Gautama who preached that enlightenment could be reached only by renouncing all desires. By this he meant the material, sensual, and even the spiritual cravings of all human beings.

mythology, descended into Hades and persuaded the god to release his dead wife Eurydice. On the journey back to earth, Orpheus could not resist turning his head to make sure that Eurydice was still following him. This was against Hades' strict command and, as punishment, Orpheus lost both his and Eurydice's lives.

Another influential Greek belief was Pythagoreanism, which was based on the teachings of the mathematician-philosopher Pythagoras. He believed that the soul had "fallen" into a bodily existence, and would have to migrate through or be reincarnated in other human and animal bodies before being set free. Pythagoras himself claimed to have had previous existences, including one as a soldier in the Trojan war.

The belief in reincarnation is strongest in Asia. In Hinduism, the religion of the majority of Indians, a person's soul is considered to be a reflection of the world-soul, and the goal of one's existence is to become one with this all-pervading divine principle, the Brahma. Before attaining this unity the soul must go through various reincarnations, both human and animal. The whole cycle of rebirths is known as the wheel of Sansara, and its turning—like the universe itself—is without beginning and without end. The Hindu believes that he can influence the nature of his next rebirth through his *karma*, the sum total of his actions in his present life. Bad karma will bring punishment in the form of reincarnation as a low caste person or a despised animal, such as a dog, or in various misfortunes during the next life. Good karma will be rewarded by reincarnation as a highly regarded animal— perhaps as a cow, the sacred animal of the Hindus—or as a Brahmin, the highest of all castes.

In between reincarnations, the soul may spend time in various heavens and hells. Some of the hells are ice cold, some boiling hot. The lot of the damned in one hell is to be boiled in oil and dismembered. The heavens provide many pleasures including music, dancing girls, and gambling houses. Of course, these fleshpot heavens have nothing to do with the soul's ultimate achievement of spiritual bliss.

Buddhism, like Hinduism out of which it developed some 25 centuries ago, teaches that humans must undergo a series of reincarnations. In the course of these various lives, some of which may be in other universes, the soul gradually learns to avoid the suffering inherent in life by giving up its craving for happiness— in fact, its craving for life itself. When one has shed all his earthly desires and achieved a state of indifference toward both pain and pleasure, he is said to have reached Nirvana. Having attained this state of supreme detachment, the soul is free from the cycle of rebirths. In fact it is no longer an individual soul as Westerners conceive it, for the whole idea is to lose the sense of self.

Such a concept takes us a long way from the idea of the spirit as an individual, which is fundamental to most Western creeds. It is almost the total opposite of Spiritualism, which holds that the spirit retains all its earthly characteristics from tone of voice to birthmarks. Whether Spiritualist, Christian, Jew, or atheist, however, the Westerner would not readily be attracted to the concept of losing his individuality.

One aspect of Eastern religions that has enjoyed some popularity in Europe and America—though not normally as part of a religion—is the belief in reincarnation. However, the fascination of this idea is, predictably, that in a sense it extends the personality. There is a time-travel aspect to it that fascinates anyone interested in the past, while those who find their present existence painful or simply dull can find solace in the possibility that they may have had a more interesting life in the past—or will have one in the future. Not all European or American believers in reincarnation are simply indulging in wishful thinking. Some have arrived at this belief through their conversion to Eastern religions. One such was the late English writer Aldous Huxley who died in 1963. In another instance, several psychiatrists practicing today have come to believe in reincarnation because some of their

Who Was Gretchen?

Mrs. Dolores Jay is an ordinary American housewife, married to a minister and the mother of four children. But when she is deeply hypnotized, Dolores Jay moves back through time past the time of her childhood and her infancy—deeper and deeper back until she whimpers in German. (When she is conscious, she neither speaks nor understands any German).

It is 1870. She is Gretchen Gottlieb, a 16-year-old Catholic girl, terrified and in hiding from anti-Catholic fanatics in a forest. "The man made my mother dead," she says. She complains that her head aches, she talks about a glittering knife, and then, desperately, evades questions. "Gretchen can't," she finally wails. And there it ends. Gretchen presumably was killed, and Mrs. Jay remembers nothing until her own life began in 1923.

Dolores Jay herself can't account for it. She doesn't believe in reincarnation. She has only heard fragments of the taped hypnosis sessions, but she can't understand the language. She has never been to Germany. She has never heard of the little town of Eberswalde where Gretchen says she lived, and which exists in what is now East Germany close to the Polish border. But Eberswalde was the scene of Germany's last stand against the Soviet Union in 1945, and the town was almost completely razed. The records that once might have proved whether or not there was such a person as Gretchen Gottlieb have been destroyed.

Who can explain it? Not the modern middle-aged woman who, under hypnosis, becomes the young 19th-century German girl — a girl who remembers her dolls, her home, and her own death.

Above: *The Resurrection* by Ferrair Gaudenzio, done in the 16th century. The resurrection of Christ—and the promise of resurrection for his faithful followers—is a fundamental teaching of Christianity. It is mentioned in all four Gospels, and in the epistles of Paul.

patients under hypnosis have recalled experiences of times before their own birth. Often the events are of such a violent nature that, according to the theory, they are traumatic enough to be retained hidden in the memory. Other more commonplace memories are entirely lost or buried too deeply to come to the surface. One man recalled being hanged for stealing by his neighbors in Colonial Massachusetts. In another case a patient recalled in great detail a previous life as a member of the Cathars, a medieval religious sect. Her recollections were full of violence, culminating in a terrifying memory of being burned at the stake for heresy.

Despite the wealth of detail that often comes from such hypnotic communications, it is usually impossible to verify the stories by referring to historical sources. When possible, investigation may disprove the case. In the 1950s a Colorado housewife, Virginia Tighe, claimed under hypnosis to have had a previous existence in Ireland as a girl named Bridey Murphy. The case received tremendous publicity until it was discovered that childhood memories, long forgotten by her conscious mind, had surfaced in the form of a "previous incarnation."

Other cases are not so easily dismissed. Some of the remembered details have been checked against reference books—in

certain cases obscure enough that the person would not have read them—and found to tally with fact.

Spiritualism was, of course, a product of a mainly Christian society whose beliefs about the afterlife, though differing slightly from one denomination to another, share the idea that the individual survives death as an individual. The Christian creed affirms "the Resurrection of the Body, and the Life Everlasting." Central to the faith is the belief that Christ rose from the dead and appeared to his disciples. Interpretations of this act vary. Some people believe that Christ appeared to them in his actual earthly body. Some interpret the story symbolically, saying that Christ was present among his followers in spirit. Still others believe that he appeared in his spiritual body, which resembled his earthly body but was subtly different from it. This difference would account for the story of the "Road to Emmaus," in which Christ walked and talked with two of his disciples for some time before they recognized him.

Christianity in its various forms has always been concerned with the life everlasting. For most of its existence, the Church held—and parts of it still hold—graphic and vivid ideas of heaven and hell, salvation and damnation. Dante's *Divine Comedy* is the

Above: *The Resurrection*, **a 20th-century view by Stanley Spencer. The scene is in the churchyard of Cookham in southeast England. It shows graves that have burst open to release their dead. The artist himself appears twice in the picture, leaning on a tomb near the porch and reclining at right. Most of the others are portraits of the townspeople of Cookham.**

outstanding expression and elaboration of these ideas. Today many theologians are less inclined to theorize about the exact nature of the afterlife, except to affirm that it is progress toward the "Vision of God." As for the nature of the body in which the soul will survive, they can quote St. Paul: "All flesh is not the same flesh: but there is one kind of flesh of men, another flesh of beasts, another of fishes, and another of birds. . . . So also is the resurrection of the dead. It is sown in corruption: it is raised in incorruption: it is sown in dishonor; it is raised in glory: it is sown in weakness; it is raised in power: it is sown a natural body; it is raised a spiritual body. There is a natural body, and there is a spiritual body." (1 Corinthians 15:39, 42–44)

What does this spiritual body look like? To this inevitable question Christianity does not offer a precise answer. It is suggested that in some fundamental way it will resemble one's earthly body so as to preserve a person's individuality, but without age or sex. More than this, few theologians would care to specify.

Many, however, have been highly critical of the Spiritualist conception of the afterlife. "I should be very disappointed," commented one Anglican clergyman, "if the afterlife were so concerned with trivia as the Spiritualists believe." To state the Christian point of view rather bluntly, we will have better things to do in afterlife than play guessing games and indulge in reminiscences with those we have left behind.

Not that all Christians would rule out the possibility of some communication from the beyond, but they would expect it to occur only for some important reason—as in some of the cases in which saints are said to have appeared to certain people. The story of Joan of Arc and her voices is probably the outstanding example of this kind. Only certain people are afforded such glimpses of the next world. Most Christians, while encouraged to prepare themselves spiritually for eternal life, are not encouraged to become preoccupied with it.

It is not suprising that some people find it difficult to adopt an attitude of patient faith. In particular those who have lost someone they love can be extremely anxious to know without a shred of doubt that that person continues to exist. Others may simply become intrigued by the possibility of discovering the truth by scientific or quasi-scientific means. Because science has solved so many of the mysteries of the universe, some people expect it to solve the mystery of possible existence beyond the grave.

After more than 125 years of gathering evidence for life after death, Spiritualism still has not arrived at a clear conception of that life. Most Spiritualists believe that there are various planes or spheres so that each spirit goes to an astral plane or sphere best suited to the stage of spiritual development the living person had reached. They also believe that there is subsequent spiritual progress open to every soul. Some Spiritualists hold that this progress entails reincarnation, while others feel that it takes place entirely in spiritual worlds. The main innovation of Spiritualism in the long history of belief in immortality is the idea that communication between the inhabitants of our world and those of the next is not only possible but relatively easy—if we on this side of the divide follow the correct procedures.

Above: Joan of Arc is a classic example of the Christian concept that communication from beyond is possible if the reason for it is of great importance. Among the spirit voices that spoke to her, Joan was able to distinguish those of St. Catherine and St. Margaret.

Right: *The Doubt: Can These Dry Bones Live?* **This painting by a mid-19th century artist draws on that period's big interest in religion and death, as well as its idealization of young womanhood. An answer is perhaps suggested by the sprouting chestnut, symbol of life, on the grave marker saying "Resurgam"—"I shall rise again."**

3

The Scientists Investigate

On a midwinter evening in England just about 100 years ago a small group of psychic investigators were sitting in a small, warm, gaslit room, eager to witness the phenomena produced by a powerful young medium named Agnes Nichol. The seance lasted for four hours, and at the end of it, a most astonishing manifestation occurred. On a bare table in the center of the room there suddenly appeared a quantity of flowers. Anemones, tulips, chrysanthemums, Chinese primroses, and ferns lay in a heap on the table.

"All were absolutely fresh as if gathered from a conservatory," wrote one of the

By the 1860s psychic phenomena were becoming so widespread that some scientists began warily to investigate the claims made by the Spiritualists and mediums.

Above: Sir William Crookes, who invented a tube that made possible the development of X-rays, was one of the first to enter the new field of psychic research.

Right: the materialization of Katie King, the spirit control of medium Florence Cook. This is a photograph taken by Crookes.

"Levitation was a common occurrence —but in an uncommon way"

witnesses. "They were covered with a fine, cold dew. Not a petal was crumpled or broken, not the most delicate point or pinnule of the ferns was out of place."

It would be easy to dismiss this report as beyond belief, and to assume that the researcher was inexperienced and gullible and the medium a brilliant fraud. However, the man who wrote those words cannot be so easily dismissed. It was Dr. Alfred Russel Wallace who, with Charles Darwin, had developed the theory of evolution. Wallace was one of the first scientists to investigate Spiritualism. The seance described was held in his own home. This fact tends to rule out the possibility of the medium having brought the flowers into the room through secret panels or doors in the ceiling, as some critics have suggested.

Dr. Wallace, like many leading scientists of his period, was strongly attracted by the idea of doing research on psychic and occult phenomena. More than a decade earlier, when he had been an unknown teacher in England's industrial heartland, he had taken a great interest in hypnosis—then known as mesmerism and considered as part of the occult. Later, during the 12 years of tropical travel, exploration, and study that led to the formulation of his theory of evolution, Dr. Wallace learned about the Spiritualism boom at home through letters. He resolved that, on his return to England, he would investigate the powers that produced the knocks, movements, and other spirit manifestations of the seances.

Dr. Wallace started his experiments in the summer of 1865. After attending a dozen seances he became convinced of, as he put it, "an unknown power." In September of that year he participated in seances with one of England's first professional mediums, Mrs. Mary Marshall. She was able to produce the raps, table levitation, and spirit writings typical of the time. Wallace is reported to have witnessed these phenomena in broad daylight, apparently satisfying himself that there was no fraud. He was particularly impressed by spirit messages spelled out through Mrs. Marshall's mediumship. Although a stranger to him, Mrs. Marshall was able to tell him his brother's name, where he died, and the last person who saw him alive.

Perhaps with the idea of ruling out fraud completely, Wallace decided to carry on his investigations in his own home. Starting in November 1866 he arranged to study at close range the extraordinary powers of young Agnes Nichol, later the well-known Mrs. Guppy. In the seances with her, levitation was a common occurrence—but in an uncommon way. Sometimes the medium was lifted chair and all onto the table. An even more astonishing aspect of her power was the ability to make delicate flowers and other objects materialize out of the thin air, in perfect form. This happened on hundreds of occasions. To confound the skeptics who insisted that the objects must have been secreted in advance, Agnes Nichol often produced specific items on request.

It is said that when a friend of Wallace asked for a sunflower, a six-foot-tall sunflower with earth clinging to its roots fell onto the table. Such experiences led Wallace to state that the existence of genuine Spiritualist phenomena did not require further confirmation. Such phenomena "are proved," he wrote, "quite as well as any facts are proved in other sciences."

Above: a six-foot Golden Lily that suddenly appeared at a seance. A spirit control named Yolande reportedly materialized it, and then was unable to de-materialize it for a week. This distressed her, for she had "only got the plant on condition she brought it back." She finally managed to dissolve it, leaving only two flowers that had fallen.

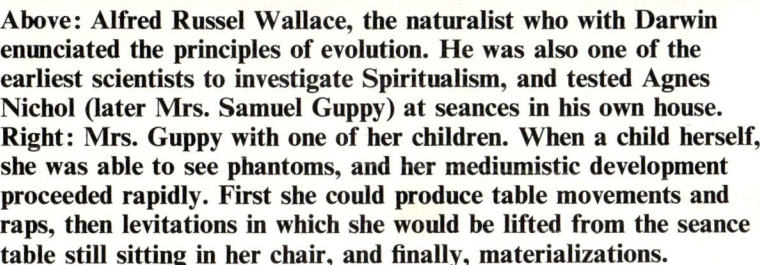

Above: Alfred Russel Wallace, the naturalist who with Darwin enunciated the principles of evolution. He was also one of the earliest scientists to investigate Spiritualism, and tested Agnes Nichol (later Mrs. Samuel Guppy) at seances in his own house. Right: Mrs. Guppy with one of her children. When a child herself, she was able to see phantoms, and her mediumistic development proceeded rapidly. First she could produce table movements and raps, then levitations in which she would be lifted from the seance table still sitting in her chair, and finally, materializations.

Above: Allan Kardec who wrote the basic text of Spiritism in France. He was born as Hypolyte Leon Denizard Rivail, but took as his pseudonym two names he believed he had used in his previous incarnations. In South America today his writings are the basis of a greatly vigorous and popular form of Spiritualism.

The public was understandably confused by the claims and counterclaims surrounding the new Spiritualist movement in the late 19th century. Many people hoped that science would eventually step in to settle the matter once and for all. The London Dialectical Society, formed in 1867, was an early attempt to do just that. Among its first minutes we find a decision to appoint a committee of eminent members "to investigate the phenomena alleged to be Spiritual manifestations, and to report thereon."

The committee's report was presented to the Society's Council on July 20, 1870, and published privately in 1871. It concluded that raps and knocks occurred without mechanical contrivance, that movements of heavy objects occurred without contact or connection with any person, and that these sounds and movements "often occur at the time and in the manner asked for by persons present, and by means of a simple code of signals answer questions and spell out coherent communications." The committee urged that the subject was worthy of more serious attention than it had hitherto received.

These conclusions did not meet with enthusiasm from the general press. For example *The Times*, then as now one of England's most influential newspapers, dismissed the report as "nothing more than a farrago of impotent conclusions, garnished by a mass of the most monstrous rubbish it has ever been our misfortune to sit in judgment upon."

Among those who wrote to the committee during its investigation was the young French astronomer Camille Flammarion, the man who is credited with having coined the word "psychic." He had embarked on a study of Spiritualism in 1861 at the age of 19 after encountering the philosophy of Allan Kardec in a book called *Le Livre des Esprits* (*The Book of the Spirits*). Kardec believed that spiritual progress can be achieved only by a series of reincarnations. He founded the Society of Psychological Studies in Paris to propagate his beliefs. Flammarion joined Kardec's Society to study psychic phenomena, and after some practice, acquired facility in automatic writing. The long-lived Flammarion believed in the immortality of the soul but, in his early days of psychic research, maintained that Spiritualist phenomena did not prove the case. By 1923, however, when he became President of the Society for Psychical Research, his views had changed. In his presidential address, Flammarion summed up his 60 years of research stating that he had been forced to moderate his views by the weight of evidence. "There are unknown faculties in man belonging to the spirit," he declared, ". . . exceptionally and rarely the dead do manifest, there can be no doubt that such manifestations occur, telepathy exists just as much between the dead and the living as between the living."

In the same month that the Dialectical Society committee gave its report—and well before publication of that 400-page document—a scientist as distinguished as Dr. Alfred Russel Wallace publicly declared himself ready to investigate Spiritualism. This was Sir William Crookes, one of the greatest physicists of the 19th century. The report and Sir William's announcement of July 1870 not only focused public attention on the field of psychical research, but also created a favorable climate in which other scientists could explore this new territory. In the 15 years after 1870, Sir William Barrett and Sir Oliver Lodge—like Sir William Crookes well-known physicists—were actively engaged in investigating the unexplained.

Crookes' decision to delve into Spiritualism was greeted with wide approval. The press felt sure that Crookes, creator of several important scientific inventions and discoverer of the element thallium, would soon show Spiritualist claims to be humbug. Crookes appeared to share that view. When he announced his investigation he stated that he had no preconceived notions on the subject, and then added: "The increased employment of scientific methods will produce a race of observers who will drive the worthless residuum of Spiritualism hence into the unknown limbo of magic and necromancy."

This statement was taken as a disclaimer of belief in Spiritualism. But, if Crookes' private beliefs had been better known, it could have been interpreted that he intended only to disprove the "worthless residuum"—perhaps the frauds—without prejudice to the basic beliefs. Crookes had first come in contact with Spiritualism in 1869 at sittings with Mrs. Marshall. He had also been intrigued by the psychic powers of another medium, J. J. Morse. In his book *Crookes and the Spirit World*, R. G. Medhurst reveals that an entry in the scientist's diary in December 1870 shows he was a firm believer in Spiritualism within months of announcing his intention of studying it. Crookes wrote: "May He [God] also allow us to continue to receive Spiritual communications from my brother who passed over the boundary when in a ship at sea more than three years ago."

Whatever his private beliefs, Crookes applied strict scientific controls during his research with the famous D. D. Home, whose levitations and other physical phenomena were celebrated throughout Europe. Crookes' meticulous testing of Home failed to produce any evidence of fraud. Though his work with Home is without doubt the most important part of Crookes' psychical investigations it is overshadowed by the more doubtful and controversial seances with Florence Cook, a young Londoner barely into her teens. Whereas Home submitted to Crookes' tests in what were virtually laboratory conditions, most of the Florence Cook seances—at least in the beginning—were held in situations in which it was far more difficult to rule out fraud. Crookes recognized this and wrote during the early days of his investigation: "On a few occasions, indeed, I have been allowed to apply tests and impose conditions; but only once or twice have I been permitted to carry off the priestess from her shrine, and in my own house, surrounded by my own friends, to enjoy opportunities of testing the phenomena I had witnessed under less conclusive conditions."

Florence Cook was an extraordinary girl, and the first English medium to produce materializations of a whole human body in the light—which at that time was gaslight. In accordance with normal Spiritualist practice, Florence sat in a dark curtained recess—usually called a "cabinet"—to protect her from the light. (Spiritualists say that bright light can be harmful to a medium during a physical seance.) After a while, a spirit form who called herself Katie King emerged from this cabinet.

During tests the medium was sometimes tied to her chair, and

Below: Camille Flammarion, the astronomer and psychic researcher, is cartooned among the stars. Although he was close to Kardec as a young man, he was skeptical about the phenomena of Spiritism as then manifested. Practicing automatic writing with Kardec's Society for Psychological Studies, he succeeded in obtaining words and phrases on astronomical subjects signed by Galileo. But he was firmly convinced that the scripts were the product of his own mind, and that Galileo had nothing to do with them. Later in his life, Flammarion softened his viewpoint, and apparently believed that some manifestations were genuine.

Above: the young Florence Cook. Below: Katie King, the materialized spirit guide of Florence Cook. The two girls looked very alike, as this picture shows, but Crookes found differences in them. For example, Florence wore earrings for pierced ears, but Katie's ears were not pierced. Katie King was also much taller.

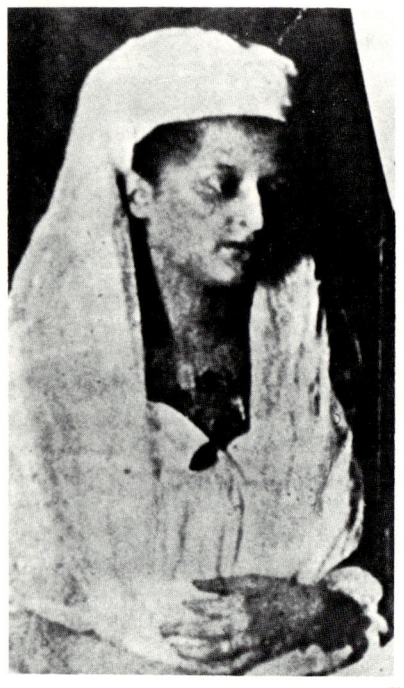

other elementary controls were introduced, but they seldom satisfied the skeptics. The disbelief was supported by the evidence of the sitters' eyes. Florence Cook and her materialization Katie King were remarkably similar in appearance. What was needed was proof that the two girls were different, and that they could both be seen simultaneously. Crookes was aware of this, and eventually furnished what he regarded as the necessary evidence. He wrote in one of the Spiritualist journals of the day that throughout the seance, while watching the materialized Katie King, he had distinctly heard "a sobbing, moaning sound . . . from behind the curtain where the young lady was supposed to be sitting." Not surprisingly, his critics were not impressed. Soon, however, Crookes furnished what he regarded as "absolute proof." In a letter to *The Spiritualist*, dated March 30, 1874, he wrote:

"On March 12th, during a seance here [at his home in Northwest London] after Katie had been walking amongst us and talking for some time, she retreated behind the curtain which separated my laboratory, where the company was sitting, from my library, which did temporary duty as a cabinet. In a minute she came to the curtain and called me to her, saying, 'come into the room and lift my medium's head up, she has slipped down.' Katie was then standing before me clothed in her usual white robes and turban headdress. I immediately walked into the library up to Miss Cook, Katie stepping aside to allow me to pass. I found Miss Cook had slipped partially off the sofa, and her head was hanging in a very awkward position. I lifted her onto the sofa, and in so doing had satisfactory evidence, in spite of the darkness, that Miss Cook was not attired in the 'Katie' costume but had on her ordinary black velvet dress, and was in deep trance. Not more than three seconds elapsed between my seeing the white-robed Katie standing before me and raising Miss Cook onto the sofa from the position into which she had fallen."

However, Crookes had still not seen the two together. The opportunity came on March 29, he said, when Katie invited him into the cabinet after he had turned out the gaslight in the laboratory. He carried with him a phosphorus lamp, by whose dim light he could see adequately.

"I went cautiously into the room it being dark [continued Crookes' letter], and felt about for Miss Cook. I found her crouching on the floor. Kneeling down, I let air enter the phosphorus lamp, and by its light I saw the young lady dressed in black velvet, as she had been in the early part of the evening, and to all appearances perfectly senseless; she did not move when I took her hand and held the light quite close to her face, but continued quietly breathing. Raising the lamp, I looked around and saw Katie standing close behind Miss Cook. She was robed in flowing white drapery as we had seen her previously during the seance. Holding one of Miss Cook's hands in mine, and still kneeling, I passed the lamp up and down so as to illuminate Katie's whole figure, and satisfy myself thoroughly that I was really looking at the veritable Katie . . . and not at the phantasm of a disordered brain. She did not speak, but moved her head and smiled in recognition. Three separate times did I turn the lamp to Katie and examine her with steadfast scrutiny until I had no

doubt whatever of her objective reality. At last Miss Cook moved slightly, and Katie instantly motioned me to go away. I went to another part of the cabinet and then ceased to see Katie, but did not leave the room till Miss Cook woke up, and two of the visitors came in with a light."

In the same letter Crookes pointed out some important differences in the appearance of the medium and the spirit materialization. Katie was six inches taller than Florence, he asserted. The spirit girl's skin was smooth on her neck, while the medium's neck was rough and had a large blister on it. Katie's ears were unpierced, but Florence Cook habitually wore earrings. The spirit's complexion was very fair, whereas the medium's was dark. Katie's fingers were longer than Florence's, and her face was larger.

Spiritualists distrusted scientists, and Crookes realized this. He and his family therefore befriended Florence Cook and gradually gained her confidence. The young girl was a regular visitor to the Crookes' house and occasionally stayed with the family, sometimes for a week at a time. The trust that developed between the scientist and the medium enabled Crookes to take a series of 44 photographs that must be among the strangest in the

Above: Katie King appearing at a seance in Philadelphia in 1874. At this time the London Katie and Florence Cook were in the midst of hectic seances with Crookes because Katie had said she was going to take her leave in a week's time. (She had said at the start that she would only manifest herself for three years.) When Crookes saw a photograph of the Philadelphia Katie, he declared her a fraud.

Private Seance by Miss Florence Cook,
OF LONDON.

Admit *Mr Banks*
3 Waverley Rd
Aston

to private Séance on *Monday April 17-99*
at *7.45* o'clock p.m. prompt,
to be held at *Mrs Pearls*
43 Avenue St New Hall Lane
Note the No. make no Inquiries

This Ticket not transferable

Above: an invitation to a Florence Cook seance. What with possible problems of publicity and the law, guests who were invited to Florence Cook's seances were politely requested to display suitable discretion.

annals of science. They show Katie King walking around Crookes' laboratory, in one case arm-in-arm with the scientist. Five cameras were used, including two stereoscopic ones. All were operated simultaneously so as to capture the spirit from various angles.

When Katie had first communicated through Florence Cook she said it would only be for a three-year period. In 1874 she announced her intended departure. The week before she was to leave for good, Crookes took the photographs. During the photographic sessions Katie is said to have covered Florence Cook's head with a shawl to protect her from the flashes.

"It was a common thing [during the photographic sessions] for the seven or eight of us in the laboratory to see Miss Cook and Katie at the same time, under the full blaze of the electric light," Crookes testified. This happened when he was asked by Katie to hold the curtain open. "We did not on these occasions see the face of the medium because of the shawl, but we saw her hands and feet; we saw her move uneasily under the influence of the intense light, and we heard her moan occasionally. I have one photograph of the two together, but Katie is seated in front of Miss Cook's head."

During the photography sessions the scientist was able to see the features of the materialized Katie in the light of the flash, and he vouched for the fact that several small marks on the medium's face were not on Katie's. He took the spirit's pulse one evening and found it beating steadily at 75 per minute, close to normal. The medium's pulse, taken a little while later, was going at its usual rapid rate of 90. He also found Katie's lungs to be sounder than Florence Cook's at a time when the medium was under treatment for a severe cough.

More proof that Florence and Katie were not one and the same had been provided by Cromwell Varley, the famous consultant electrician who worked on the Atlantic cable. An ardent

Above: this drawing of Crookes shows him looking at Katie King and Florence Cook with a phosphorus lamp while the medium is in trance. The scene is the library of Crookes' home, used as a cabinet during seances. Most mediums used cabinets to condense the psychic energy necessary for manifestations, they explained. Right: a photograph by Crookes showing himself with Katie King on his arm. He took many photos of Katie, but few now survive.

Spiritualist, Varley devised a test designed to prove that Florence Cook was inside the cabinet when Katie paraded around the seance room. Florence was placed in an electrical circuit with wires connected to coins placed on her arms so that a small current was running through her body. A large *galvanometer*—an instrument that detects and measures small electric currents—was placed 10 feet away from the cabinet. It was placed on a mantelpiece in full view of the sitters so that the flow of the electrical current could be monitored. If the medium broke the circuit in order to leave the cabinet dressed as Katie, the galvanometer would register violent fluctuations. Katie appeared as usual, and there was no change in the current. Crookes asked Katie to plunge her hands into a chemical solution that would cause a change in the current flow if Florence managed to dress as Katie and leave the cabinet without removing the wires. Again the galvanometer showed no significant fluctuation of current.

At her last materialization Katie allowed Crookes to witness the touching farewell between her and her medium Florence Cook. Crookes sent an account of this to *The Spiritualist*:

"After closing the curtains she conversed with me for some time, and then walked across the room to where Miss Cook was lying senseless on the floor. Stooping over her, Katie touched her and said, 'Wake up, Florrie, wake up! I must leave you now.' Miss Cook then woke and tearfully entreated Katie to stay a little time longer. 'My dear, I can't; my work is done. God bless you,' Katie replied, and then continued speaking to Miss Cook. For several minutes the two were conversing with each other, till at last Miss Cook's tears prevented her speaking. Following Katie's instructions I then came forward to support Miss Cook, who was falling onto the floor, sobbing hysterically. I looked round, but the white-robed Katie had gone. As soon as Miss Cook was sufficiently calmed, a light was procured and I led her out of the cabinet."

Was Sir William Crookes the victim of an extremely clever fraud? He was fully aware that many people assumed so, but he felt that he was not. He defended his experiences with these words:

"Every test that I have proposed she [Florence Cook] has at once agreed to submit to with the utmost willingness; she is open and straightforward in speech, and I have never seen anything approaching the slightest symptom of a wish to deceive. Indeed, I do not believe she could carry on a deception if she were to try, and if she did she would certainly be found out very quickly, for such a line of action is altogether foreign to her nature. And to imagine that an innocent schoolgirl of 15 should be able to conceive and then successfully carry out for three years so gigantic an imposture as this, and in that time submit to any test which might be imposed upon her, should bear the strictest scrutiny, should be willing to be searched at any time, either before or after a seance, and should meet with even better success in my own house than at that of her parents, knowing that she visited me with the express object of submitting to strict scientific tests—to imagine, I say, the Katie King of the last three years to be the result of imposture does more violence to one's reason and

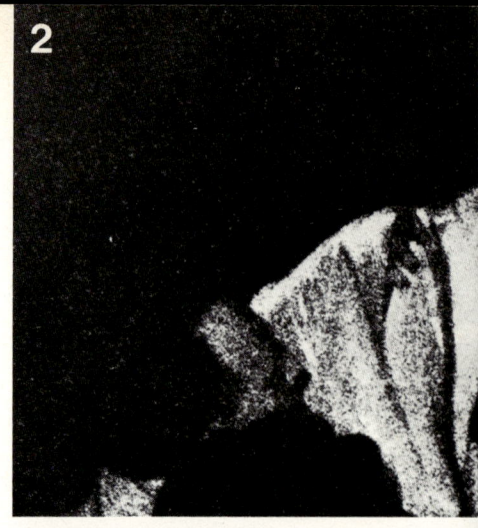

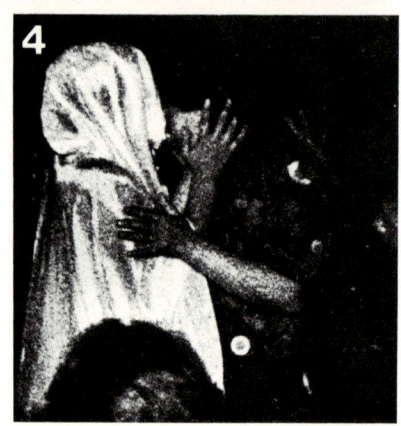

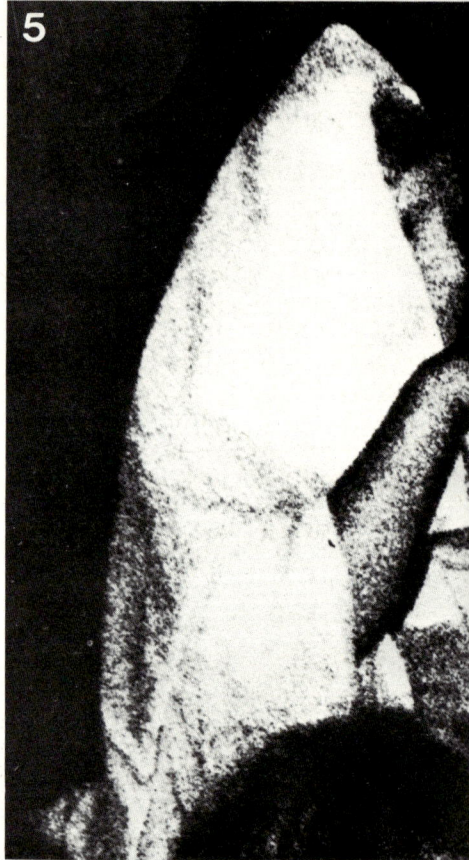

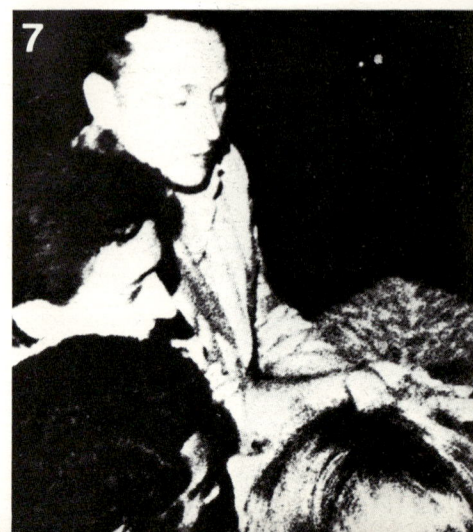

After the reports Crookes made of his sensational work with Florence Cook and Katie King, Katie became a kind of psychic celebrity. It was claimed that she appeared not only at the Philadelphia seance, but in Winnipeg as well. More recently, she reportedly materialized in Rome in July 1974, appearing to a circle of 23 sitters. The seance was held under strong red light that made strange photo lighting. The medium was Fulvio Rendhell.

common sense than to believe her to be what she herself affirms.''

Crookes' experiments with Florence Cook were not as rigidly controlled as today's psychic researchers would demand. Nonetheless they leave few areas of doubt. There are three possible conclusions: either Katie King was in fact a spirit being, in which case Crookes' research is probably the most important on record; or Florence Cook deceived everyone about her mediumistic powers, in which case she must be regarded as the most accomplished imposter in Spiritualism's history; or Crookes and the young medium were in collusion. The third alternative touches the distinguished scientist with scandal. It is based on a statement by a man named Anderson, who claims that Florence Cook made a confession of fraud to him during her later life. According to Anderson, she also said that Crookes was having an affair with her. This statement was not made public until after Anderson's death. Most researchers regard it as flimsy evidence either of fraud or of a sexual alliance between Florence Cook and Sir William Crookes. It seems unlikely that a scientist of Crookes' standing would risk his career and reputation by fabricating evidence. However, his predisposition to believe in Spiritualism must be taken into consideration. Whatever the explanation, the story of the scientist, the medium, and the spirit girl remains one of the most fascinating and puzzling enigmas in the Spiritualist saga.

While Crookes was photographing Katie King, another prominent scientist was embarking on a study of psychic phenomena. This was Sir William Barrett, professor of physics

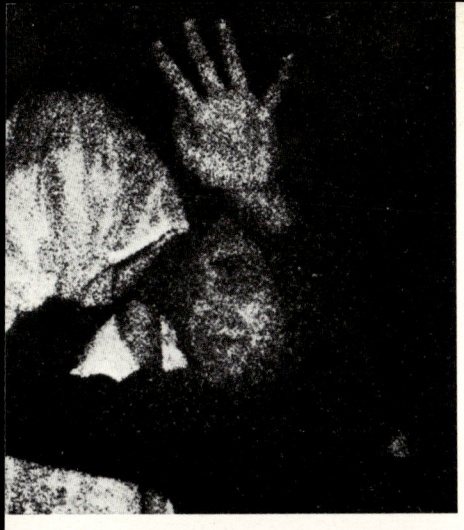

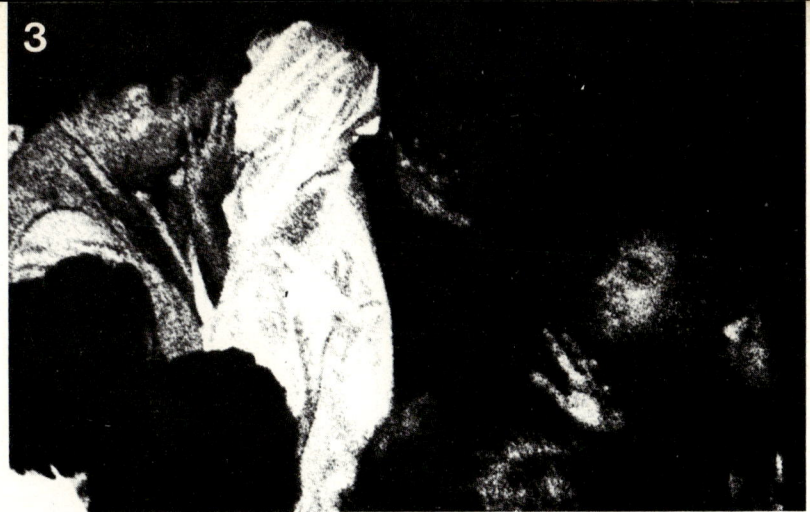

Katie materialized gradually (2), and then walked around the outside of the circle touching several sitters and kissing a few. She materialized gladioli and rose petals (3 & 6), which she held during the full half hour of her appearance. Katie permitted a doctor to check her heartbeat and temperature; both were normal. Then she embraced her medium, and dematerialized on his chest, leaving an empty chair (7) and the flowers behind.

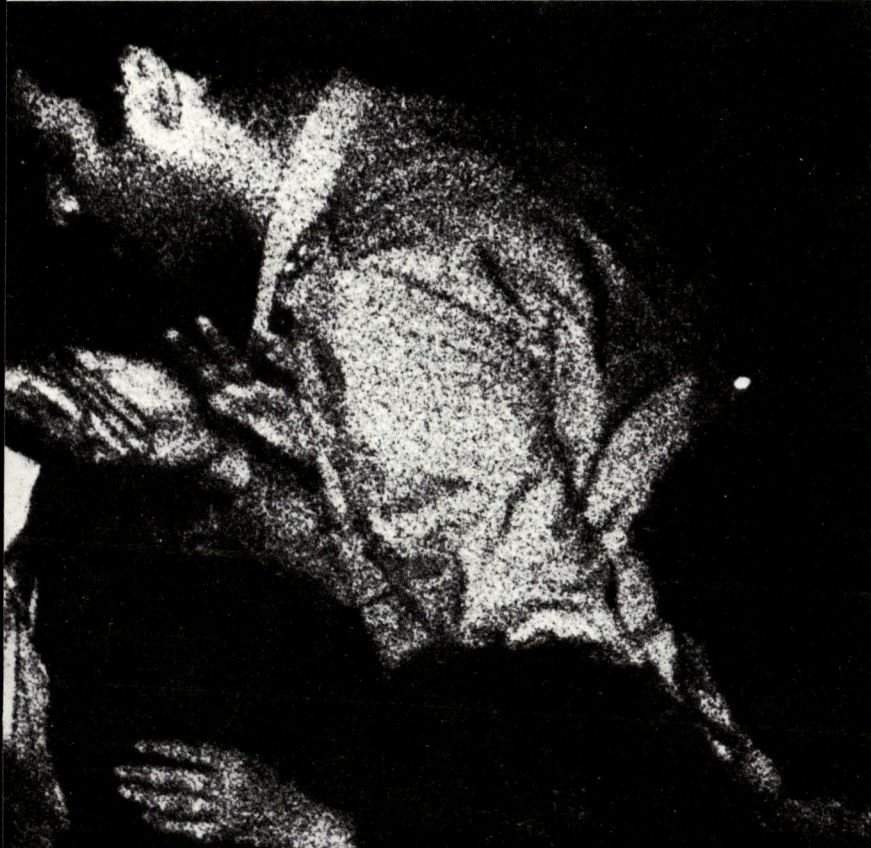

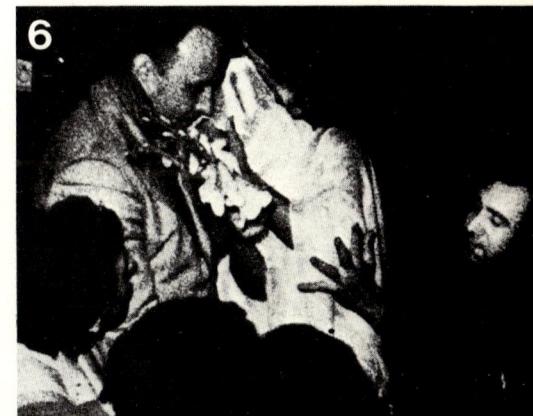

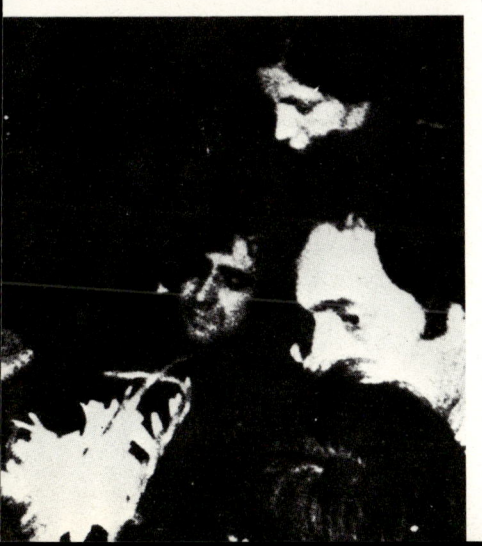

at the Royal College of Science in Dublin. His first experiments centered on hypnotic trances, but he went on to study many aspects of Spiritualism including physical phenomena. During the course of his research, he heard raps in broad daylight in circumstances that ruled out fraud. After that he was inclined to consider raps as possible indication of spirit activity. But he still at first dismissed the more dramatic phenomena—such as levitation—attributing them to hallucination. He later revised his thinking on the subject when he discovered that some of his friends possessed mediumistic powers that caused levitation. They were above suspicion, and with their help he carried out tests in daylight which satisfied him that such powers were genuine.

In January 1882 Barrett called a conference in the offices of the British National Association of Spiritualists. Out of this was born the Society for Psychical Research (SPR). Its objectives were to examine a variety of phenomena including telepathy, hypnotism, apparitions, and the physical phenomena of Spiritualism, and to collect and collate material on these subjects. The SPR, still active today, holds no corporate view on any of these phenomena, but many of its members, and its own publications, have been responsible for presenting much of the best-authenticated evidence for Spiritualist phenomena. Professor Barrett was one of the original members of the Society, along with other eminent researchers and Spiritualists. Three years later, during a visit to the United States, Barrett gave impetus to the foundation of the American Society for Psychical Research.

Crookes once wrote that he "intended only to devote a leisure month or two to ascertain whether certain marvelous occurrences . . . would stand the test of close scrutiny." He discovered, however, that "the subject is far more difficult and extensive than it appears," and those months soon became years. The same was probably true of Barrett, who spent over half a century investigating Spiritualism and similar subjects. In a paper included in the SPR's *Proceedings* in 1924 entitled "Some Reminiscences of Fifty Years of Psychical Research," Barrett summed up his conclusions. He stated that there is evidence for the existence of a spiritual world, for survival after death, and for occasional communications from those who have died—or "passed over" as Spiritualists say.

As the founders of the SPR were launching a systematic study of the psychic world, the world-famous physicist Sir Oliver Lodge was independently becoming involved in experiments in telepathy. While teaching at Liverpool University, Lodge was asked by a local merchant to supervise some tests of two of his salesgirls who had shown telepathic powers. The tests were conducted along lines suggested by the SPR, and Lodge submitted a report of the findings to the Society. Soon afterward he became a member of the organization.

His interest in psychical research having been aroused, Lodge continued such study for the remaining 56 years of his life. He became convinced of the existence of thought-transference. He also encountered convincing evidence of the continued existence of the personality after death—called "survival" by Spiritualists—in the work of the remarkable Boston medium Mrs. Leonore

Piper. This American medium visited England in 1889–90 purposely to give test seances for the SPR. She and her daughters, who were met in Liverpool by Lodge, stayed with the Lodge family for some time. During seances in their home she went into trance and produced information about distant and deceased relatives of Lodge. She included details that she could not have learned merely from talking to the Lodge family, or even from family letters and records. Lodge became, in his own words, "thoroughly convinced not only of human survival, but of the power to communicate, under certain conditions, with those left behind on the earth."

Having satisfied himself about the value of Spiritualism, Lodge became a crusader, sharing his findings with any who would listen to him or read his words. It was not until World War I that his belief in communications with the spirit world received its greatest publicity, however. This was through a very personal book, *Raymond, or Life and Death*. In it Lodge related the events surrounding the tragic loss of his son Raymond, who was killed in action in September 1915. He said that, before learning of his son's death, he had received a cryptic message in automatic writing from Mrs. Piper, then on her third visit to England. The message was from Dr. Richard Hodgson, a pillar of the SPR who had died in 1905. Through Mrs. Piper he wrote in part: "Myers says you take the part of the poet and he will act as Faunus. Faunus. Myers. Protect." (Frederick Myers, one of the founders of the SPR, had been dead since 1901). A classical scholar recognized the reference to Faunus as coming from a poem by the Roman writer Horace. In his poem, Horace describes how the woodland god Faunus saved his life by cushioning the blow when a tree fell on him. Shortly afterward Lodge received the news of his son's death. He then interpreted the message as both a prediction of the event and as an effort by the spirits to cushion him from the blow. Lodge gave other examples in his book of the numerous communications he and his wife received from their dead son through mediums.

Before he died Lodge left a sealed message with the SPR. He let it be known that the message contained details he had never revealed to anyone, and that he hoped to reveal from beyond the grave. Although many messages were allegedly received from the great physicist after his death in 1940, none has been the one Lodge intended to communicate as the proof of survival.

Whereas scientists usually accept the conclusions of their colleagues on scientific matters, they have always been reluctant to concur on psychic matters without having personal experience. This is probably partly because the evidence violates well-established natural laws, and partly, no doubt, because emotional factors can influence the evaluation of evidence. And so, although Dr. Alfred Russel Wallace, Sir William Crookes, Sir William Barrett, and Sir Oliver Lodge had all accepted the evidence in favor of Spiritualist claims after their own research, other scientists scoffed at their findings.

For example, Professor Cesar Lombroso, a famous Italian criminologist, wrote an article in 1888 in which he ridiculed Spiritualism. As a result, he was publicly challenged to a seance with a famous medium, and in 1891 he accepted the invitation.

Above: the American medium Mrs. Leonore Piper. Almost all her work was done under strict scientific control. Her powers were almost entirely mental, her one physical accomplishment being to withdraw scent from flowers which then withered. Below: an example of automatic writing as done by Leonore Piper.

Above left: Cesar Lombroso, the skeptical Italian criminologist who was convinced that at least some Spiritualistic manifestations were genuine after sitting with the medium Eusapia Paladino. Above right: Eusapia Paladino. Right: a 1909 cartoon from the *American Journal-Examiner* during Eusapia Paladino's American tour, when she was detected in the act of producing fraudulent effects at her seances. Her exposure caused a sensation in the press. Below: a table levitating at one of Eusapia Paladino's seances. When her feet were not held, she would lift the tables with her knees. However, even when she was put under tight restraint, the tables still unquestionably rose.

He was accompanied by three other professors and five doctors. Afterward he wrote: "I am ashamed and grieved at having opposed with so much tenacity the possibility of the so-called spiritistic facts; I say the facts because I am still opposed to the theory. But the facts exist, and I boast of being a slave to facts."

Lombroso continued to investigate Spiritualism, and eventually accepted the idea that the dead could communicate through mediums. In his book *After Death—What?* he gave an account of a seance with the medium who had convinced him of the genuineness of psychic powers:

"The medium, who was seated near one end of the table, was lifted up in her chair bodily, amid groans and lamentations on her part, and placed (still seated) on the table, then returned to the same position as before, with her hands continually held, her movements being accompanied by the persons next to her."

The medium in question was Eusapia Paladino, an almost illiterate peasant woman of Neapolitan birth. For 20 years she was the center of intensive research by almost every psychical researcher of importance in Britain, in America, and on the Continent. She was often exposed in fraud, but nearly every scientist who investigated her came to the conclusion that she could also produce a wide variety of genuine manifestations. Sir Oliver Lodge was one of the scientists who sat with Eusapia Paladino. Another was Dr. Charles Richet, Professor of Physiology at the Faculty of Medicine in Paris. Professor P. Foa, Professor of Pathological Anatomy at the University of Turin, and several other Italian scientists also tested the medium and published a report of their findings.

Although a curtained cabinet was used by Eusapia Paladino, she always sat outside and the manifestations—hands and faces sometimes—appeared inside the cabinet. During the seance with Professor Foa and his colleagues, a photographic plate was used in an attempt to register radiations associated with the phenomena. The presence of this plate, according to the report, aroused the spirits' hostility:

"The 'hand' . . . made an effort to seize the plate by snatching it unexpectedly, and renewed this attempt repeatedly, but without success. Dr. Foa seized the hand which was covered with the curtain, and had the impression of pressing real fingers; the fingers escaped him, however, and gave him a blow . . . Dr. Aggazotti, who held another plate over the medium's head, had in his turn to struggle in order to prevent its escaping him.

"At this juncture the medium told . . . Foa not to be alarmed whatever might happen, and advised all present not to touch the objects which would be suspended in the air, otherwise she would be unable to restrain the movements and might hurt somebody.

"Table No. 1 rose in the air many inches high, and passed once over the head of Prof. Foa; returning to the ground and, keeping all the time outside the cabinet, it turned over, then stood up again. . . .

"After table No. 1 had stood upright, Dr. Arullani approached it, but the piece of furniture moving violently toward him, repulsed him; Dr. Arullani seized the table, which was heard to crack in the struggle . . . [the table] passed behind the curtain . . .

The Spirit Hand that Slapped

During his investigation of the powers of Eusapia Paladino, the Italian medium noted for bang-up seances, Professor P. Foa tried to use a photographic plate to register radiations. Eusapia Paladino's spirits apparently resented the interference. As the medium sat in trance outside the curtained cabinet, a hand shot out and tried to snatch the plate. Dr. Foa seized the hand as it retreated behind the curtains and felt the fingers, but the hand wriggled loose and hit him squarely.

The spirits then turned their attention to a table, which they sailed over the heads of the company. When one sitter attempted to approach it, the spirits whisked it behind the curtain where it began to break up noisily. Dr. Foa saw the table turn over on its side, and one leg snap off. At that point it shot back out of the cabinet and continued to break up noisily under the fascinated gaze of the entire circle. One of the sitters asked for a handshake, and Eusapia Paladino invited him to approach the cabinet. He had hardly reached it when he felt himself attacked by hands and pieces of wood.

The entire circle heard the noises of the blows, and saw the hand moving in the ghostly half-light.

Left: Baron A. Shrenck-Notzing, a physician from Munich, Germany who did much pioneering work in psychical research. He was particularly interested in the nature of ectoplasm. He spent several years investigating the phenomenon of a young girl medium known as Eva C.

Right: Eva C. and Bien Boa, one of her materializations. He was supposed to be a Brahmin Hindu who had died 300 years before. Eva C., whose real name was Marthe Beraud, was discovered by a General Noel and his wife, while in Algeria. They were both greatly interested in psychical research. Eva C. had been engaged to their son before his death in the Congo. She was tested under stringent conditions, but the results were dubious. After a few years all her psychic powers apparently disappeared entirely.

Left: Eva C. producing ectoplasm. Her hands are holding apart the curtains of the cabinet. The photograph was taken by flashlight.

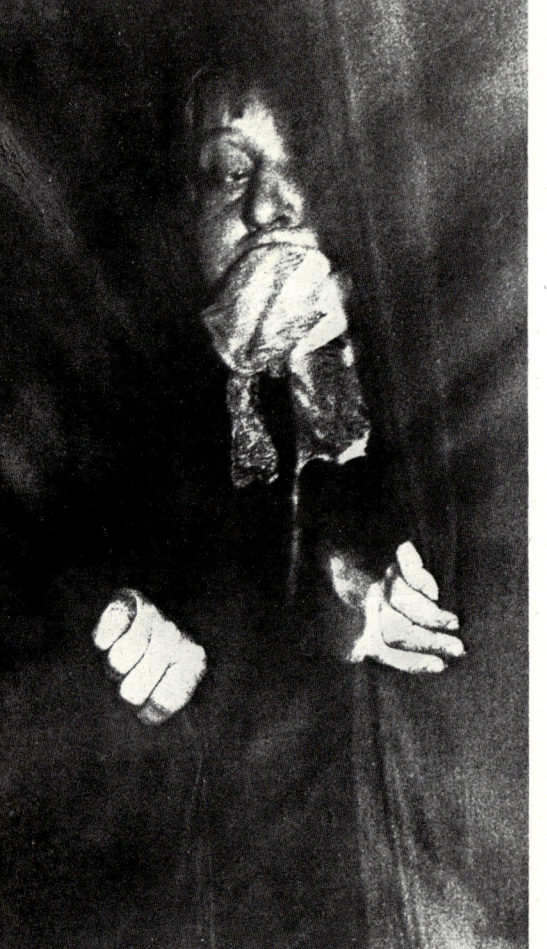

Dr. Foa saw it turn over and rest on one of its two short sides, whilst one of the legs came off violently, as if under the action of some force pressing upon it. At this moment the table came violently out of the cabinet, and continued to break up under the eyes of every one present. Dr. Arullani asked for [a] handshake, and was invited by the medium to approach the cabinet. He had hardly reached it when he felt himself hit by pieces of wood and hands, and we all heard the noise of the blows."

No one slept when Eusapia Paladino was giving a seance!

All the European investigators of Eusapia Paladino knew that the medium sometimes used trickery, and also knew her tricks. However, when she went to the United States during 1909–10, she was given much bad publicity on being exposed in her well-known frauds, in spite of her performance of many genuine phenomena. Her defenders said that she was so fearful of her American investigators that she often did not allow herself to go into trance in case she might be hurt. She herself explained to one newspaper reporter: "Some people are at the table who expect tricks—in fact they want them. I am in a trance. Nothing happens. They get impatient. They think of the tricks—nothing but the tricks. They put their minds on the tricks and I automatically respond. But it is not often. They merely will me to do them."

Psychic magazine sums up Eusapia Paladino's extraordinary career in these words: "No scientist then or now . . . has been able to explain many of [her] dizzying feats in any way that does not of necessity imply the existence of some force as yet completely unknown to science . . . she is one of history's unresolved paradoxes."

The ability of mediums to produce physical manifestations has been attributed to a curious substance called ectoplasm. This substance, produced from the medium's body, is believed to be capable of assuming various forms. Sometimes, according to Spiritualists, it is able to cause raps and knocks though invisible. At other times, it takes on the appearance of a misty cloud floating around the room. Spiritualists believe it can also become as solid as a human being, taking on all the human characteristics of color and texture. Baron A. von Schrenk-Notzing, a Munich physician and psychical researcher, was able to obtain and preserve a small piece of ectoplasm and submit it for analysis. It was found to contain leukocytes—white or colorless blood cells—and epithelial cells—those from various protective tissues of the body. Ectoplasm was, he said, "an organized tissue which easily decomposes—a sort of transitory matter which originates in the organism in a manner unknown to us, possesses unknown biological functions and formative possibilities, and is evidently peculiarly dependent on the psychic influences of the medium."

Between 1917 and 1920, Dr. W. J. Crawford, lecturer in mechanical engineering at Queens University, Belfast, conducted many experimental seances with the Goligher family in an attempt to define the nature of ectoplasm. He discovered that during seances, the medium, Kathleen Goligher, and the sitters all lost weight. The medium's body shrank perceptibly. Placing the medium on a set of scales, he measured her loss of weight when ectoplasm was experimentally withdrawn in fluxes from her. The maximum loss was $54\frac{1}{2}$ pounds, nearly half her normal weight. By contrast, during table levitations her weight increased. Strict test controls prevented her from touching the table, so the increase could not be explained by her bearing the weight. Dr. Crawford put forward the theory that the medium threw out ectoplasmic supports, like cantilevers. He was able to take flash photographs that appear to show ectoplasmic rods issuing from Kathleen Goligher, some of them reaching to the table. Dr. Crawford had reached no final conclusion at the time of his death on July 30, 1920.

Sir William Barrett was a witness at one of the Goligher seances. He described later how he had seen the table suspended 18 inches in the air with no one touching it. He was unable to press the table down, using all his strength. When he climbed onto it to force it down, he was promptly thrown off. After this the table turned upside down on the floor. He was asked to lift it up, but was unable to move it. It "appeared screwed down to the floor," he attested.

It is now many years since these eminent scientists investigated Spiritualism and, although many of them declared themselves 100 percent convinced of the authenticity of some of the psychic phenomena, we are today no nearer a scientific understanding of what really happens at a seance. The case for the authenticity of physical phenomena rests largely on the research of these early pioneers, for today there are few mediums who claim power to produce such phenomena. Mediums at some Spiritualist camps still offer to give materialization seances, but the ease with which the manifestations appear makes their genuineness more than a little suspect.

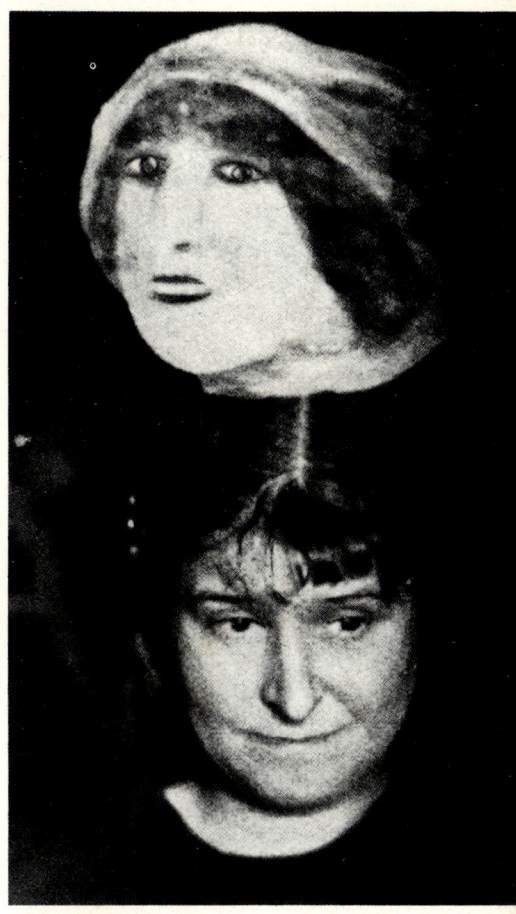

Some of the spirits materialized by Eva C. had a distinctly flat, two-dimensional appearance, and skeptics suggested they were simply pictures on cardboard. This is certainly indicated by the materialization above with its striking resemblance to a photo in a magazine (below) which had appeared just four weeks earlier.

4

Frauds and Fraud-hunters

On a cold night in January 1880, Marie, a "spirit girl", was singing and dancing before some distinguished guests. Round and round the darkened seance room she danced. Suddenly one of the guests reached out and grabbed her by the wrist. Surprisingly, the spirit struggled and fought with him—and the seance ended abruptly when gaslight revealed that Marie was really the medium herself, dressed only in undergarments.

An even more embarrassing aspect of the exposure was the fact that the medium was the same Florence Cook whose Katie King materialization had walked arm-in-arm with Sir William Crookes a few years earlier.

As Spiritualism developed, the phenomena became more dramatic and the opportunities for fraud more abundant. Investigators of a skeptical turn of mind looked for cheating, and found it. Above: Harry Houdini, one of the most famous of all stage magicians, hunted Spiritualist frauds. He wrote that he had truly sought an example of communication from the next world, but in 30 years had not "found one incident that savored of the genuine." This picture of Houdini and a crown of spirits was taken by a Denver spirit photographer, A. Martin, in 1923. Houdini dismissed the picture as a double exposure. Right: an illustration from the *London Graphic* in 1880, showing the famous seance where the spirit girl Marie turned out to be the medium in her underwear.

The preliminaries are not at all unpleasant

Just a going to begin

SPIRITUAL GARMENTS

AWFUL!!

Be thou a Shirik or health or godlin whem

59

"Many genuine mediums will resort to fraud"

Below: Dr. Henry Slade, the American slate-writing medium. His calamitous visit to England had originally been planned simply as a stopover on his way to St. Petersburg. There he was to demonstrate his supernormal phenomena to the University investigators Madame Blavatsky and Colonel Olcott, who had been asked to find a suitable medium.

That famous scientist had affirmed his belief in the genuineness of the phenomena Miss Cook had produced under his supervision. Even now, when she was caught in an act of fraud, he continued to believe in her psychic powers. Others, too, continued to believe in her. As for Florence Cook's reaction to the exposé, she was apparently untroubled by it, for she gave another seance the following day.

All professional mediums cheat. That was the view of Camille Flammarion, the French psychic researcher. However, Flammarion was also convinced after nearly 60 years' study of psychic phenomena that mediums could be genuine. His views on fraud were shared by many of his fellow researchers. "It is unfortunately true," wrote the English psychic investigator Hereward Carrington, "that many genuine mediums will frequently resort to fraud when their powers fail them, or when phenomena are not readily forthcoming." He said that the Italian medium Eusapia Paladino, whom he considered to possess genuine powers of a high order, "would constantly trick whenever the occasion for her to do so was presented."

Spiritualists learned to live with a certain amount of fraud as, one after another, even the most respected mediums were caught impersonating spirits. Like some of the scientists, they believed a single case of fraud was not enough proof that a medium had no genuine powers. This permissive attitude toward occasional fraud explains why, even after an exposure, most mediums were able to continue filling their seance rooms.

Although many researchers could easily detect even clever fraud, and could take it into account in their conclusions, it was disputed whether the careful investigator could never be fooled. A lively debate on this subject arose during discussion of Sir William Crookes' paper on mesmerism and Spiritualism, read before the British Association for the Advancement of Science in 1876. Crookes was confident that the controls he applied in testing mediums would make fraud impossible. Sir William Barrett of the SPR disagreed, arguing that a skilled magician or fraudulent medium could be equipped with devices which, whatever the conditions imposed, could be used to deceive.

In spite of the fact that controls in the early days of psychical research were rather slack by modern standards, a great many mediums were exposed in fraud. In 1876—the same year that Crookes and Barrett debated the subject—three British mediums who had attracted large followings were caught red-handed.

Francis Ward Monck, a clergyman turned medium, was challenged by a magician who insisted on searching the medium during a seance in Huddersfield, England. Monck ran into a room, locked himself in, and escaped through a window. Later a pair of stuffed gloves were found among his belongings. Monck was apprehended and put on trial for fraud. Dr. Alfred Russel Wallace, the scientist who had investigated Agnes Nichol and others, was one of the defense witnesses. He claims to have seen Monck produce the spirit form of a woman without trickery. However, Monck had been caught in a flagrant fraud before by none other than Sir William Barrett. On that occasion Sir William found Monck simulating a partially materialized spirit with a piece of white muslin on a wire frame.

Above: a contemporary drawing showing Henry Slade's trial. The man testifying in the witness box is Professor Lankester, who had seized Slade's slate and found writing already prepared. Slade asserted that just as the slate was snatched he heard the spirit writing, and said so, but his words were lost in the commotion.

Above: Henry Slade and a sitter. General messages were written clearly and punctuated carefully, as might be expected if they were prepared in advance, but answers to on-the-spot questions were vague, clumsily written, and difficult to read. In short, they bore unmistakeable traces of hasty work under pressure.

Above: a slate used in seances with its red wax seals visible. (The College of Psychic Studies)

1 2 3

Above: contemporary drawings exposing the methods of fraudulent mediums to produce startling fake effects at their sittings. Almost all seances were held in the dark, since strong light was believed to be harmful to mediums in trance, but the darkened rooms offered a perfect opportunity for the fraudulent medium and his tricks. 1. Simulating levitation. The medium creeps around the circle, pretending he is floating above the sitters' heads as he knocks a few with the heels of shoes. 2 and 3. Two views of a "spirit hand" at work mystifying the credulous would-be believers.

On the present occasion, Monck was found guilty of fraud and sentenced to three months in prison.

Dr. Henry Slade, an American medium known for spirit writing on slate blackboards, visited Britain in the same year. Professor Ray Lankester was determined to expose Slade as an imposter. Together with another investigator he visited the American medium and observed his techniques. During his second visit to Slade, Lankester suddenly seized the small blackboard before the writing was to take place. He found a message already written on it and secreted. After exposing Slade in a letter to *The Times* on September 16, 1876, Lankester brought an action against the medium for obtaining money under false pretences. The case was heard on October 1. Once again, as in Monck's trial, Dr. Alfred Russel Wallace was a witness for the defense. Despite this distinguished support, Slade was found guilty and sentenced to three months' imprisonment with hard labor. In the course of the appeal the sentence was quashed on technical grounds, and Slade left England quickly for the Continent before Lankester could obtain a fresh summons. When he returned to London two years later he did so under the assumed name of Dr. Wilson.

William Eglinton was the third medium to be revealed as a fraud in 1876. The accounts of his seances are among the most dramatic in the annals of psychic science, and include a number of materializations that occurred out of doors in bright daylight. Eglinton was exposed by Thomas Colley, the Archdeacon of Natal in Southern Africa and the Rector of Stockton in England. The Archdeacon, an eager psychical researcher, cut off pieces of the white robe and beard of a spirit materialized by Eglinton. Later investigation showed that these exactly matched some muslin and a false beard found in the medium's suitcase. His exposure of Eglinton did not make Archdeacon Colley discredit all mediums. He was a firm believer in the genuineness of Monck, for example, and challenged J. N. Maskelyne, a famous magician and anti-Spiritualist, to duplicate Monck's materialization performances by trickery. Archdeacon Colley offered a large sum of money if the magician were successful. Maskelyne attempted to produce a materialization, but failed.

This underlines the enigma of mediumship—that although

4

5

6

three well-known mediums such as Monck, Slade, and Eglinton were exposed in fraud, many scientists and investigators of repute did not doubt that all three were also capable of extraordinary mediumistic feats without evidence of trickery.

From the earliest days of Spiritualism there has been a running battle between mediums and magicians. In 1853, just five years after the Hydesville rappings had taken the public by surprise, the first challenge was issued by magician J. H. Anderson of New York. He offered a handsome monetary reward to "any poverty stricken medium" who could produce raps in the public hall where he gave his performances. The Fox sisters were among those who accepted Anderson's challenge, but Anderson backed out and, amid hisses from the audience, refused to allow the mediums on the stage.

The magician-medium rivalry reached a peak in the case of the Davenport brothers. Their home in Buffalo, New York, had had an outbreak of raps, bumps, and assorted other noises in 1846—two years before the more publicized Hydesville rappings. In 1850 the two boys, Ira and William, and their young sister Elizabeth, tried table turning. The table moved, conveying messages, and some force caused Ira's hand to write automatically. Some witnesses at the same session claimed that the three children levitated simultaneously.

The two young Davenport brothers decided to go professional and give theater performances. They used a special cabinet that had three doors at the front and a bench running lengthwise inside. The center door had a small diamond-shaped opening covered by a curtain, through which various phenomena could manifest. Before each performance members of the audience were free to inspect the cabinet, and also to check that the Davenports, who sat astride the bench facing each other, were securely tied and immobile. Within seconds of the doors being closed, the brothers were able to produce raps, musical sounds, and a variety of other phenomena. During part of the performance a member of the audience was allowed to sit on the bench between the brothers.

Although the phenomena were typical of Spiritualist seances of the day, the brothers maintained an ambiguous stance in regard to their powers. They never presented themselves as

Seance procedure was usually for the members of the circle to hold—or at least touch—hands. This not only united their psychic energies, but could also serve as a rudimentary control on the medium. However, it was easily bypassed by any deft and unscrupulous medium, as many exposures have shown.
4. The medium starts out with both hands in contact with those of the sitters on either side.
5. Note the hands. One is now free for banging the tambourine.
6. The trustful sitters, still hand in hand, are duly impressed by the amazing spirit activity.

THE DAVENPORT BROTHERS'
PUBLIC CABINET SÉANCE.

NOW BEING HELD AT

THE QUEEN'S CONCERT ROOMS,
HANOVER SQUARE.

Right: the Davenport brothers in their famous cabinet with three doors. The two gentlemen in the middle are a medium and Robert Cooper, who wrote a book about the wonder workers. He said he was certain that they were only "passive instruments."

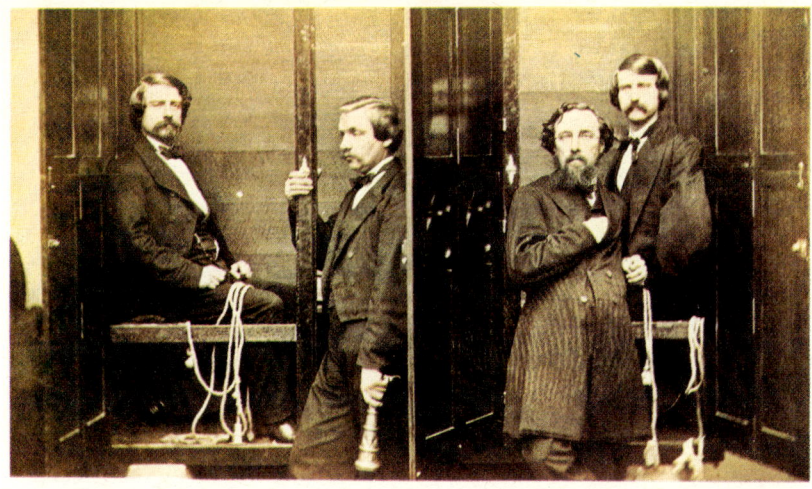

MR IRA DAVENPORT.   MR FAY.   MR COOPER.   MR WM DAVENPORT

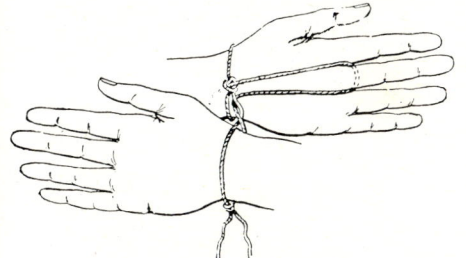

Above: the Davenport knot as explained by W. E. Robinson, a contemporary investigator. He claimed that the Davenports always used a smooth hard-finished rope, which made it impossible for a really secure knot to be tied. The brothers would also influence the person who did the tying to use a particular procedure. This was to tie the left hand first with two or three good knots around the wrist as the two faced the audience. Then, as the brothers put their left hands behind their backs and turned their backs to the audience, the person tying them up was to tie the right hands to the left hands with as many knots as he or she saw fit. But— according to Robinson—they had always managed to catch a little slack between the two hands, and by looping their fingers in the cord between the hands, made certain that the slack did not pull away. Once safely in the cabinet, they simply bent the fingers and, with enough slack to get one hand free, untied the other and produced the noises.

Left: a poster advertising one of the performances by the two Davenport brothers. Their public seances were well advertised and well attended, in spite of— or perhaps because of—the similarity of their rope effects to a nonpsychic conjuring act.

Spiritualists; on the other hand, they insisted on the genuineness of the phenomena. In 1857 they responded to a challenge from the *Boston Courier*, which had offered a big prize to anyone producing genuine physical phenomena. A committee of professors from Harvard University conducted the tests. The brothers were tied in their cabinet with no thought for their comfort; the ropes around them were drawn through holes bored in the cabinet, firmly knotted outside, and tied again with linen strips. Professor Benjamin Pierce, a committee member, sat in the cabinet between the brothers. According to the brothers' biographer, as soon as Professor Pierce entered an invisible hand shot the bolt, the din of musical instruments filled the tiny room, and a phantom hand moved in and out of the diamond-shaped window in the center door. The professor also felt the hand touching his face. At the end of the session the brothers were found released from their ropes, and the ropes were found twisted around the professor's neck. This last statement was hotly denied by the sponsoring newspaper, but it was neither verified or denied by the committee. Aside from a brief negative statement, it never published a report of its findings. However, the prize money was not awarded, so we may surmise that the professors were unconvinced.

In 1864 the Davenports went to England where they soon became a center of controversy. They held seances every night for more than two months in a public hall in London. Various committees studied these demonstrations without finding evidence of fraud. Nevertheless, there was widespread public opposition and even hostility. The Davenports were not helped by the fact that the long ropes and other paraphernalia they used were typical of magicians' acts.

When the Davenports visited Liverpool two members of an inspection committee selected by the audience used a complicated knot to secure the brothers. The Davenports protested that the knot was too tight and inhibited their circulation, but a doctor who examined them disagreed. They refused to sit, and asked one of their helpers to cut the knot. The following night a riot broke out, and the Davenports hastily left Liverpool.

In Hull, Huddersfield, and Leeds, the brothers encountered

openly threatening and antagonistic audiences. Feeling that police protection was inadequate, they broke off further engagements. Writing of these events to an associate, the Davenports said: "Were we mere jugglers we should meet with no violence, or we should find protection. Could we declare that these things done in our presence were deception of the senses, we should no doubt reap a plentiful harvest of money and applause. . . . But we are not jugglers, and truthfully declare that we are not, and we are mobbed from town to town, our property destroyed and our lives imperilled."

Life was not all unpleasantness for the Davenports. They went to France where, after some initial opposition from the authorities, they gave a number of successful performances. Before leaving Paris they were summoned to appear before Emperor Napoleon III and Empress Eugénie at the Palace of St. Cloud. There they performed for an astonished gathering of the nobility. They went on to Belgium and then to St. Petersburg, now Leningrad, where the Czar received them in the Winter Palace.

The brothers must have had their private beliefs about the nature of the phenomena they produced, assuming that they were not fraudulent, but they remained resolutely noncommittal in speaking of them. One obvious reason for such a policy was that the speculation and controversy on their attitude created tremendous publicity—and therefore larger audiences. In a letter to Harry Houdini, one of the world's most famous magicians, Ira Davenport said: "We never in public affirmed our belief in Spiritualism. That we regarded as no business of the public, nor did we offer our entertainment as the result of sleight-of-hand or, on the other hand, as Spiritualism. We let our friends and foes settle that as best they could between themselves, but, unfortunately, we were often the victims of their disagreement."

Houdini believed that he could produce all the Davenport's amazing effects by trickery. He claimed that in 1911 he tracked down the surviving brother, Ira, then in his 70s to discover the secret behind one puzzling aspect of their performance. One of the conditions sometimes imposed on the brothers by a member of the audience was that they had to hold flour in their hands throughout the performance. They were able to produce the phenomena without spilling the flour. Houdini claimed that Ira admitted to fraud, revealing that they simply held the flour in the palms of their hands while using their teeth and thumbs to manipulate the ropes and musical instruments. However, there is only Houdini's word for this.

Houdini rode to stardom on the Spiritualist bandwagon, throwing out challenges to mediums wherever he went. According to the British Spiritualist weekly *Psychic News*, Houdini was himself a fraudulent medium for five years before achieving fame as a magician. His subsequent campaign against mediums was accompanied by a wealth of publicity. Part of his act was to give a seance in which he duplicated by trickery the effects presented as genuine by mediums.

Houdini said he believed it was his mission to protect the public from fraudulent mediums. But it also seems that he would

Above: Ira Davenport in his old age with Harry Houdini. (William died in 1877 during a tour of Australia.) Houdini claimed that in 1909 Ira had quite willingly explained to him exactly how the brothers had faked their effects.

HARRY HOUDINI THE JAIL BREAKER

INTRODUCING HIS LATEST & GREATEST

PRISON CELL & BARREL MYSTERY

HOUDINI is strapped & locked in a barrel placed in a police cell which is also locked and in less than 2 seconds changes places.

£100. WILL BE PAID TO ANYONE FINDING TRAPS, PANELS OR FALSE DOORS IN THE CELL.

Above: a poster advertising one of Houdini's fantastic escape performances. As an expert at mystifying audiences, Houdini was himself a very difficult man to fool, although he did not win all his attempts to expose mediums.

go to any lengths, fair or foul, to prove trickery in psychic phenomena. In 1922 he agreed to be a committee member for the *Scientific American*, which offered a huge prize for proof of genuine mediumship. Margery Crandon, wife of a professor of surgery at the Harvard Medical School, was one of the mediums to be tested. She conducted several convincing seances for the committee in Houdini's absence, and it seemed that they were about to award her the money in 1924.

Houdini hurried back to challenge the decision. Three more sessions were arranged, during which Houdini imposed strict conditions. He designed a cabinet in which the medium could be enclosed with only her head and hands visible. This was used for two of the seances. During the second seance Mrs. Crandon's spirit control Walter accused Houdini of planting incriminating evidence in the cabinet. When the session came to an end, a folding rule was found in the cabinet. Houdini in turn accused Margery Crandon of having smuggled it into the cabinet so that she could use it to manipulate a small box containing a bell which, supposedly, was rung by spirit hands. After Houdini's death in 1926, his assistant confessed that he himself had put the ruler in the cabinet on Houdini's instructions. Whether Houdini exposed Margery Crandon or whether the spirit control exposed Houdini is still a matter for debate.

When the famous illusionist died in 1926, he left a code word with his wife Beatrice in order to prove his identity if anyone claimed to get messages from him. Just over two years later, Beatrice Houdini announced that she herself had received a

Left: a spirit photograph faked to show the spirit of Lincoln and Houdini brooding together. It became part of the collection of Harry Price, an amateur conjurer and a respected investigator into dubious psychic phenomena.

message from her dead husband through a young medium named Arthur Ford. In sworn testimony she declared:

"Regardless of any statements made to the contrary, I wish to declare that the message, in its entirety, and in the agreed-upon sequence, given to me by Arthur Ford, is the correct message prearranged between Mr. Houdini and myself."

The witnesses to the statement were H. R. Zander of the United Press; Mrs. Minnie Chester, a lifelong friend of Mrs. Houdini; and J. W. Stafford, associate editor of the *Scientific American*.

Beatrice Houdini had not accepted Ford's mediumship without prior evidence, and had arranged a seance with him only after a previous series of sittings attended by Houdini's mother. In those seances separate words were given, presumably by Houdini, through Ford's spirit control or guide—which is a spirit that relates principally to one medium and introduces other spirits wanting to communicate with the living through that medium. First came "Rosabelle." Four weeks later, the word "lock." Then, after various other clues, Ford declared the entire message as: "Rosabelle — answer — tell — pray — answer — look — tell — answer — answer — tell." The dead magician asked the sitters to convey the message to his widow, adding, "I know she will be happy because neither of us believed it to be possible."

After the message was given to her, Beatrice Houdini arranged a sitting with Ford. During this seance, Ford conveyed intimate information to her from Houdini. Mrs. Houdini released the affidavit the next day, only to be greeted by sneers and abuse from Houdini's former colleagues, who accused her of fraud. This upset her so much that she wrote a long letter to newspaper columnist and radio reporter Walter Winchell, who published it.

"This letter is not for publicity," she began. "I do not need publicity. I want to let Houdini's old friends know that I did not betray his trust. I am writing because I wish to tell you emphatically that I was no party to any fraud. Now, regarding the seance: for two years I have been praying to receive the message from my husband; for two years every day I have received messages from all parts of the world from people professing to have received them. I have got the message I have been waiting for from my beloved, how, if not by spiritual aid, I do not know."

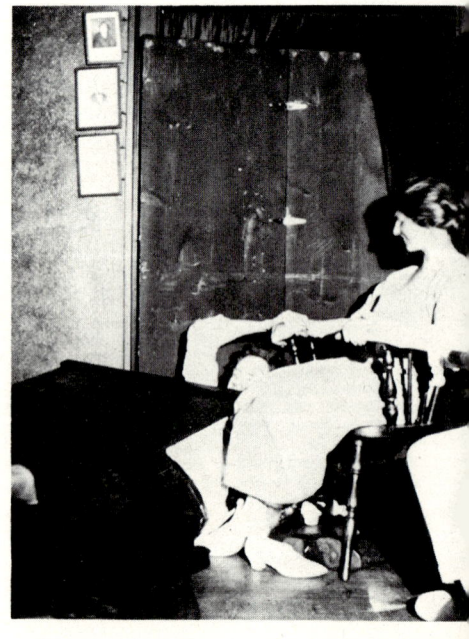

Years later, the truth of the affidavit and of the letter to Winchell came into question. When the British Broadcasting Corporation made a television film of Houdini's life in 1969, it referred to his interest in Spiritualism, but made no mention of his widow's sworn testimony. When a reporter for the *Guardian* newspaper asked the program's producer the reason for this omission, the producer replied: "We spent months researching the subject in America, but Mrs. Houdini's sister, Marie, told us that Houdini's widow had admitted to her that the affidavit was a complete fabrication; that she had signed it because Arthur Ford, her boyfriend at that time, had persuaded her to do so for personal publicity." By this time, Beatrice Houdini had died, and was unavailable for comment on this statement. However, if she had lied in issuing the affidavit, she was certainly guilty of a Spiritualist fraud as great as any of those of a similar na-

Above: Mina Crandon, who became known in Spiritualist circles under the pseudonym Margery. Her control was her brother, Walter, who had died in a train accident in 1911. Margery first gained international notice when she applied for the substantial prize offered by the *Scientific American* to any medium who could —under test conditions—produce a "visible psychic manifestation." Left: the fraud-proof wooden cage which Houdini devised to test Margery Crandon. It was uncomfortable and restrictive for anyone.

Left: a Margery Crandon seance. Malcolm Bird has been thrown to the ground by a panel of the seance cabinet which the spirit control had apparently ripped off, although it had been secured with three strong angle brackets. Right: a technique was developed for the spirit guide Walter to make his thumb print in dental wax. One of the investigators, checking Walter's print (left) against those of the sitters, found it was identical to that of Margery's dentist (on the right). He had helped her to develop the method of taking the prints. It was believed that the dentist was apparently innocent of any part in the business. Who was guilty, unless it was Walter, was never decided.

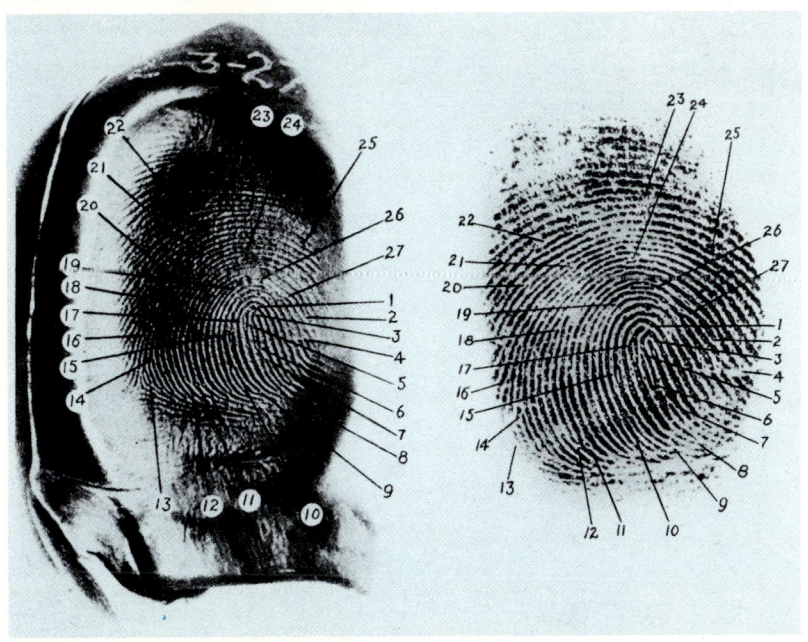

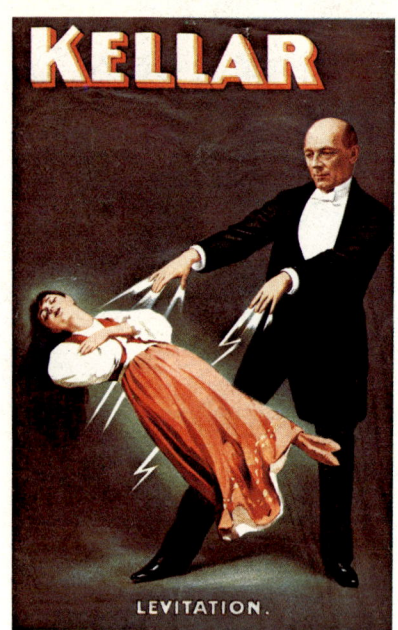

KELLAR

LEVITATION.

Above: Houdini was not the only successful professional magician who devoted himself to unmasking fake mediums. Harry Kellar also used his expert knowledge of skillful illusion to challenge frauds claiming psychic gifts. Right: Houdini with Kellar.

ture exposed by her crusading husband during his lifetime.

Another member of the Houdini team, press agent Cal Harris, also signed a statement that he had heard Houdini's voice at a seance with medium Frank Decker. "I am satisfied the medium was not speaking," said Harris, "because I had one hand over his mouth." The message Harris received was said to be personal. In the years since Houdini died, the magician Joseph Dunninger has gained valuable free publicity by holding a seance every year on the anniversary of the great man's death. Houdini never communicates—but his silence might be due to the fact that Dunninger is not a medium.

The medium who is said to have broken the Houdini code, Arthur Ford, became America's most famous mental medium— that is, one who contacts the spirits through mental processes without producing physical phenomena. The peak of his career came in a televised seance with Bishop James Pike, the former Episcopal Bishop of California. It was conducted for Toronto TV by Allen Spraggett, and was shown throughout America and in Britain. It caused a sensation. In the seance, the Bishop's dead son, James Jr., apparently communicated with his father via Ford. Later, the seance was proved to have been fraudulent. Spraggett and Canon William V. Rauscher, Ford's confidant, wrote a biography entitled *Arthur Ford: The Man Who Talked With the Dead*. In it they revealed damning evidence found in Ford's private papers after his death in January 1971.

Although he had been convinced of the genuineness of the televised seance, Bishop Pike had admitted that much of the evidence could have been obtained through the most elementary research. He was impressed mostly by obscure details in messages said to come from his predecessor, the Right Reverend Karl Morgan Block, fourth Bishop of California, and the Reverend Louis W. Pitt, former rector of an Episcopal church. All of these particular details were found in obituaries cut from newspapers and kept among the medium's private papers. Ford's biographers say that he had a remarkable memory, and used it to memorize masses of details from obituaries he collected. Yet in surveying Ford's career, Spraggett concludes: "I think the evidence supports the hypothesis that Arthur Ford was a genuine gifted psychic who, for various reasons, scrutable and inscrutable, fell back on trickery when he felt he had to."

Harry Houdini made people believe that his campaign against mediums was a trail-blazing effort to dispel public ignorance about fraudulent mediumship. But in fact, exposure had been done effectively and earlier by two books that must have been essential reading for psychical researchers in those days. In 1907 Dr. Hereward Carrington published his *The Psychical Phenomena of Spiritualism,* and in the same year David P. Abbott his *Behind the Scenes with the Mediums*. They did a thorough job of revealing the conjuring techniques used by fraudulent mediums to produce a variety of effects. Between them the two books gave no less than 100 versions of trickery in slate writing alone.

Abbott, a magician and a member of the American Society for Psychical Research, based his book on personal observation of many fraudulent mediums. In one example he describes the seemingly astonishing performance of a woman medium who gave seances in a theater. She asked her audience to write questions and sign their names on bits of paper, and to keep the papers in their possession. Then, from the stage, she answered the questions. The effect was startling, but Abbott revealed that it was relatively easy to do with the aid of accomplices. Because many members of the audience had not brought paper, assistants handed out pads of paper for their use. These pads were scored into sections so that each person could tear off the square on which he had written his question, keep it, and pass the pad to someone else. These tablets were especially prepared with wax so that the base could be easily developed and the impression left by the pressure of a pen or pencil read.

Assistants collected the pads and apparently placed them in front of the medium on the stage. In fact, however, they switched the pads, giving her blank ones and smuggling the used ones under the stage. These were quickly developed and handed to a confederate with a telephone. The medium had a small receiver hidden in her hair, which was connected to carefully concealed wires running down to copper plates in her shoes. When she stepped on two nails hammered into the stage floor, she was able to complete the telephone circuit and hear her accomplice read the questions. In addition, other assistants in the hall picked out the people who wrote questions on their own paper, and read their questions while collecting the pads throughout the audience. At the earliest opportunity they wrote out the questions they had spotted, and sent them below stage to

Below: Arthur Ford, the medium who claimed to have communicated the code that Houdini had given his wife before his death with the idea that it would, if transmitted correctly, prove that his spirit had survived death. Like most mediums, Ford seems to have resorted to unethical means to create fake paranormal effects, mainly by memorizing published information which he later presented as transmitted from those in the spirit world.

Above: a catalog of fakery for mediums in need of earthly assistance for their miracles in the seance room. According to Harry Price, the investigator, this catalog was available only on loan to mediums who had to return it when they had made their choice of goods. There were both effects, which were illustrated, and secrets. For the complete novice, there was a kit—the "Complete Spiritualistic Seance"—which included slate writing; table turning, rapping, and lifting; fire-resisting effects; and reading of sealed letters, all at a bargain price.

be read with the others. Most people came away convinced that the performance was supernormal.

A similar trick was used to astound some theater audience members. The audience was invited to write questions on pieces of paper, addressing the questions to a dead friend or relative. They were also asked to sign their names. Each question was sealed in an envelope, and given to a blindfolded medium. She or he would remove the piece of paper, read the message without removing the blindfold, and convey an answer from the spirit world. This trick is extremely simple, because even with adhesive tape and absorbent cotton beneath a blindfold, a person can see a sufficiently large area down the sides of the nose to be able to read what is written on a piece of paper. Many gullible people are convinced by this demonstration, never dreaming that in this case they themselves could do the same.

Fifty years after Abbott wrote about the question-and-answer trick, a British medium was making a fortune with the same method but more sophisticated equipment. William Roy has been described as the most audacious Spiritualist crook of modern times. Before his exposure in 1955 he was the best-known medium in Britain. He was denounced as a fraud by the Spiritualist publication *Two Worlds*. The following account of his methods is taken from Simeon Edmunds' book *Spiritualism, A Critical Survey:*

"Much of Roy's success in duping quite critical sitters was due to his clever development of the microphone-relaying technique whereby he was able to demonstrate the 'direct voice' in full light, an achievement quite beyond the capabilities of his rivals. To do this he ran wiring under the carpet from the microphone and amplifier to two brass tacks, the heads of which protruded through the carpet and were ostensibly securing it to the floor. He adapted the hearing aid as a miniature loudspeaker and attached it to his cuff, running wires from it up his sleeve, inside his jacket and down his trouser legs into his shoes. Here they connected through the soles with two metal plates, one on each shoe, so that when he stood on the tacks a circuit was completed and the confederate could produce voices from the loudspeaker." The voices would issue from the area around Roy's wrist—far enough away from his mouth to avert suspicion.

Roy, whose real name was William George Holroyd Plowright, was paid handsomely by a British newspaper, the *Sunday Pictorial*, for a five-installment confession in 1958. He posed for photographs with his ingenious apparatus, which eventually found its way into the museum at the Metropolitan Police Detective Training School. He also boasted that he had made wealth out of grief-stricken people. The success of his performance was partly due to the thoroughness with which he researched his victims. He examined voters' lists, visited the National Registry office to pore over records of births, marriages, and deaths, and gleaned a wealth of information from wills. All this information he kept in a card index file. Some details were supplied by fellow frauds. "We phony mediums traded information—like swapping stamps," he confessed.

When sitters arrived for a seance they were asked to leave their coats and handbags outside in the hall. Roy listened to their

Right: a page from *Gambols with the Ghosts*, the marvelous catalog issued by Ralph E. Sylvestre & Co. of Chicago in 1901. Notice at the bottom of the page item 140, the 20th-century Rapping Hand.

Below: the self-rapping hand. It was used at many fraudulent seances to produce spectacular effects undetected in the customary dark. It was probably controlled pneumatically by rubber tubing.

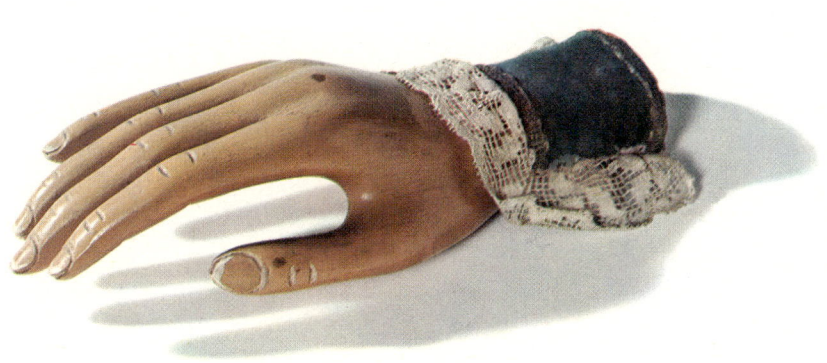

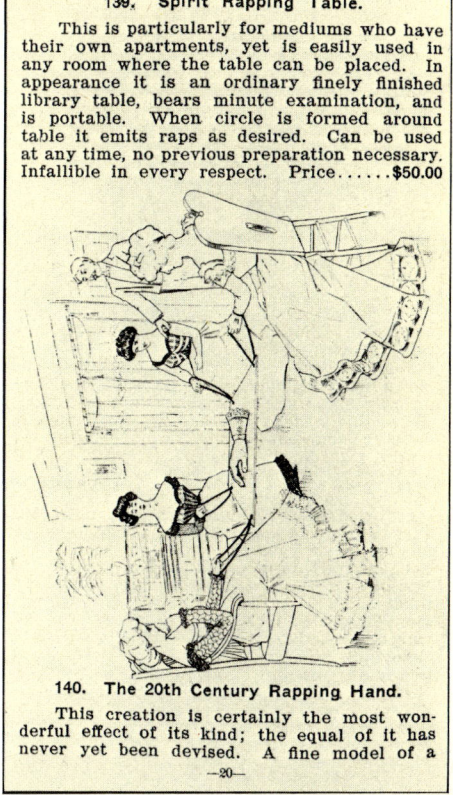

139. Spirit Rapping Table.

This is particularly for mediums who have their own apartments, yet is easily used in any room where the table can be placed. In appearance it is an ordinary finely finished library table, bears minute examination, and is portable. When circle is formed around table it emits raps as desired. Can be used at any time, no previous preparation necessary. Infallible in every respect. Price......$50.00

140. The 20th Century Rapping Hand.

This creation is certainly the most wonderful effect of its kind; the equal of it has never yet been devised. A fine model of a

—20—

conversation via a concealed microphone before he entered the seance room. Meanwhile a confederate searched handbags and coat pockets for further clues in letters, tickets, or notebooks. The phony phenomena usually started with the movement of a light cardboard trumpet coated with bands of luminous paint—a prop commonly used to condense the voice in producing direct voice phenomena. He achieved the voices by attaching a telescopic tube, invisible in the darkness, through which he spoke. He would then remove a hearing aid from his pocket and plug it into what looked like a normal wall socket. This linked him to the confederate who supplied him with information. Roy, in turn, gave the information to the sitters in the guise of a trance message from his American Indian spirit guide, Tinka. Next, by using the hearing aid as a miniature loudspeaker attached to the end of the trumpet, he was able to relay voices from his confederate, while continuing to speak at the same time through another trumpet. The sitters were greatly impressed to hear two spirit voices speaking simultaneously. Masks and cheesecloth were also used by Roy to create materializations.

Spiritualists knew Roy was a fraud as early as 1951 but agreed not to reveal it in return for his promise to stop conducting seances and to leave the country. Roy did so, but soon returned and continued his fraudulent practice. After *Two Worlds* labelled him a fraud in 1955 he issued a writ for libel. Once the matter went to court, the newspaper was prevented from making further comment. When Roy abandoned the lawsuit in February 1958, he agreed to pay the court costs in 24 monthly installments to the editor, Maurice Barbanell. Immediately afterward the newspaper published all its evidence for fraud. At first Roy

Above: demonstration of a fake medium at work. Her hands and legs are tied to the stool. but a spring releases a section of the stool and gives her free movement to use instruments and the voice trumpet on the table.

73

Left: two pictures of William Roy taken to illustrate his confession. After making a fortune as a fraudulent medium, Roy got a handsome fee for his personal story, run in five parts by a newspaper. Above Roy is shown in the black darkness in which he conducted his seances. Behind him, and separated by a brick wall, is his accomplice. The picture below shows the same scene with the lights on. Roy is producing one voice from the trumpet (invisible in the gloom). The accomplice does the second voice with a microphone in his hand connected by wires through what looks like an ordinary wall socket to a speaker hung on Roy's telescopic rod. The confederate also has an earphone connected to a microphone behind the curtains to pick up voices in the seance room. Among the other equipment in his room is an amplifier, a tape recorder, and a pile of stage props, all of which the medium successfully used for his marvelous effects.

denied the charges. Then, having been offered a substantial fee by the *Sunday Pictorial* for his story, he cheerfully confessed. By the time the story was published Roy had left the country again.

His final remark in the series of *Pictorial* articles was: "Even after this confession, I know I could fill seance rooms again with people who find it a comfort to believe I am genuine." Ten years later in 1968 those words were proved right. A medium using the name Bill Silver and working under a wealthy man's patronage was discovered to be William Roy. Once again it was a Spiritualist newspaper, *Psychic News*, that exposed him. Moreover, the paper revealed that some of the sitters knew the real identity of Silver as Roy, but were still convinced by his phenomena, which were said to include voice communications from beings living on Venus. The sitters included a bishop and the Beatles. When challenged by another Sunday newspaper, William Roy had the gall to claim that his earlier confession had been a pack of lies, and that he had always been genuine.

Not all mediumistic fraud is as coldly calculated as that practiced by Roy. Some, in fact, seems to be unconscious.

Above: Harry Price, the psychic investigator, with a trick blackboard used by fraudulent mediums. Two apparently plain slates are placed together by the medium. When taken apart, one slate has a spirit drawing on it and the other some writing. The secret is a strong hidden spring, which releases a previously prepared surface and conceals the blanks. Price was the director of the National Laboratory of Psychical Research, and spent a great deal of time and money on the testing and exposure of fake mediums.

Professor James Hyslop, an American psychical researcher, discovered a woman medium who, in complete darkness, made tambourines play and bells ring. She willingly agreed to his taking flash photographs of these phenomena. When the pictures were developed she was dumbfounded to see that she was producing these effects with her own hands. They plainly showed her ringing the bells and banging the tambourine. Subsequent investigation showed that her hands and arms were completely numb during seances, and she had no conscious knowledge of their movements and actions.

The long contest between mediums and magicians has included many challenges and counterchallenges. Many, if not most, of these encounters served to confirm the magicians' disbelief in Spiritualism. In some cases, however, magicians have become convinced that spirits could communicate through mediums, and some have even become Spiritualists themselves.

In 1930 the British psychical researcher Harry Price challenged any magician who could duplicate the phenomena of medium Rudi Schneider under the same conditions. Schneider, an Austrian, was subjected to extensive testing. During his seances, held in the National Laboratories of Psychical Research, he produced levitation of various objects, musical sounds, and partial materializations in a cabinet some five feet away from where he was sitting. Various controls were imposed to eliminate any contact between Schneider and the manifestations. No one came forward to accept Price's challenge—perhaps because of the strings attached. Although he offered a large money prize to the successful challenger, Price made it part of the deal that any unsuccessful ones contribute the same sum to his organization.

Will Goldston, one of the greatest professional magicians in Europe, said after witnessing Schneider's phenomena: "I am convinced that what I saw at the seance was not trickery. No group of my fellow magicians could have produced these effects under such conditions." Goldston told the story of his conversion to Spiritualism in his book *Secrets of Famous Illusionists* published in 1933.

The great exposés are, for the most part, a thing of the past. This is mainly because physical phenomena, the featured attraction of most late 19th century seances, are now rarely produced. Although advancing technology has provided fraudulent mediums with more sophisticated methods of duping the public—as in the case of William Roy and his voice-up-the-sleeve act—it has also provided investigators with more sophisticated means of detection. Infra-red photography in particular has made it possible to reveal the machinery behind physical phenomena without affecting the darkness of the physical seance room. Technological expertise, say the skeptics, is the reason behind the virtual disappearance of old-style physical mediumship. The recent emergence of spiritual healing, including psychic surgery, will no doubt call forth a new breed of investigators, bent on discovering the tricks—if they are tricks—behind some of today's astonishing manifestations. In the meantime, most Spiritualists look to a different kind of medium—the kind who relies entirely on mental processes to establish that link between this world and the next that Spiritualists continually seek.

The Medium and the Message

Two days after the huge British airship, the R101, had crashed in flames on a hillside in Beauvais, France—killing 48 of its 54 passengers—the hesitant, anxious voice of a man claiming to be its captain spoke through the lips of a medium in London. In short disjointed sentences he described the horrifying last moments before his incineration. His account of the crash included a wealth of technical information that was confirmed six months later by an official inquiry. The disaster, which occurred on October 4, 1930, included two high ranking aviation officials among its victims. It shook the government's confidence in dirigibles, and ended British

The raps, table turnings, and blasts of seance trumpets faded away with the beginning of the 20th century, and in their place messages began to appear. Spoken or written, they conveyed often precise, evidential information apparently from those who had died. Much more difficult to prove fraudulent than physical manifestations, they were also much harder to explain away.

Above: Eileen Garrett, medium at the extraordinary seance of October 7, 1930, when the spirit of the captain of the R101— the dirigible developed by the British for passenger service, which had crashed just two days before—broke into the sitting.

Right: the charred wreckage of the R101 after the disaster.

"A dramatic moment in psychic history"

efforts to develop the lighter-than-air craft for commercial use.

The seance in which the dramatic communication was received took place at the National Laboratory of Psychical Research set up four years earlier by Harry Price, a well-known psychic investigator. Price, his secretary, and journalist Ian D. Coster, had arranged a sitting with the talented young medium Eileen Garrett. The purpose was to attempt a spirit contact with the recently deceased writer Sir Arthur Conan Doyle, the report of which was to be published in a magazine. Sir Arthur, the creator of Sherlock Holmes, was also a Spiritualist.

Shortly after the sitters had gathered in the seance room, Eileen Garrett went into a trance. Instead of making contact with the novelist, however, the sitters heard a voice announcing himself as Flight Lieutenant H. Carmichael Irwin. In anguished tones, the voice said: "I must do something about it . . . The whole bulk of the dirigible was entirely and absolutely too much for her engines' capacity. Engines too heavy. It was this that made me on five occasions have to scuttle to safety. Useful lift too small. Gross lift computed badly—inform control panel. And this idea of new elevators totally mad. Elevator jammed. Oil pipe plugged . . . Flying too low altitude and never could rise. Disposable lift could not be utilized. Load too great for long flight . . . Cruising speed bad and ship badly swinging. Severe tension on the fabric which is chafing . . . Engines wrong—too heavy—cannot rise. Never reached cruising altitude—same in trials. Too short trials. No one knew the ship properly. Weather bad for long flight. Fabric all waterlogged and ship's nose is down. Impossible to rise. Cannot trim. Almost scraped the roofs of Achy. Kept to railway. At enquiry to be held later it will be found that the superstructure of the envelope contained no resilience and had far too much weight in envelope. The added middle section was entirely wrong . . . too heavy, too much overweighted for the capacity of engines . . . ."

The reporter who took this amazing communication in shorthand at first resented the intrusion of Irwin, captain of the R101, when he had expected the voice of Sir Arthur Conan Doyle. But he was soon to realize that he had unwittingly been part of a dramatic moment in psychic history. He published the story, and it was read by, among others, a Mr. Charlton, who had been involved in the R101's construction. Charlton asked Harry Price for a copy of the seance report. After studying it he and his colleagues described it as "an astounding document," containing more than 40 highly technical and confidential details of what occurred on the airship's fatal flight. "It appeared very evident," said Charlton, "that for anyone present at the seance to have obtained information beforehand was grotesquely absurd."

Charlton was so impressed by the evidence that he began his own psychic investigation, and ultimately became a Spiritualist. The only hypothesis that he could put forward to explain all the evidence was that "Irwin did actually communicate with those present at the seance, after his physical death."

Before the official enquiry into the crash, Major Oliver Villiers of the Ministry of Civil Aviation participated in a seance with

Above: a newstand poster advertising one newspaper's account of the R101 seance. Because of the worldwide interest in the crash of the airship, the seance also attracted worldwide attention. A reporter present at the seance had put the news story out at once.

Above: an aerial view of the R101 wreck on the hillside in Beauvais just north of Paris.

Left: Flight-Lieutenant H. C. Irwin, captain of the airship. He had had a naval background, and some of the terms used in the seance communication were naval terms he might well have used.

Left: the Court of Inquiry, chaired by Sir John Simon, "to hold an investigation into the causes and circumstances of the accident which occurred on October 5th, 1930, near Beauvais in France, to the Airship R101." This Court started its work on October 28, three weeks after the memorable seance with Eileen Garrett. Much of the technical information given then by the airship's captain was confirmed during the inquiry, and would not have been available to the public before the seance. But if the captain's communication had been made out of his desire to make sure that future airships were safer, it was in vain: after the crash of the R101 the British government gave up its airship program.

Eileen Garrett. Through the medium he heard the testimony of others who had lost their lives in the disaster. Here is part of the verbatim account of the conversation during the seance between Villiers and crew member Scott, one of the victims:

"Villiers: What was the trouble? Irwin mentioned the nose."

"Scott: Yes. Girder trouble and engine."

"Villiers: I must get this right. Can you describe exactly where? We have the long struts numbered from A to G."

"Scott: The top one is O, and then A, B, C, and so on downward. Look at your drawing. It was the starboard of 5C. On our second flight after we had finished we found the girder had been strained, not cracked, and this caused trouble to the cover . . ."

Later Villiers asked Scott if the girder had broken and gone through the airship's covering:

"Scott: No, not broke, but cracked badly and it split the outer cover . . . The bad rent in the cover on the starboard side of 5C brought about an unnatural pressure, forced us into our first dive. The second was even worse. The pressure on the gas bags was terrific, and the gusts of wind were tremendous. This

Above: Sir Arthur Conan Doyle in 1927 in a portrait by H. L. Gates. The seance that produced the amazing R101 material was arranged originally as an attempt to contact Conan Doyle, who had died the previous July. He was a convinced Spiritualist for nearly 30 years of his life, and largely gave up his writing to travel and lecture as a kind of Spiritualist missionary.

Right: a *Punch* cartoon of Sir Arthur chained to his creation Sherlock Holmes, but with his head in the Spiritualist clouds. After he tired of his popular detective hero, he tried to kill him off, but the outcry was so tremendous that Conan Doyle reluctantly resurrected him.

external pressure, coupled with the fact that the valve was weak, blew the valve right off, and at the same time the released gas was ignited by a backfire from the engine."

The Court of Inquiry report showed that practically every one of these statements was correct; none were incorrect.

One important aspect of Eileen Garrett's work is that she respected psychical investigators and actively encouraged their work. In fact, she founded the New York-based Parapsychology Foundation, which was financed by a wealthy woman politician, Congresswoman Frances Payne Bolton of Ohio. On Eileen Garrett's death in 1970 at the age of 77, Archie Jarman, a researcher and writer who had known her for nearly 40 years, paid tribute to her in the columns of *Psychic News*. He revealed that she had asked him to "dig into the famous R101 airship case as deep as I could delve." He agreed to do so and pledged he would take neither fee nor expenses, so that whatever his investigation disclosed, it would be seen that he had worked "without fear or favor." He continued:

"The completed saga, so often briefly mentioned, turned out to be a pretty massive affair. It took nearly six months and finally filled 455 pages of typescript and blueprints. It involved two trips to France, seeking the few remaining witnesses at Beauvais, where the R101 crashed. There were conferences with aeronautical experts, such as the designer of the R101's heavy diesel engines (which were partly responsible for the fatal crash), and with the aging but active captain of the sister-ship, R100.

"Technical witnesses were interrogated; ordnance maps scrutinized; Eileen's own aeronautical knowledge investigated (result, nil, she knew hardly enough to float a toy balloon). At close range I became familiar with meteorology, geodetics, with prewar political maneuvering and with certain conspiracy at a Ministry, with aerodynamics and with scandalous decisions which took nearly 50 brave men to their deaths.

"It was the technical aspect of this case which makes it unique in psychic history—and I mean *unique* . . . My opinion is that greater credulity is demanded to believe that Eileen obtained her obscure and specialized data by mundane means than to accept that, in some paranormal manner, she had contact with the remembering psyche of the 'dead' Captain Irwin to the moment of his incineration with his vast airship."

No one materialized in Eileen Garrett's presence. There were no physical manifestations such as raps or levitations, so beloved of early Spiritualists and psychical investigators. Why, then, is the R101 case so important to the Spiritualist case? The reason is that many of the scientists who risked ridicule by declaring their belief in materialized figures were equally adamant that these seance phantoms were not proof of an afterlife. They felt that mental mediumship might provide the proof.

Professor Charles Richet, a French physiologist and psychical researcher, for example, eventually came to believe in the genuineness of some physical phenomena—after having first ridiculed the idea. But Richet found it difficult to believe in life after death. He described materialization phenomena as "absurd but true," and argued: "Even if (which is not the case) a form identical with that of a deceased person could be photographed

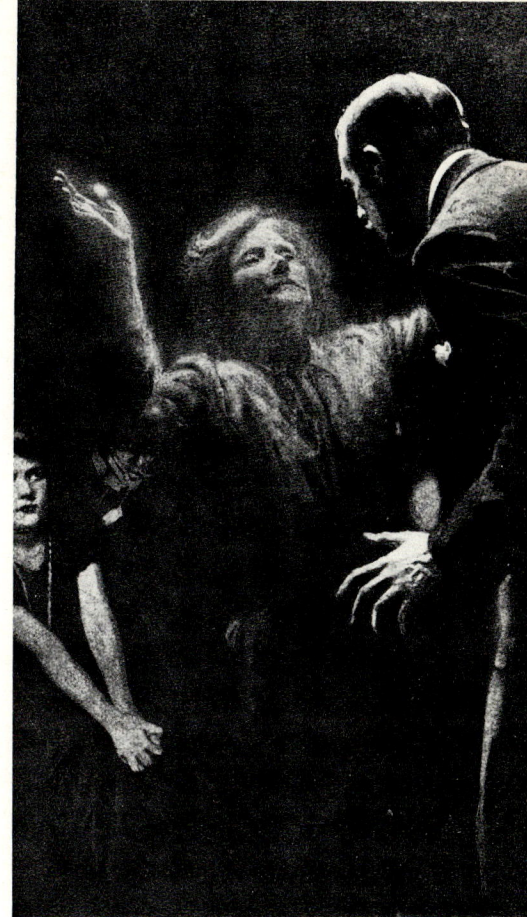

Above: an illustration from one of Conan Doyle's stories, which was serialized in an English magazine. Called "The Land of Mist," it had a theme of Spiritualists and seances. Here the hero is astonished by the materialization of his dead mother. Conan Doyle himself desperately wished to communicate with his own dead mother or with his son, killed in World War I.

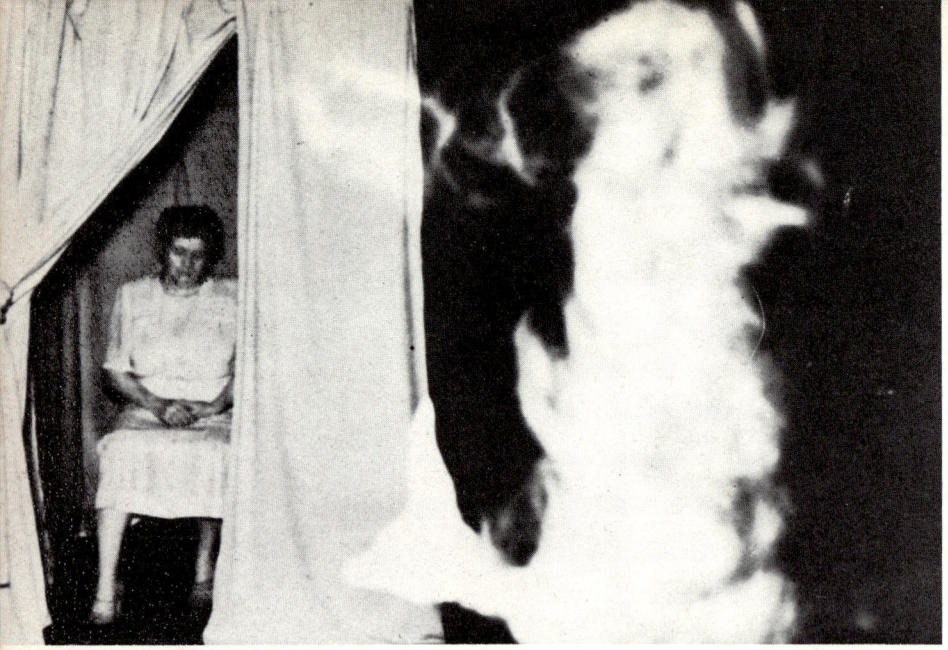
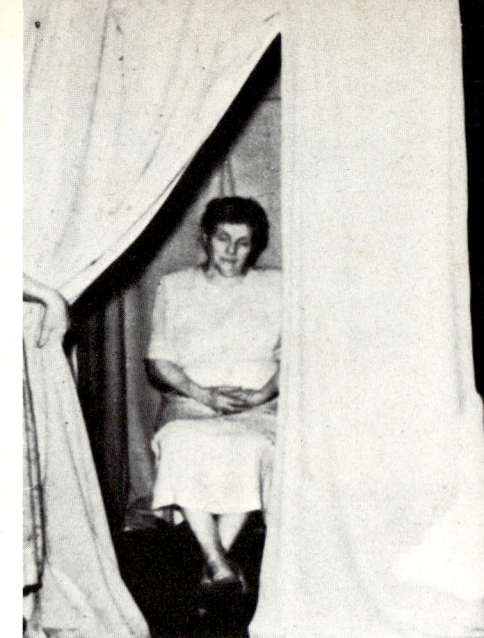
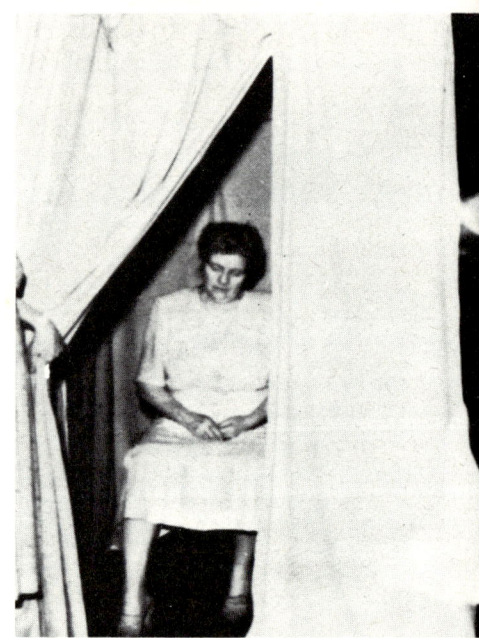

Materializations are not usual in seances today, but they still occur. Here is the materialization of a spirit, Silver Belle, photographed by infrared light at 50-second intervals, during a seance that took place at a Spiritualist summer camp in Ephrata, Pennsylvania, in 1953. The medium, sitting in her curtained cabinet, is Ethel Post-Parrish. Silver Belle was her spirit control or guide. During this manifestation, Silver Belle was reportedly witnessed by 81 people. Some of them apparently walked arm-in-arm with her.

I should not understand how an individual 200 years dead, whose body has become a skeleton, could live again with this vanished body any more than with any other materialized form."

Baron A. von Schrenck-Notzing, German pioneer in investigation of psychic phenomena, conducted experiments with every leading medium until his death in 1929. He discovered the amazing powers of Willi and Rudi Schneider. One hundred formerly skeptical and often hostile scientists who witnessed his tests with Willi Schneider signed a statement that they were convinced of the reality of telekinesis—the moving of objects by mental power—and of ectoplasm. Yet the Baron maintained: "I am of the opinion that the hypothesis of spirits not only fails to explain the least detail of these processes, but in every way it obstructs and shakes serious scientific research."

Other scientists accepted materializations as proof of an afterlife. But who was to say they were right? Richet and Schrenck-Notzing believed that, in a way we do not understand, and probably subconsciously, the medium shaped the phantom forms from the ectoplasmic material exuding from his or her body, controlling it through an extension of the nervous system. That may seem to be a far-fetched or fantastic theory, but to some it is more satisfactory than to admit the existence of a soul—and the far-fetched idea of a soul materializing itself.

If, however, a medium were to communicate information known only to the dead person and to the sitter, this would be more convincing evidence that the person's spirit had survived death. Still, many investigators would maintain that the medium

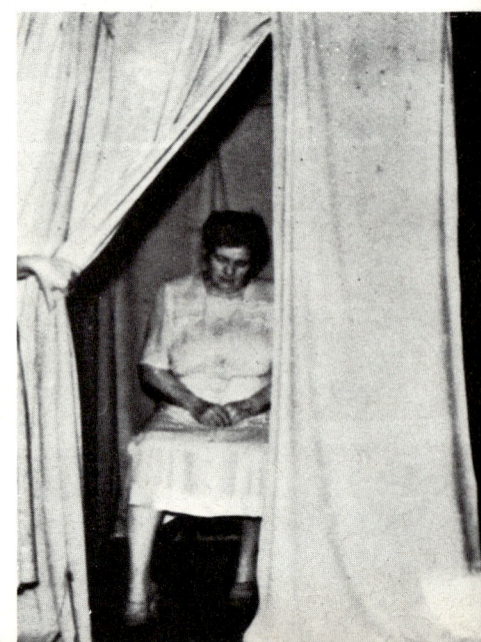

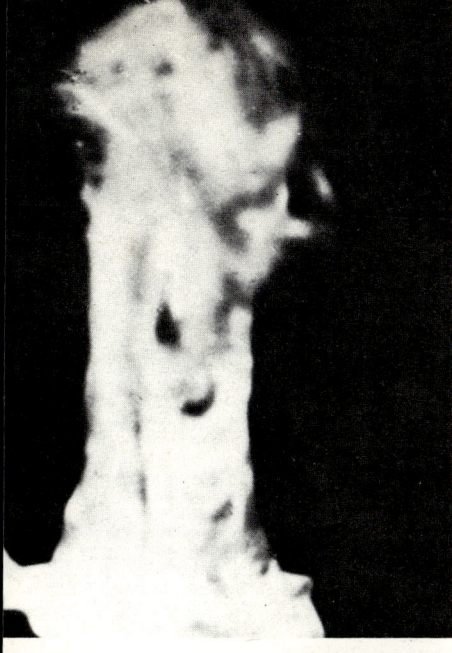

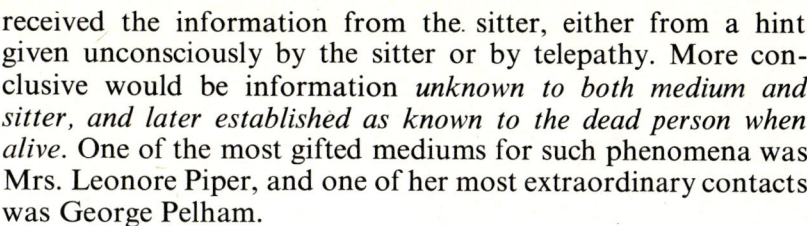

received the information from the sitter, either from a hint given unconsciously by the sitter or by telepathy. More conclusive would be information *unknown to both medium and sitter, and later established as known to the dead person when alive*. One of the most gifted mediums for such phenomena was Mrs. Leonore Piper, and one of her most extraordinary contacts was George Pelham.

"The case of George Pelham," said Richet, "though there was no materialization, is vastly more evidential for survival than all the materializations yet known."

Pelham was the pseudonym of George Pellew, a young New York lawyer who had given up the law to become a writer. He had known Dr. Richard Hodgson of the SPR—a brilliant researcher who devoted much of his life to the study of Mrs. Piper's mediumship—and the two men had often discussed survival. Pelham argued that the idea of life after death was not only improbable but inconceivable. Hodgson said that if it was not probable it was at least conceivable. Pelham then promised that if he died first, he would return and "make things lively." He apparently kept his promise, and much sooner than he could have anticipated; for in February 1892 at the age of 32, he was killed in a fall from his horse.

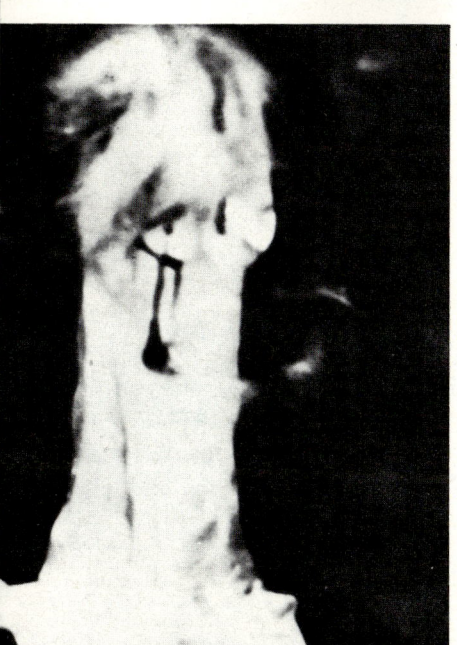

A month later the first of a series of communications from Pelham began. Dr. Hodgson had arranged a sitting with Mrs. Piper for an intimate friend of Pelham's, using the pseudonym "John Hart" for the sitter. Mrs. Piper went into a trance, her spirit control Phinuit made various vague statements before announcing that there was a "George" present who wanted to speak. According to Dr. Hodgson, who took notes, Pelham took over the seance, giving his real name in full as well as the first names and surnames of several of his most intimate friends, including the one under an assumed name at the seance. He mentioned in particular a Mr. and Mrs. Howard and gave a message to Katherine, their daughter. When the Howards were told of the message, it was instantly recognized by the family as a reference to a conversation he had had with the girl some years earlier. The Howards later attended sittings with Mrs. Piper, and plied George Pelham with questions. His

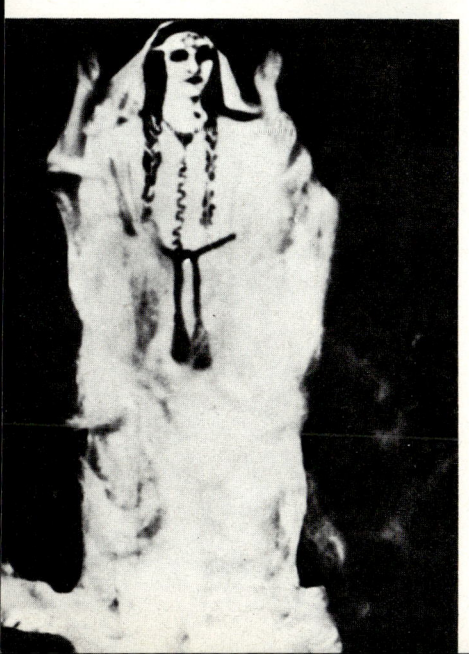

Above: Dr. R. Hodgson shown in a faked photograph he had taken to demonstrate the ease of fakery. He was a very capable, but skeptical, investigator who undertook a systematic study of the medium Mrs. Leonore Piper. Below: Madame Blavatsky, mystic and medium, who was exposed as a fraud in India by Dr. Hodgson.

answers were full and detailed in most cases, but Mr. Howard pointed out that Pelham had failed to answer some points. This failure caused him to have doubt about the identity of the alleged spirit. He therefore challenged George Pelham to "tell me something in our past that you and I alone know."

Mrs. Piper's hand then began writing a message which Dr. Hodgson later said contained too much of the personal element in Pelham's life to be made public. Hodgson watched as the medium's hand rapidly covered the paper, and Mrs. Piper allowed him to read what was written until the word "private" appeared. At that point she gently pushed Dr. Hodgson away.

"I retired to the other side of the room, and Mr. Howard took my place close to the hand where he could read the writing," Dr Hodgson recounted. "He did not, of course, read it aloud, and it was too private for my perusal. The hand, as it reached the end of each sheet, tore it off from the block book and thrust it wildy at Mr. Howard, and then continued writing. The circumstances narrated, Mr. Howard informed me, contained precisely the kind of test for which he had asked, and he said he was 'perfectly satisfied, perfectly.'"

Having apparently established his identity, George Pelham stayed on as one of Mrs. Piper's regular spirit controls along with Phinuit. During a six-year period he spoke to 150 sitters, 30 of whom were old friends. He recognized all 30, although each had been introduced to the medium under a pseudonym. He not only addressed them all by name, but also used with each the tone and manner he was accustomed to use with that person when alive. Never once did he mistake a stranger for a friend. When his father and stepmother heard of Pelham's alleged posthumous activities, they decided to attend a seance. They used false names, but the moment George Pelham spoke through the medium he said, "Hello, father and mother, I am George." The conversation that followed was, according to the father, exactly what he would have expected from his living son.

Dr. Richard Hodgson was one of the mainstays of the SPR in its early days. He had a reputation as a talented investigator with a critical and skeptical mind. In 1887 he was sent to America by the SPR to act as secretary for the American Society for Psychical Research in Boston—a post he held for the rest of his life. He became a close friend of the American philosopher and psychologist William James, who brought him and Leonore Piper together. Professor James had been persuaded to attend one of Mrs. Piper's seances by some female relatives who had been greatly impressed by her. James expected to be able to explain the medium's feats logically, but was soon convinced that she possessed supernormal powers. He began a systematic study of Mrs. Piper, and introduced her to Hodgson. When James had to terminate his studies temporarily because of pressure of other work, Hodgson took up the project. Being extremely skeptical, he had Mrs. Piper watched by private detectives to learn whether she tried to collect information she could use at seances. He also took every precaution to prevent her from acquiring knowledge about her sitters in advance, and introduced them anonymously or by pseudonyms to protect their identities. Hodgson finally became convinced not only that Leonore Piper was genuine but also that spirit beings were communicating through her mediumship.

Typical of the evidence which helped him reach this decision was that provided at a seance attended by Professor Herbert Nichols of Harvard University. The sitting with Mrs. Piper was arranged by Hodgson at the request of Professor James. Professor Nichols was extremely skeptical at the outset. After the seance he wrote a letter of praise to James declaring, "she is the greatest marvel I have ever met . . . I asked her scarcely a question, but she ran on for three-quarters of an hour, telling me names, places, events, in a most startling manner. Then she suddenly stopped talking and began writing—this was far less satisfactory and about an entirely different set of matters— mostly about Mamma (who recently fell and was killed) and messages to her grandchildren. One thing here, however, will interest you. Mamma and I one Christmas exchanged rings. Each had engraved in their gift the *first word* of their favorite proverb. The ring given me I lost many years ago. When Mamma died a year ago the ring I had given her was, at her request, taken from her finger and sent to me. Now I asked Mrs. Piper, 'What was written in Mamma's ring?' and as I asked the question I held the ring in my hand and had in mind *only that ring*, but I had hardly got the words from my mouth till she slapped down on paper the word on the *other ring*—the one Mamma had given me, and which had been lost years ago while traveling. As the word was a peculiar one, doubtfully ever written in any ring before, and as she wrote it in a flash, it was surely curious."

Time and again, Dr. Hodgson witnessed similar astonishing phenomena produced by Mrs. Piper. In his second report on her mediumship, published in 1897, he stated:

"At the present time I cannot profess to have any doubt that the chief communicators to whom I have referred in the foregoing pages are veritably the personages that they claim to be, that they have survived the change we call death, and that they have directly communicated with us whom we call living, through Mrs. Piper's entranced organism."

On Hodgson's death in 1905 the investigation into Leonore Piper's psychic powers was continued by James Hervey Hyslop, Professor of Logic and Ethics at Columbia University, New York. Within days of taking up the task he was studying communications received from his former colleague Dr. Hodgson, who became a regular communicator. Professor Hyslop had first encountered Mrs. Piper in 1888, and his initial skepticism about her mediumship soon dissolved. After 12 sittings, the personalities of the communicators who spoke through Mrs. Piper—and the evidence they provided—were so strong that he declared: "I have been talking with my father, my brother, my uncles. Whatever supernormal powers we may be pleased to attribute to Mrs. Piper's secondary personalities, it would be difficult to make me believe that these secondary personalities could have thus completely reconstituted the mental personality of my dead relatives. To admit this would involve me in too many improbabilities. I prefer to believe that I have been talking to my dead relatives in person; it is simpler."

Eastern Miracles by Western Hands

It was evening in Benares, India. The legendary Madame Blavatsky—the small dumpy Russian mystic and medium with a strangely magnetic personality—was surrounded by several Indian scholars, a German professor of Sanskrit, and her devoted disciple Colonel Olcott.

The professor observed with regret that the Indian sages of old were supposed to have been able to perform amazing feats, such as making roses fall from the sky, but that people said the days of such powers were over. Madame Blavatsky stared at him thoughtfully. "Oh, they say that, do they?" she demanded. "They say no one can do it now? Well, I'll show them; and you may tell them from me that if the modern Hindus were less sycophantic to their Western masters, less in love with their vices, and more like their ancestors in many ways, they would not have to make such a humiliating confession, nor get an old Western hippopotamus of a woman to prove the truth of their Shastras!"

She set her lips together firmly, and made a grand imperious sweep of her right hand. With a swish, exactly one dozen roses came cascading down.

Madame Blavatsky returned calmly to her conversation.

Above: William Stainton Moses, English medium who had been a clergyman. He produced a famous series of automatic scripts, which he wrote while in trance. They were interspersed with words written by the spirits themselves. (The College of Psychic Studies)

Sunday Feb 1. 1874. Dglas House.

Who was with Charley last night?

The guides were there: but the inspiring you - it was Benjamin Cooke who is much concerned with the boy. Others too were present.

Who then?

We will shew.

Felix

Who is it? I never heard of Felix.

Mendelssohn

The same conclusion was reached by the vast majority of Mrs. Piper's sitters. Because her mediumship was so accurate and detailed, and because men with critical and skeptical natures believed that fraud had been ruled out, the case of Mrs. Leonore Piper has become one of the most significant in psychic history. It established within 40 years of Spiritualism's beginnings that evidence for an afterlife could be provided through the mind of a medium, without the need for darkness, raps, levitations, or spirit forms. What is more, the quality of the evidence was in most cases far superior to the laboriously spelled out messages that were banged out by tilting tables, or the indistinct materializations that appeared at many seances.

At its best, mental mediumship appears to offer a kind of psychic telephone link between this world and the next, using the medium as a receiver. In some cases, the medium goes into a trance and speaks with the voice of the communicator. More often mediums remain conscious and relate in their normal voice what they are hearing mentally. The telephone analogy is a useful one, for it points to some of the difficulties that can occur. Suppose, for example, that you had been abroad for 20 years and, on returning home, decided to call up some friends. They would not be able to see you, so to establish that it really was you, you would probably talk about events in your life before you had left, and about which they knew or in which they had shared. This is what most spirit communicators do.

This raises an immediate objection, however. The communications seem trivial, and the sitters usually know the facts that are given to establish identity. Therefore, telepathy between sitter and medium is postulated as the explanation. Also, sometimes the evidence provided is not right, dates or names are wrong, and doubt is thrown on the authenticity of the entire communication. Here is where the comparison with telephoning breaks down, for conveying information through a medium is not as simple as the telephone analogy indicates. F. W. H. Myers, an early SPR researcher, is supposed to have spoken through a famous medium to give this posthumous description of his efforts to communicate:

"The nearest simile I can find to express the difficulties of sending a message—is that I appear to be standing behind a sheet of frosted glass which blurs sights and deadens sound—dictating feebly—to a reluctant and somewhat obtuse secretary. A feeling of terrible impotence burdens me—I am so powerless to tell what means so much."

We are used to atmospheric interference in television and radio communications and more or less accept it. So perhaps we should allow for distortions through mediumistic communication. Spirit communicators indicate that—in a way we do not understand—they have to use the medium's mind to control vocal cords or move a hand to write a message. The medium's

Left: a sample of automatic writing by William Stainton Moses. The scripts began in 1872 and went on until 1883, getting scarcer after 1877. Altogether, they fill 24 books. The Felix referred to in this message is apparently Mendelssohn; his signature shows clearly at the bottom of the page. (The College of Psychic Studies)

own mind can therefore color the communications. It seems reasonable that if contact really is established between the living and another realm of existence, then difficulties could easily arise. If we accept this, the wonder is not that inaccuracies and misunderstandings creep into many seance messages, but that on occasion a communicator is able to convey accurate information at length—as in the R101 seances.

A set of seance messages called the Cummins-Willett Scripts provide us with the best evidence of this kind. They were received through the mediumship of one of the best modern exponents of automatic writing, an Irishwoman named Geraldine Cummins. The presumed sender of the messages was Mrs. Winifred Coombe Tennant who, during her life, also produced automatic writing under the pseudonym of "Mrs. Willett." Her real name came to light as a result of what she wrote through Geraldine Cummins.

Mrs. Winifred Coombe Tennant was an energetic, practical, and highly intelligent person. She was appointed a Justice of the Peace in 1920, and was the first woman magistrate to sit on the Glamorganshire, Wales, County bench. In 1922 she ran unsuccessfully as a Liberal Party candidate for Parliament. Later, however, she became the first woman to be appointed by the British Government as a delegate to the League of Nations Assembly. With this background, it is perhaps not surprising that she kept her psychic talents secret, and her work as a medium, under the name Mrs. Willett, became known only when she communicated with Geraldine Cummins.

Mrs. Winifred Coombe Tennant died in August 1956. A year later W. H. Salter, honorary secretary of the SPR, wrote to Geraldine Cummins asking if she would cooperate in an experiment. She agreed to do so, but only after she had returned to her home in County Cork, Eire. Two weeks later Mr. Salter sent a second letter to her in Ireland. In it he gave her the name of Major Henry Tennant, who hoped to receive a message from his mother.

During the next two years Geraldine Cummins received 40 scripts, ostensibly from Mrs. Tennant, Major Tennant's mother. Most of them she included in her book *Swan on a Black Sea*, published in 1965 and edited by Signe Toksvig. These scripts represent one of the most important contributions to psychical research in the last few decades. In them, the spirit of Mrs. Tennant discusses her life, her relationships with others, and her involvement in psychic work. The writings are peppered with names, dates, and details which, with few exceptions, were found to be accurate.

Skeptics might claim that Geraldine Cummins could have researched all or most of this material when she got the name of Major Tennant, or that she was acquainted with the family. Either theory is questionable in view of comments in a letter

Above: during her life Mrs. Winifred Coombe Tennant was a Justice of the Peace—and, under the secret name Mrs. Willett, a medium who produced automatic writing while fully conscious. After her death she sent a series of detailed communications.

Right: Geraldine Cummins, an Irish medium whose automatic writings on mainly theological themes have shown remarkable knowledge. She was asked by the bereaved son of Winifred Coombe Tennant (Mrs. Willett) to try for a message, and for three years after received scripts that were full of details only the immediate family had known.

that Geraldine Cummins wrote to Signe Toksvig on August 31, 1957, a few days after receiving Salter's second letter. She refers to the experiment, saying in an aside that the letter from Salter contained the name of a major. "The name meant nothing to me. But I realized I must tackle the job the next day. Otherwise these critical people would say I spent time making inquiries about this blasted major." The first communication from Mrs. Winifred Coombe Tennant was received on August 28, 1957, five days after Salter's second letter. The medium was not happy with the result, and she commented: "I don't care if it's all wrong. It seemed to me an impossible task." She referred to the test scripts in another letter four days later adding, "I'm sure the script message is a failure." In her introduction to *Swan on a Black Sea*, Signe Toksvig observes: "It can be seen that Miss Cummins is by no means an automatic believer in her automatic or transmitted scripts."

Professor C. D. Broad, Fellow of Trinity College, Cambridge, wrote a long and masterly foreword to the Cummins/Toksvig book. He examines many alternative explanations for the scripts and comments: "I found them of great interest, and I believe that these automatic scripts are a very important addition to the vast mass of such material which *prima facie* suggests rather strongly that certain human beings have survived the death of their physical bodies . . ."

The scripts are too long and complicated to condense meaningfully. Instead, here is part of one of the scripts addressed to her son Major Tennant, dated October 29, 1958:

"I am back again in my married life. It is different, though in appearance to my perceptions it is the same outer world of reason, order, and sensible arrangements. But it is different, humanly speaking. I am much with Christopher [another son], who is a darling, while your father pairs off with Daff [her daughter]. That is a new experience to me.

"What is novel also is that I appear to be in a kind of kindergarten, and in my working hours I relive in memory what earth time has snatched away from me. So in the study of memory I do not remain at Cadoxton [their home in Gloucestershire]. I enter the film of past events and make excursions into different times in my past earth life so as to assimilate it.

"I perceive again my budding public life, my immense enthusiasm for the Welsh Wizard, Lloyd George. He has even visited me in the disguise of his past earthly personality so blazing with fire and force when in its prime. . . ."

Major Henry Tennant, initially a skeptic, wrote to Geraldine Cummins after receiving the first communication to say, "The more I study these scripts the more deeply I am impressed by them." He pointed out only one incorrect name and added, "every other name and reference is accurate, and to me very evidential and at times surprising. There was no tapping of my mind because much appears that I never knew."

Geraldine Cummins was highly critical of her own gift. She admitted shortly before her death in 1969 that it was not until she had received the Willett scripts that she felt she had produced what she demanded as irrefutable proof of survival. It had taken her 35 years of mediumship to achieve that goal.

Right: Grace Rosher, who does automatic writing with a pen lying lightly on her hand. Her gift first made itself manifest after her fiancé died when, pausing after finishing a perfectly normal letter, she discovered to her surprise that the pen was moving by itself. The handwriting was that of her dead fiancé Gordon Burdick.

Below: Grace Rosher ready for writing. Each of the spirits that communicates through her apparently uses the lightly propped pen to produce its own distinctive style of handwriting.

Left: Miss Rosher comparing a spirit message she claimed to receive from Sir William Crookes with a facsimile of his normal handwriting during his life.

6

Mediums and Machines

As the technology of the 20th century has developed, ingenious minds have found ways to employ it in the search for a method to prove the existence of a dimension to life beyond those of which we are normally aware.

Right: this dead nettle leaf, photographed by the Kirlian method, is visibly surrounded by a brilliantly glowing corona.

Below: the Swedish film maker and painter Friedrich Jurgenson with his tape recorder, on which he is convinced he has captured multilingual voices of the dead.

Friedrich Jurgenson switched on his tape recorder one day in 1959 expecting to hear the recording of bird calls he had made in a Swedish forest. Suddenly the voice of his dead mother addressed him. He heard her saying: "Friedel, my little Friedel, can you hear me?" That was all. Astonished, Jurgenson replayed the tape to check that his ears had not deceived him. His mother's voice was distinct and unmistakable. Jurgenson, a Russian-born writer, painter, and film producer living in Sweden, began a long series of experiments to record spirit voices following his first experience. Since then, hundreds of voices mysteriously appeared on his tapes.

93

"One of the most exciting manifestations of recent years"

Usually they uttered just a word or two at a time. After Jurgenson received his first tape phenomena, other experimenters also began receiving spirit voices on tape. The most notable of these was Dr. Konstantin Raudive, a Latvian-born psychologist who was living in Sweden at the time of Jurgenson's first tape voices.

Spirit recording had arrived—and it seemed to be what psychical research had been waiting for: a simple, fraud-proof means of contacting the next world without the vagaries of mediumship. The phenomenon, whatever it proves in the long run, is one of the most exciting manifestations of recent years.

For 14 years Jurgenson let it be thought that the startling voice of his mother on the bird-call recording was an unexpected event. He now admits that he had been experimenting for several months before with the aim of receiving "something" on electromagnetic tape. "Somehow, and completely without any known reason," he has said, "there grew in me an overwhelming desire to establish electronic contact with somebody unknown. It was a strange feeling, almost as if I had to open a channel for something which was still hidden and wanted to get into the open. At the same time I remember feeling skeptical, amused, and curious."

When the late Dr. Raudive heard about Jurgenson's mysterious phenomena, he began his own experiments. He used various techniques from simple recording with a microphone to more complex electronic systems for which he had certain equipment especially designed. The results in numerical terms alone have certainly been impressive. By 1968 Raudive had recorded more than 70,000 voice effects. He wrote about these in his book published that year. Known as *Breakthrough* when it appeared in the United States and Britain in 1971, it was originally entitled *Unhorbares wird Horbar* (*The Inaudible Becomes Audible.*) As a result of the publicity surrounding Dr. Raudive's work, voice phenomena have been dubbed "Raudive voices."

"In one 10-minute recording I got 200 voices," Raudive once said. "With patience there is no reason at all why anyone cannot tape the voice phenomena. But the experimenter must develop his hearing by constant listening to tapes. What at first seems like atmospheric buzzing is often many voices. They have to be analyzed and amplified, of course."

Raudive was convinced that the voices were of the dead, as the voices themselves claimed. "There is no doubt that we have established communication with another world," he said. He was also fascinated by the mixture of languages the voices used. Often, he said, one message would be made up of words from more than one language. Since Raudive spoke Latvian, Russian, German, Swedish, French, and Spanish, and could understand most Slavonic dialects, he was usually able to interpret the most curious sounds into meaningful messages.

The problem is that different individuals listening to the recordings seldom hear the same words. Often the listener has to be told what the voice allegedly is saying before he can make out the words. This subjective factor is well illustrated in a message that Raudive claimed came from Sir Winston Churchill. Raudive wrote down the message as "Te Mac-Cloo, mej dream, my dear, yes"—a combination of Latvian, Swedish, and English words. Two British researchers thought the message was en-

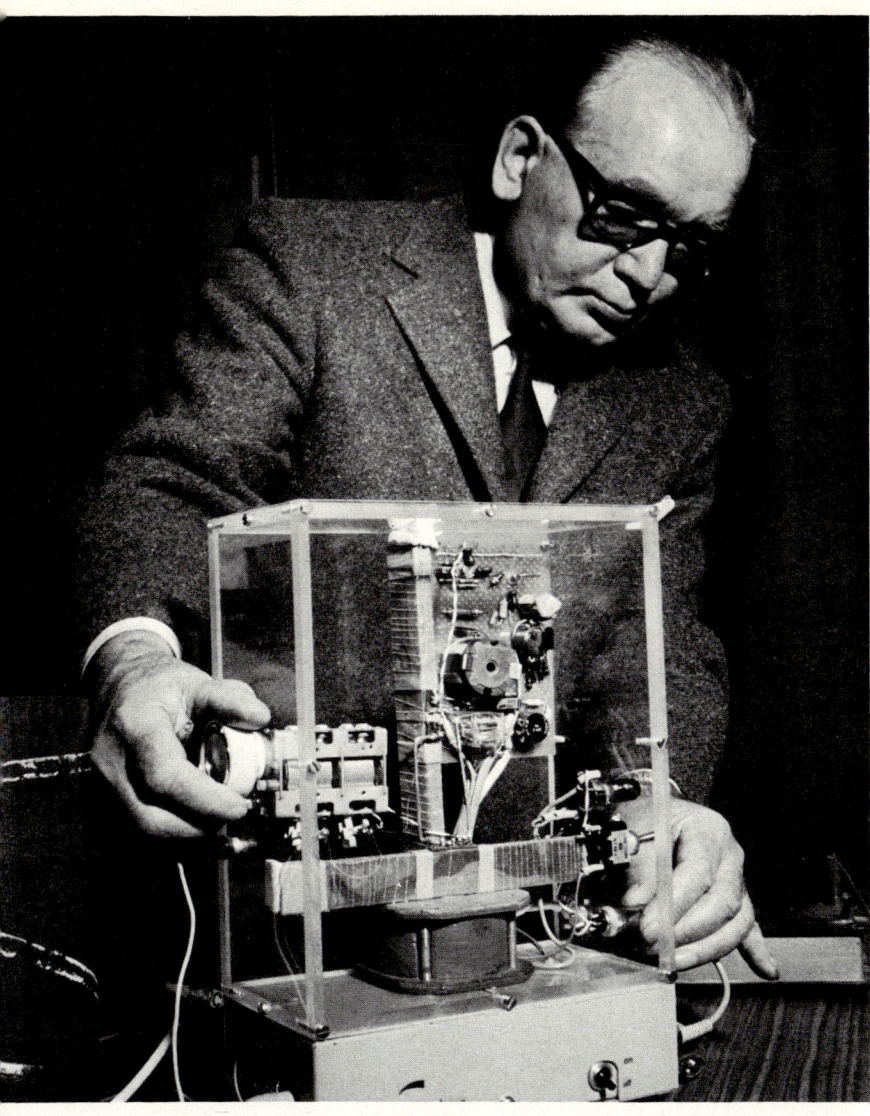

Left: Konstantin Raudive with the goniometer, a recording device built especially for him by an interested electronics engineer to receive the voices Raudive believed were coming from the dead. Raudive himself had no technical background, and reportedly relied entirely on his collaborators to develop and supply recording equipment.

Below: Dr. Hans Bender, the German parapsychologist who has investigated both Jurgenson and Raudive believed were coming the voices on the tape recorder.

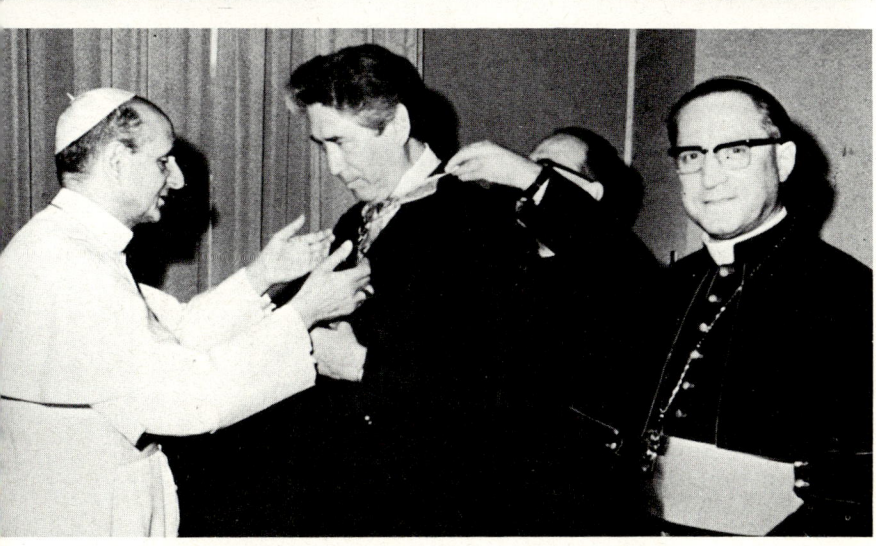

Above: Pope Paul VI decorating Jurgenson. This honor was for his work as a film maker, although supporters have claimed that the Vatican has taken an interest in his taped voice recordings.

tirely in English, which is more plausible inasmuch as Churchill did not speak either Swedish or Latvian. One of them thought he said, "Hear, Mark you, make believe, my dear, yes," while the other thought the British leader was saying, "Mark you, make thee mightier yet." In either case the message is something of a stylistic deterioration for a man who was arguably the greatest master of rhetoric of our time.

Churchill is not the only famous personality alleged to have communicated on Raudive's tapes. The spirits of Tolstoy, Nietzsche, John F. Kennedy, Hitler, and Stalin have also come through electronically according to Raudive.

Many of the voices seemed to want to communicate specifically with Raudive, and would address him by name: "The dead live, Konstantin;" "Kosti we are;" "Please believe." At times when another researcher was doing the taping, the voices would ask for Dr. Raudive: "We need Kosti."

David Ellis, an English college student who received a special grant from Cambridge University to study recorded voice phenomena, spent two short periods with Dr. Raudive in Germany in 1970 and 1971. Although inclined to believe in the possibility of spirits communicating electronically, Ellis expressed some reservations about the actual source of some of the voices he heard on Raudive's tapes. Writing in an article for *Psychic* magazine in February 1974, Ellis said that he thought many of the sounds could easily have been radio transmissions. "The air is full of broadcast transmissions—commercial and amateur radio, radio telephony, scrambled speech—no wavelength in the normal range can be guaranteed to be clear . . ." Ellis reported that one message was eventually translated as some chat from a Radio Luxembourg program: "Hello, this is Kid Jenson reminding you about Dimensions. Later on tonight on 208: soft rock, hard rock, jazz, and blues . . ."

Above: Thomas A. Edison, inventor of the phonograph and the light bulb. He shared the enthusiasm of many of his generation for contact with unseen forces, and worked on a device that would locate a frequency between long and short waves to be used as a telepathic channel between the worlds of the living and the dead.

Left: Guglielmo Marconi. He was another notable scientist—the inventor of the wireless radio—who believed modern technology would hold the key to expanding man's knowledge and understanding of time and the universe. He hoped to find a way to capture Christ's last words on the cross.

Not all of the voices can be accounted for in this way. There are many instances when they apparently reply to questions put by the experimenter. Ellis thinks that in some way, Raudive may have himself telekinetically produced the voices. "How else," he asks, "could the extraordinary mixture of languages, many of which the purported communicators did not know in their earthly life, be explained?"

Ellis says that his theory of telekinesis would not necessarily rule out the possibility that the messages *originated* with spirits. But, he goes on, it does mean that, instead of speaking directly onto the tape, the spirit voices would first be received telepathically by the experimenter and then "clothed in words from his own unconscious mind before being imparted to the tape."

Above: a cartoon lampooning the antics of amateur mediums and the spirit manifestations that were popular. It was captioned "Alarming effect produced by imprudently trying the hat and table-moving experiments." Below: another early method of contacting spirits. The sitters each place a finger on an up-turned wineglass on a table with the letters of the alphabet written around the edge. (The most common early 19th-century table was a round one, with a central pedestal support). The glass whizzed around the table, spelling out the spirit message.

The Ellis theory is similar to that of Dr. Hans Bender, a German professor of psychology who studied the voices received by Jurgenson. He is satisfied that the voices are genuine, but not necessarily spirits. He believes that the operator's subconscious mind somehow imprints the messages on the tape.

Another experimenter in the field of taping spirit voices is Raymond Cass, a British hearing aid specialist. On June 18, 1974, he recorded a voice which is reputed to have said, "Raudive, man of oak, toward the tomb." He sent copies of this cryptic message to three researchers who were also studying the phenomena. Three months later, at the age of 63, Raudive died.

The possibility of a form of spirit radio was predicted in 1936 by Sir Oliver Lodge, a former President of the SPR. Lodge, whose work on wireless transmission formed a basis for Marconi's invention of the radio, believed that some way would be found to link this world with the spirit world. In 1930 a voice believed to be that of Sir Arthur Conan Doyle, speaking through the medium Eileen Garrett, had indicated that the initiative in experimenting with communication methods was being taken by spirit scientists. Today many people believe that the modern tape recorder has enabled spirits to establish contact.

Marconi and Edison both hoped to achieve some form of contact with the unseen through electronic means. In 1920 Edison was busily constructing a device that he believed would put him in touch with people who had died. He believed there would be a radio frequency between the long and short waves which would make possible a form of telepathic contact with the other world. Until his death in 1937, Marconi worked secretly on a highly sophisticated device that he hoped would receive voices from the past. A devout Roman Catholic, he wanted in

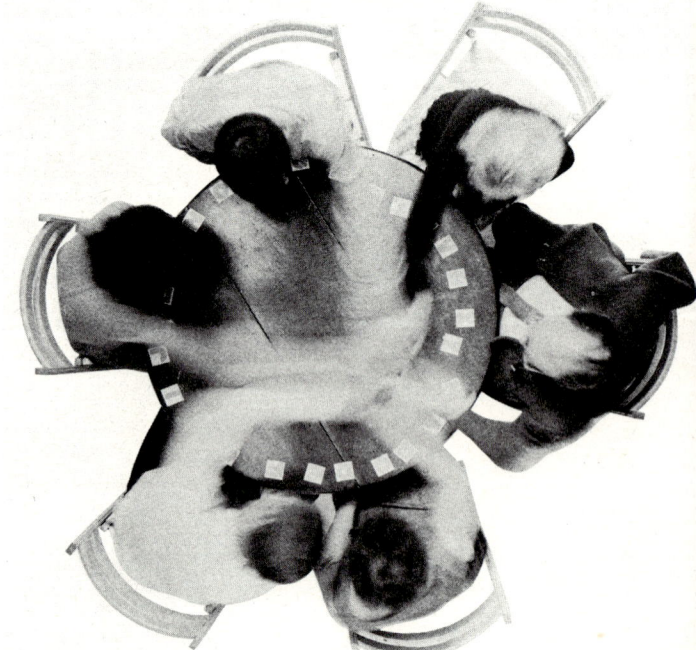

particular to record the words spoken by Jesus on the Cross.

Mechanical means of establishing a dialogue between the two worlds have been sought for many centuries. According to one historical account, Pythagoras, the famous Greek mathematician and philosopher attempted spirit contact. He held frequent gatherings for his followers at which "a mystic table, moving on wheels, moved toward signs which the philosopher and his pupil, Philolaus, interpreted to the audience as being revelations supposedly from the unseen world."

Pythagoras' moving table was apparently an early ouija board (from the French *oui* and the German *ja*, both meaning "yes"). The ouija is a small wooden pointer mounted on rollers. It is placed on a board marked with the letters of the alphabet and with the words "yes" and "no." The questioner's hand rests lightly on the pointer, which moves around the board, spelling out a message. Similar results can be obtained with the use of an inverted drinking glass on a table around which the letters and words have been arranged.

Compared to direct speech through the medium, ouija board communication is rather slow and laborious. However, in the hands of Hester Dowden, one of Britain's foremost automatic writing mediums of the early 20th century, the ouija board method produced some impressive results. According to one witness, "The words come through so quickly that it is almost impossible to read them, and it requires an experienced shorthand writer to take them down when the traveler moves at its maximum speed." Hester Dowden was usually blindfolded so that she could not see the letters and pointer.

In 1853 a French Spiritualist had devised an improvement on the ouija board, incorporating a pencil. Known as a planchette,

Right: the ouija board in use. Here Patience Worth, the spirit control of medium Mrs. John H. Curran, has materialized and is serving as the second guide for the board. Experts claimed that the spirits were able to speak exceedingly fast by means of the board, so perhaps a materialized spirit got even better results.

Adoption by the Ouija Board

At the turn of the century the ouija board craze swept the country. In St. Louis, the ouija board of medium Mrs. John H. Curran began spelling out a message in quaint English. The spirit said it was Patience Worth, a Puritan girl who had died 300 years before. She said she had always wished to write books and to be a mother, but had done neither.

Using the ouija board, Mrs. Curran produced four novels by Patience Worth.

Motherhood was more complicated. Patience Worth was determined that Mrs. Curran adopt a baby girl with red hair and blue eyes. The Currans finally found a young widow, due to deliver her baby, who agreed that they could adopt her baby if she did not survive childbirth. The baby girl—red-haired and blue-eyed — was born, and the young widow died. Patience Worth had her baby. The child was named Patience Worth Wee Curran.

Mrs. Curran died in 1938 and after that, Patience Worth never spoke again through any other medium. But mysteriously, the child Patience Worth Wee died of an apparently mild heart ailment five years later.

Had Patience Worth claimed her own?

this simple instrument was used to write messages automatically. The medium's hand would rest lightly on the planchette, which would then roll over the paper and write the message. However, mediums who produced automatic writing soon dispensed with the planchette and simply held a pen or pencil normally.

All these forms of communication can be explained in terms of unconscious muscular movements. Though the people using the devices are not aware of their actions, their subconscious minds may be controlling the movements of their hands. This makes the resulting messages no more than a reflection of the thoughts stored in the deeper levels of the mind. Of course, this theory is slightly less believable in the case of several operators working with a glass on a table because each operator would have different subconscious thoughts that might tend to cancel each other out. Even in this case, however, one could suppose that one operator might be influencing the thoughts of the others.

The "subconscious mind of the operator" theory cannot satisfactorily explain a case in which the message contains information not known to anyone present. Dr. Reginald Hegy, a former ship's surgeon and founder member of the College of Physicians of South Africa, told about his early experiments with the glass and alphabet in his book *A Witness Through the Centuries*. He and a small group of friends tried the glass-and-table method of contact with spirits, and received a series of messages. Some were in English, but many others were in French, Hungarian, and various provincial German dialects—languages not known by the sitters. It took some time to have the messages translated and their information checked. Many of the messages to the questioners seemed to come from complete strangers, who helpfully gave their names and information about their deaths. "Among the hundreds of names, dates, and other facts given," Hegy reports, "not one proved to be incorrect on investigation."

To prevent unconscious control of the glass, the group appointed one person to rearrange the letters so that they would be out of order. The sitters were then led in blindfolded. During the seance they held their heads turned away from the table, probably to avoid seeing the board down the sides of their noses. The messages continued as before, just as accurate, but were given even more rapidly than usual.

These various mechanical methods of contacting spirits—the ouija board, planchette, glass and table—are fairly sophisticated compared to table turning, which was one of the most widespread methods in the early days of Spiritualism. In this technique, the participants sit or stand around a table and place their hands lightly on its surface, sometimes with their fingers touching so as to complete a human circuit around the table. The table then rocks, and by means of a simple code—one tilt for "yes," two for "no," for example—is able to answer questions or, if the alphabet is recited, to spell out messages.

This crude method is open to the same criticism of subconscious influence levelled at ouija boards and planchettes. In addition, fraud is relatively easy. Table turning is only occasionally used by Spiritualists today, and then generally as an elementary introduction to the subject of contact with the next world.

Early in Spiritualism's short history mediums dispensed with

Below: a planchette, which is a ouija pointer equipped with a pencil so that instead of indicating letters to make up a message, the spirits can write out what they have to say directly. At first it was a fascinating novelty, but soon mediums turned to direct writing.

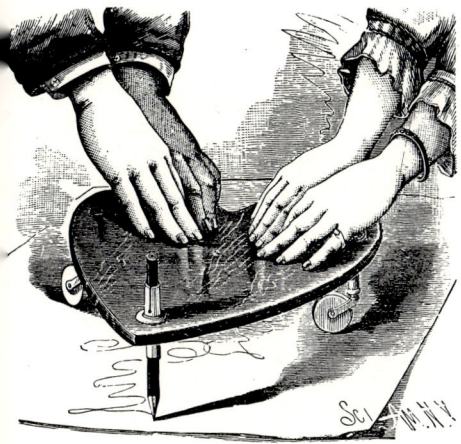

some of the cumbersome techniques, preferring to use trance control or direct voice. In the former method no mechanical device is involved, but the latter generally makes use of a trumpet or megaphone. The theory is that a spirit larynx can form itself out of ectoplasm and attach itself to the narrow end of the trumpet. The trumpet then acts as an amplifier and travels around the circle of sitters, pausing to allow a communicator to speak to particular individuals. Some witnesses claim to have heard voices so like the earthly voices of the communicators that they recognized them instantly. An explanation for this extraordinary phenomenon, allegedly from a spirit, was given by J. Arthur Findlay in his book *On the Edge of the Etheric:*

"From the medium and those present a chemist in the spirit world withdraws certain ingredients which for want of a better name is called ectoplasm. To this the chemist adds ingredients of

Below: a contemporary view of the courtroom during the highly publicized Cavendish case in 1903. The complainant was Henry Cavendish, a wealthy young man whose estate had fallen into the control of a Major and Mrs. Strutt through their influence over him. He told the court that Mrs. Strutt had given him planchette messages from his dead mother and the archangels Gabriel, Michael, and Uriel, all persuading him to sign his property over. Cavendish was able to identify a planchette, but could not swear it was the one Mrs. Strutt used.

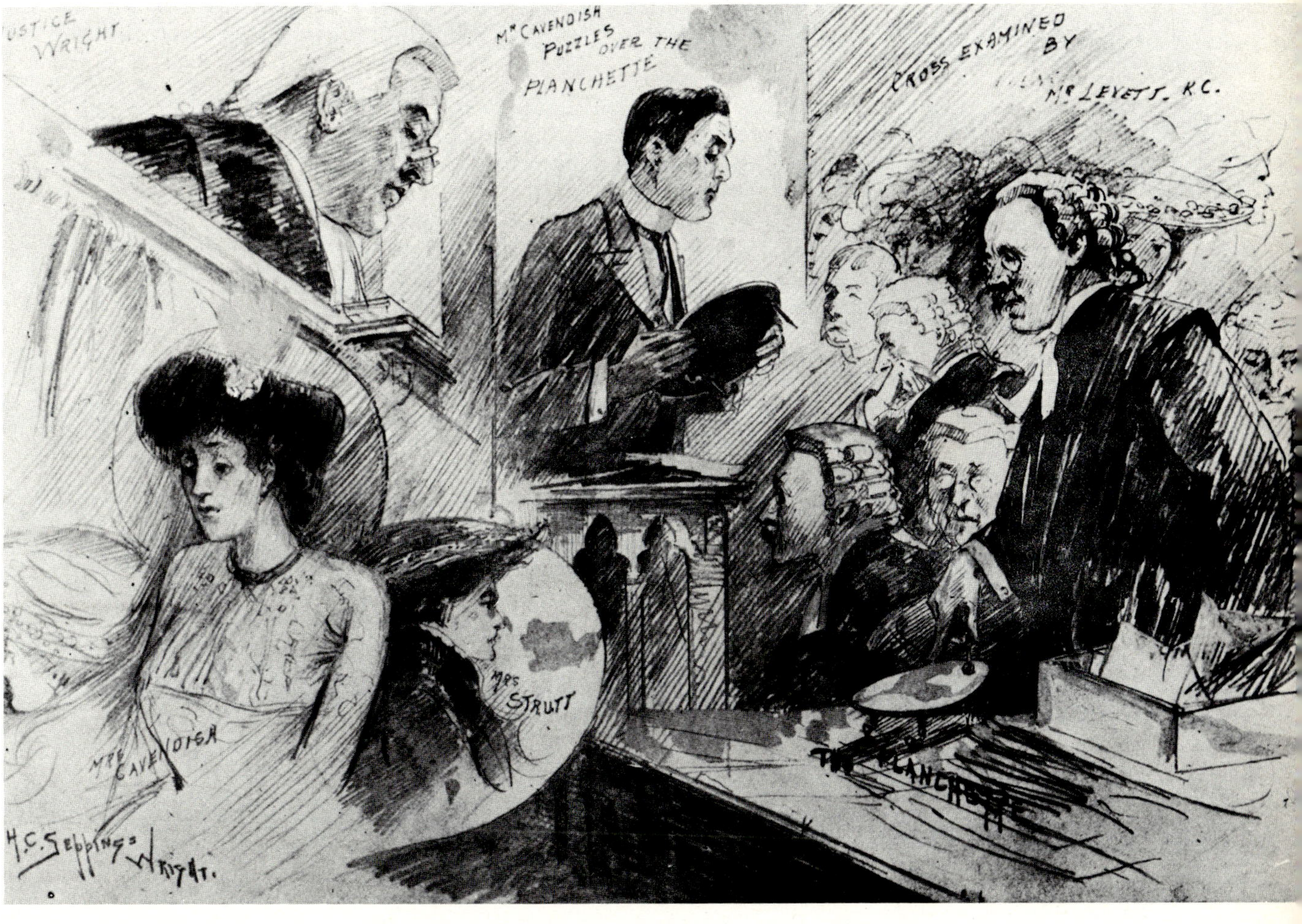

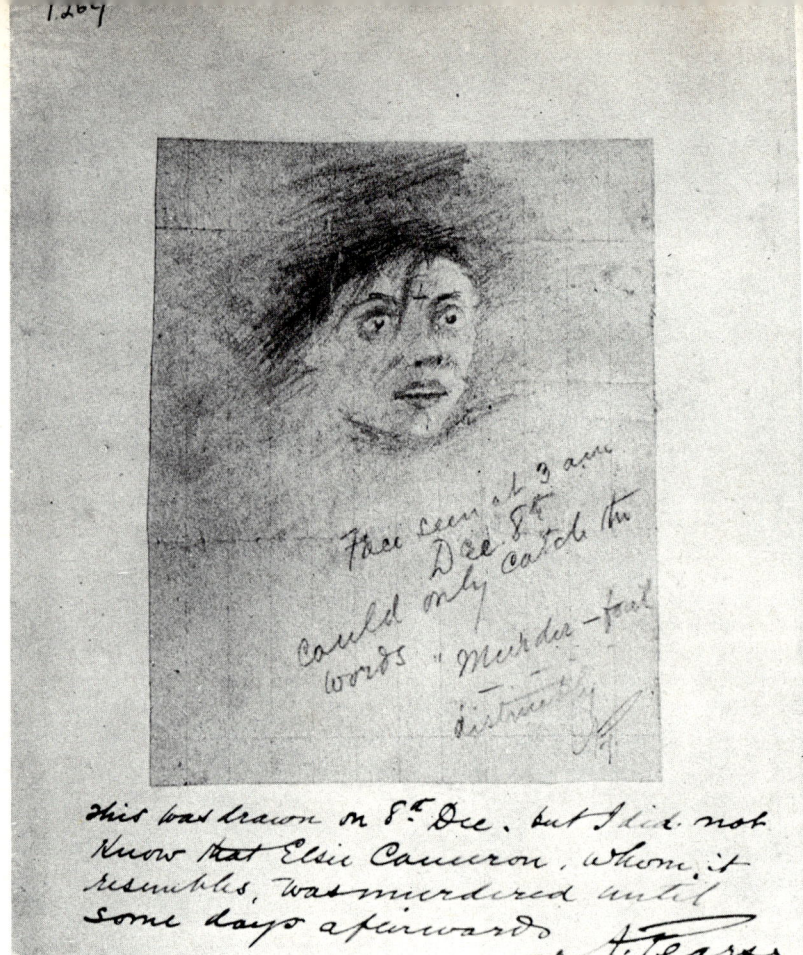

This was drawn on 8ᵗʰ Dec. but I did not know that Elsie Cameron, whom it resembles, was murdered until some days afterwards. A. Pearse

Left: a drawing executed in a trance by Captain A. Pearse on December 8, 1924. It resembled Elsie Cameron, a young London typist who had left home on December 5. Two days after the drawing was made, Mr. Cameron started to make inquiries of poultry farmer Norman Thorne, in whom his daughter had been interested. Thorne denied having seen her; but on January 15, the mutilated dead body of the girl was found buried under one of his poultry runs. Thorne was tried for Elsie Cameron's murder, found guilty, and hanged.

Right: a psychic drawing done by Ethel Le Rossignol, a British artist. She did a good number of automatic drawings and paintings in the late 19th century, presenting in them visions which she saw in her trance. In this particular drawing she has portrayed her vision of the Spirit of Wisdom enfolding men and women who love spiritually.

Right: one of Miss Le Rossignol's later spirit paintings. *The Unsealing of the Mysteries.* The most striking characteristic of most automatic artists is the tremendous speed with which they work, so capturing the power of their psychic visions.

his own making. When they are mixed together a substance is formed which enables the chemist to materialize his hands. He then, with his hands, constructs a mask resembling the mouth and tongue. The spirit wishing to speak places his face into this mask and finds it clings to him, gathers round his mouth, tongue and throat. . . . The etheric organs have once again become clothed in matter resembling physical matter, and by the passage of air through them your atmosphere can be vibrated and you hear his voice."

That was the spirit world's explanation according to Findlay. Another method of producing spirit voices was for the medium to crawl around on all fours in the darkness, whispering through the trumpet. More than one medium was caught in this fraud. However, there were some convincing direct voice seances. Mrs. Etta Wriedt of Detroit, Michigan often held seances in daylight. On these occasions the trumpet did not float on air to a sitter, but was held to the ear by the sitter, whereupon a spirit voice apparently issued from it. Mrs. Wriedt did not sit in a cabinet, nor did she enter a trance, so she was able to converse with the voices along with the sitters. Sometimes voices were heard independently of the trumpet. One sitter is said to have heard three

voices together. One spoke in each ear, and the third addressed him through the trumpet.

During one of her visits to England, Etta Wriedt was invited by the Dowager Duchess of Warwick—who had been the mistress of the late King Edward VII—to visit Warwick Castle, which was troubled by strange phenomena. Mrs. Wriedt was taken directly to her room on arrival at the castle, but some of her luggage was left in the hallway outside her door. Among the pieces was her seance trumpet. While waiting for her guest, Lady Warwick noticed the trumpet. She picked it up out of curiosity and placed it to her ear. Immediately she heard the voice of King Edward speaking in his characteristic slightly German accent. She conversed with him, partly in German.

At later seances held by Etta Wriedt in the castle, the King

Above: Mrs. Etta Wriedt, the American direct voice medium. She did not sit in a cabinet, did not go into a trance, and frequently entered into brisk conversation with the voices and her sitters. Although Etta Wriedt herself only spoke English, the voices were a multilingual lot, speaking just about every western European language, some eastern languages, and Arabic. When they were speaking in a language the medium did not understand, she generally appeared to take little interest in the proceedings. (The College of Psychic Studies)

Above right: a seance trumpet. Often in the early days of Spiritualism they were painted with a luminous paint so that a ghostly shape seemed to float around the darkened seance room.

often communicated, sometimes in German. He became so persistent that no other communicator was able to speak to Lady Warwick. Apparently resenting this possessiveness on the part of her deceased lover, Lady Warwick terminated the seances.

Foreign languages were a feature of Mrs. Wriedt's seances. On one occasion, two European sitters were addressed in their native languages of Serbian and Croatian. The medium herself appeared to have no interest in such communications. While the foreign spirits spoke she usually sat knitting.

Early in the 20th century, the English writer Dennis Bradley made an enthusiastic forecast regarding direct voice contact: "Communication with the spirits in their actual voices may, within this century, become as simple as the telephone or wireless. In fact, it seems to me that it is a new and phenomenal form of wireless communication."

As it turned out his prediction was wrong, for direct voice contact has virtually disappeared—along with other physical phenomena. Perhaps tape recording is the new improved method of tuning in the direct voice. It remains to be seen whether everyone who tries for long enough with a tape recorder and a blank tape will get the Raudive voices, or whether only those with psychic gifts—as Raudive himself seems to have had—will be able to do so.

Photography, which was in its infancy when Spiritualism was born, offered a unique opportunity to prove the existence of spirits by mechanical means. It also offered lucrative opportunities for tricksters, thanks mainly to the double exposure.

The first spirit photograph was produced by William Mumler in Boston in 1862. Mumler, an engraver by trade, tried to take a picture of himself by focusing a camera on an empty chair, and then jumping into a pose beside the chair after uncapping the lens. When developing the plate, he discovered the transparent figure of a young girl sitting in the supposedly empty chair. Below the waist, the figure seemed to dissolve into a mist. Mumler recognized the girl as a cousin who had died 12 years earlier. He repeated the experiment, and obtained other spirit images. Soon his work was attracting the interest of Spiritualists, and he set up a business producing photographs of the bereaved with their departed loved ones. The widowed Mary Todd Lincoln visited Mumler's studio under an assumed name, and obtained a photograph of herself with Lincoln by her side.

Later Mumler was accused of trickery. One spirit, for example, turned out to be the picture of a living man whom Mumler had photographed a few weeks earlier. Accusations of fraud must have hurt the business of the first psychic photographer, for he died in poverty in 1884.

Meanwhile, of course, other practitioners of spirit photography had appeared on the Spiritualist scene in America and Britain. Some sitters reported receiving pictures of long-dead relatives who had never had their photographs taken during their lifetime. A prominent English spirit photographer even succeeded in capturing the image of a spirit rabbit—perhaps a forebear of the rabbits that he kept in his backyard.

Despite the frequent errors to which these artists were prone—

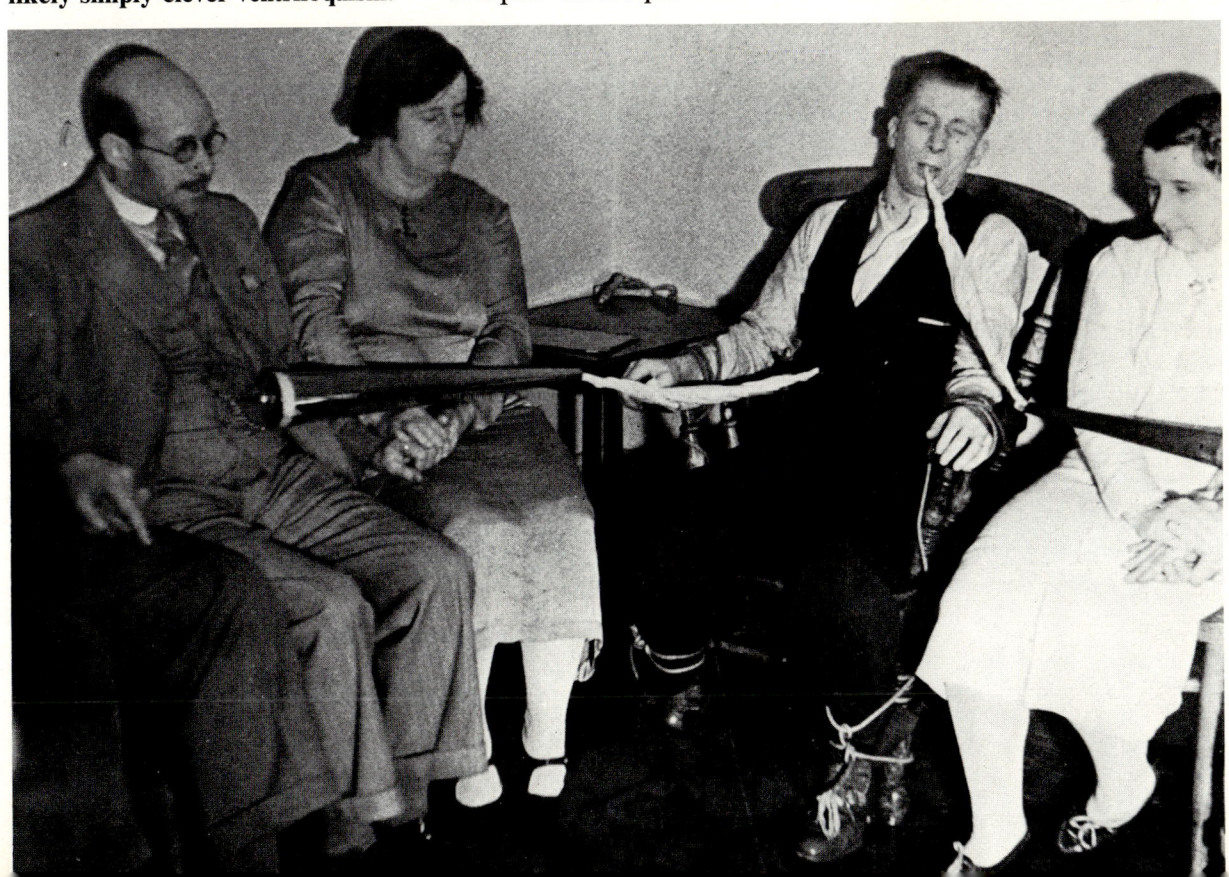

occasionally the spirits appeared upside down, suggesting a certain carelessness in loading the camera—many people were convinced that the images could be genuine, particularly when they themselves imposed safeguards against trickery. The Marquess of Donegall, for example, carried out a test seance with John Myers, a former London dentist and one of England's well-known psychic photographers. In the presence of several witnesses, including a leading magician, Lord Donegall loaded Myers' camera—which he examined closely—with his own marked plates. He took six photographs in bright light while Myers simply stood by. Lord Donegall then developed the plates himself. Two of them showed extra, unidentifiable, nondescript men whose presence could not be accounted for. Lord Donegall published his findings in the *Sunday Dispatch* on October 9, 1932. The following week, however, he published the results of a further sitting with Myers in which he accused Myers of substituting plates.

While psychic photographers tried to capture the spirits of the dead, a doctor at St. Thomas' Hospital, London, was developing a method of making one aspect of a person's spirit visible *before* death. Dr. Walter J. Kilner was intrigued by the possible existence of the aura—a permanent radiation long believed to surround the human body. The belief that saints had a visible aura has been given expression by artists in many religious paintings. Clairvoyants often claimed to be able to use the colors of a person's aura to diagnose diseases or read character. Dr. Kilner thought that if such radiation existed, it should be possible to detect it by modern technology—and he set about experimenting with various techniques.

In 1911 Dr. Kilner published the results of his research in a book entitled *The Human Atmosphere*. Enclosed with each copy of the book was a special screen that was said to render the aura visible to normal sight. The screen consisted of two hermetically sealed pieces of glass enclosing some coal tar dye. By looking through this screen in daylight, and then looking at a naked person standing in front of a dark background in dim light, one could see three distinct radiations around the person's body. According to Kilner, these radiations lay in the normally invisible ultraviolet end of the spectrum. They varied in depth, with the outer aura extending as much as a foot from the body. Their depth could be affected by a magnet, and was also sensitive to electric currents. Illness was found to affect both the size and color of the aura. Mental deterioration caused a marked reduction, and the approach of death made the aura shrink to almost nothing.

Today some striking advances in the study of auras have been made by a Russian husband-and-wife team, Semyon and Valentina Kirlian. Some 30 years ago Kirlian, an electrical engineer, happened to see a demonstration of high frequency electrotherapy machinery at a research institute. As he watched, Kirlian noticed a tiny flash of light between the electrodes of the machine and the patient's skin. He wondered what would happen if he placed a photographic plate between the patient and the electrode. He knew that glass electrodes would fog the plate through exposure of light, so he decided to use a metal electrode. This was

Above: the French photographer Buguet, who cashed in on the general enthusiasm for spirit photography. When a client arrived at the studio, Buguet's secretary would discreetly ask about the age and appearance of the dead person being sought. Buguet would place a plate in the camera and start waving his arms around, complaining of pains in his head from the spirits. Pains were soothed only when a convenient healing medium made "magnetic passes" at his head. After all this, the plate was developed, and with luck there would be a spirit lurking in the gloom. Buguet prudently insisted on prepayment, but in time the police took note of a multitude of complaints. When the studio was raided they found dolls to represent dead babies and 240 heads neatly cut out of photos made for ordinary clients. Buguet was fined and sent to prison for a year.
Right: nine spirit photographs by Thomas Hudson, the first British psychic photographer. Like the others, he was detected in fraud. Apparently sometimes he used double exposures; other times he dressed up to play the part of the ghost himself.

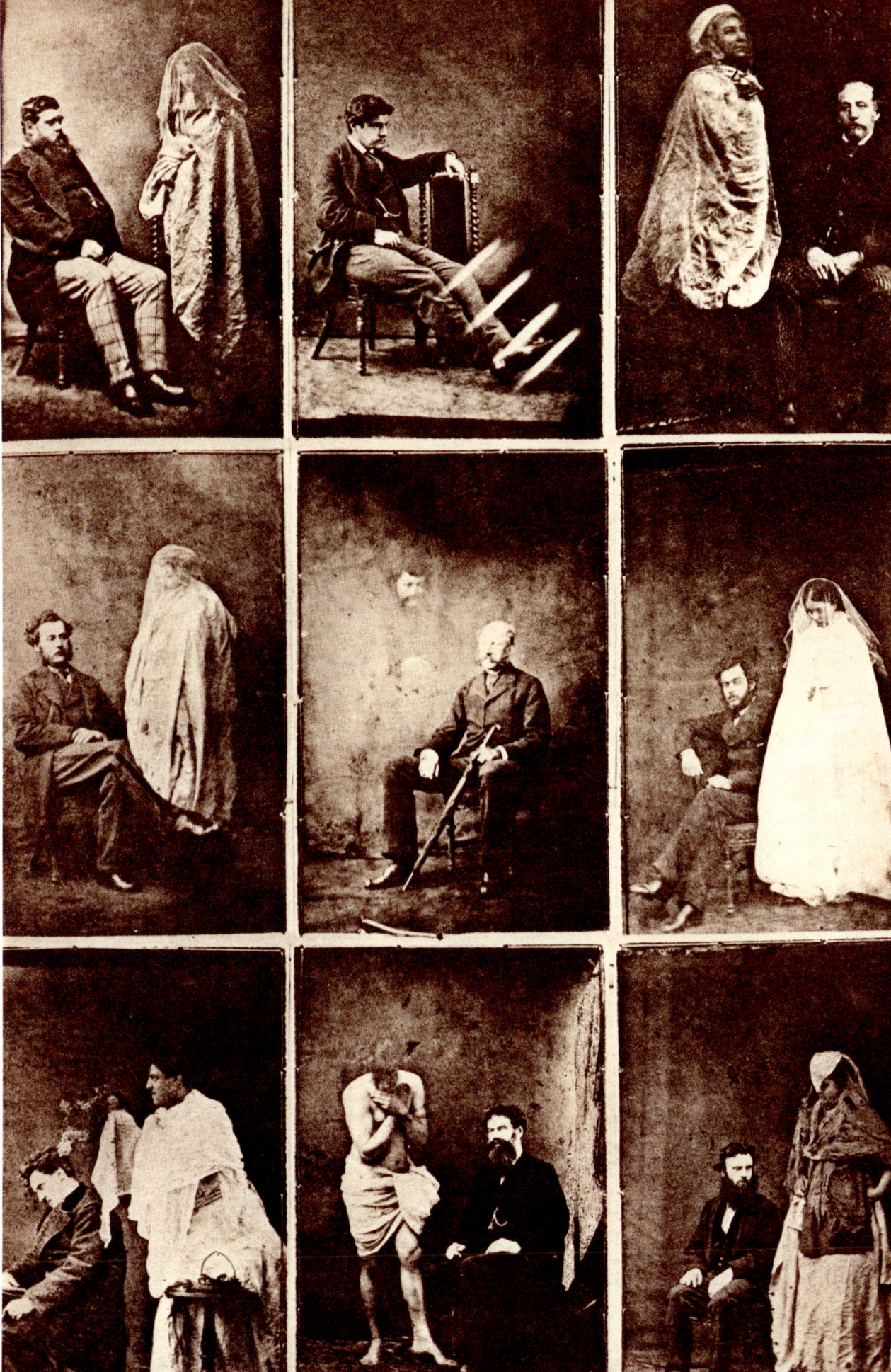

risky, however, and for this reason, Kirlian used himself as a guinea pig. He placed his hand beneath the electrode and switched on the machine. For three seconds he withstood the stabbing pain in his hand, and then he hurriedly placed the plate in emulsion. On the developing plate he saw a strange luminescence in the shape of his fingers.

Kirlian and his wife set to work developing a more satisfactory method of recording the phenomenon. Eventually they invented and perfected a technique that achieves astonishing results. No camera is required for the process, which is now called Kirlian photography. The object to be photographed—which can be organic, such as a finger or a leaf, or inorganic such as a stone—is placed on photographic paper. The paper then goes underneath a specially constructed high frequency spark generator that produces 75,000 to 200,000 oscillations per second. When the generator is switched on, the radiation from the object is transmitted to the paper. The Kirlians also invented a special optical instrument so that they could observe the phenomenon in motion. A description of Kirlian's hand as seen through this instrument appeared in the book *Psychic Discoveries Behind the Iron Curtain* (1970), by Sheila Ostrander and Lynn Schroeder:

"The hand itself looked like the Milky Way in a starry sky. Against a background of blue and gold, something was taking place in the hand that looked like a fireworks display. Multicolored flares lit up, then sparks, twinkles, flashes. Some lights glowed steadily like Roman candles, others flashed out, then dimmed. Still others sparkled at intervals. In parts of his hand there were little dim clouds. Certain glittering flares meandered along sparkling labyrinths like space ships traveling to other galaxies."

Research by other Russian scientists revealed even stranger phenomena. They took a leaf and photographed it by Kirlian photography. Then they cut part of the leaf away and rephotographed it. To their astonishment the Kirlian machine produced a complete image of the leaf. It seems that this special energy—called "bioplasma" by the Soviet psychic researchers—will remain even though the physical object is mutilated.

The question immediately arises whether bioplasma proves the existence of a human spirit, capable of surviving death. On the face of it, the evidence seems to give a negative answer. If a leaf posses bioplasmic energy—not to mention inorganic objects—it seems likely that what the Kirlians have revealed is a purely physical phenomenon. On the other hand, it is possible that this energy field plays some part in telepathic, extrasensory, and physical phenomena such as poltergeist activity. At present, Dr. Thelma Moss of Los Angeles and other American investigators of paranormal phenomena are making important contributions to the field of Kirlian photography, and in the years ahead we can probably expect to hear of further developments in this new area of psychic research.

If man does possess a soul, it may well be that proof of its existence may one day be provided not by Spiritualists, but by people like Friedrich Jurgenson and the Kirlians—people who have stumbled on fascinating aspects of the unseen through the unconventional use of modern technology.

Above: Semyon and Valentina Kirlian, the husband-and-wife team working in the USSR. They have experimented with high-frequency electrical current photography for over 30 years.

Right: two Kirlian photographs of a man's finger. The picture above shows the normal condition. In the bottom picture, the man has taken a drug that slows down his metabolism, and this makes the color of the corona around his fingertip change. Further Soviet research at the Kazakh State University in Alma-Ata has found that illnesses tend to show up in advance— before any symptoms appear—as a disordered play of flares.

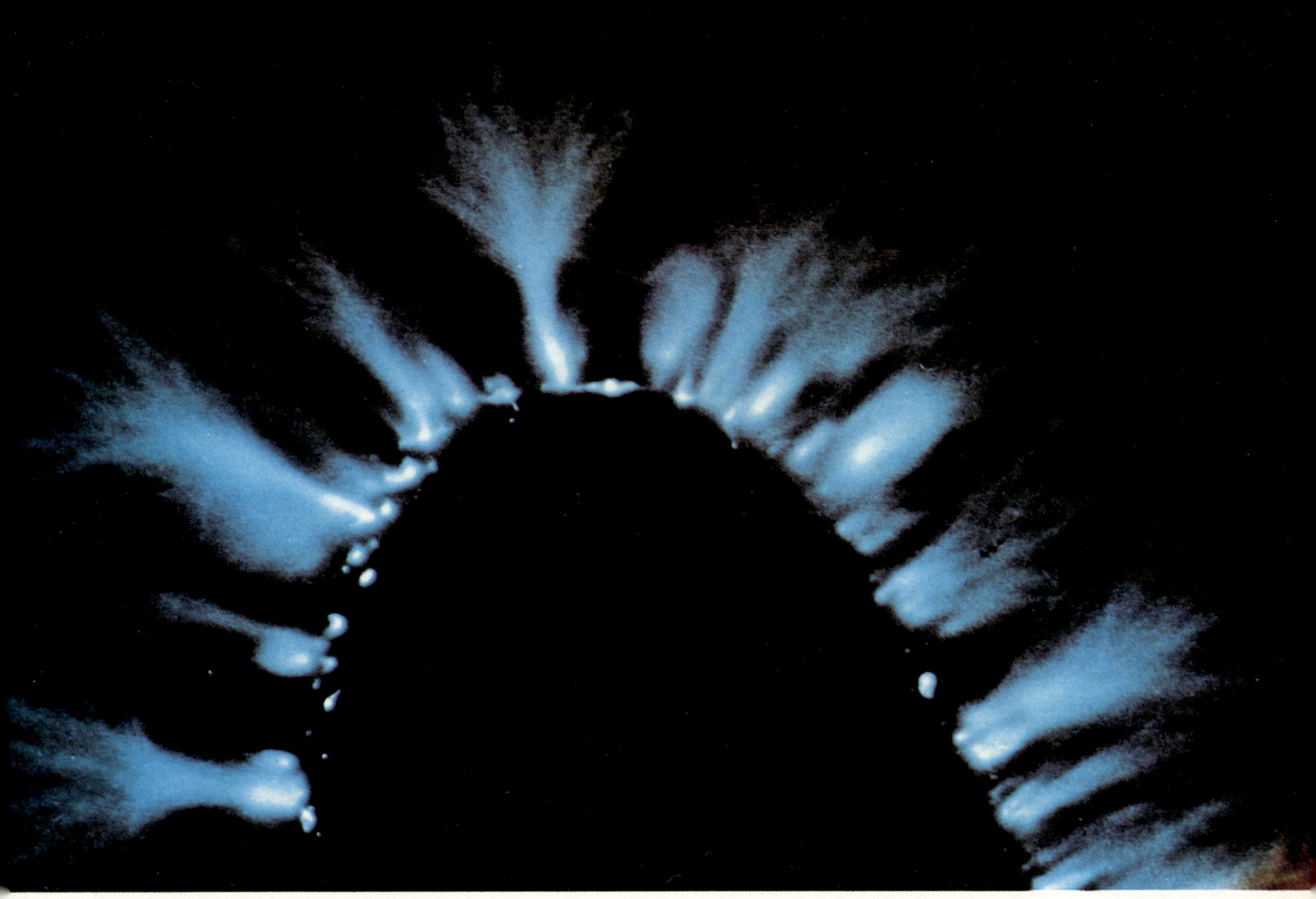

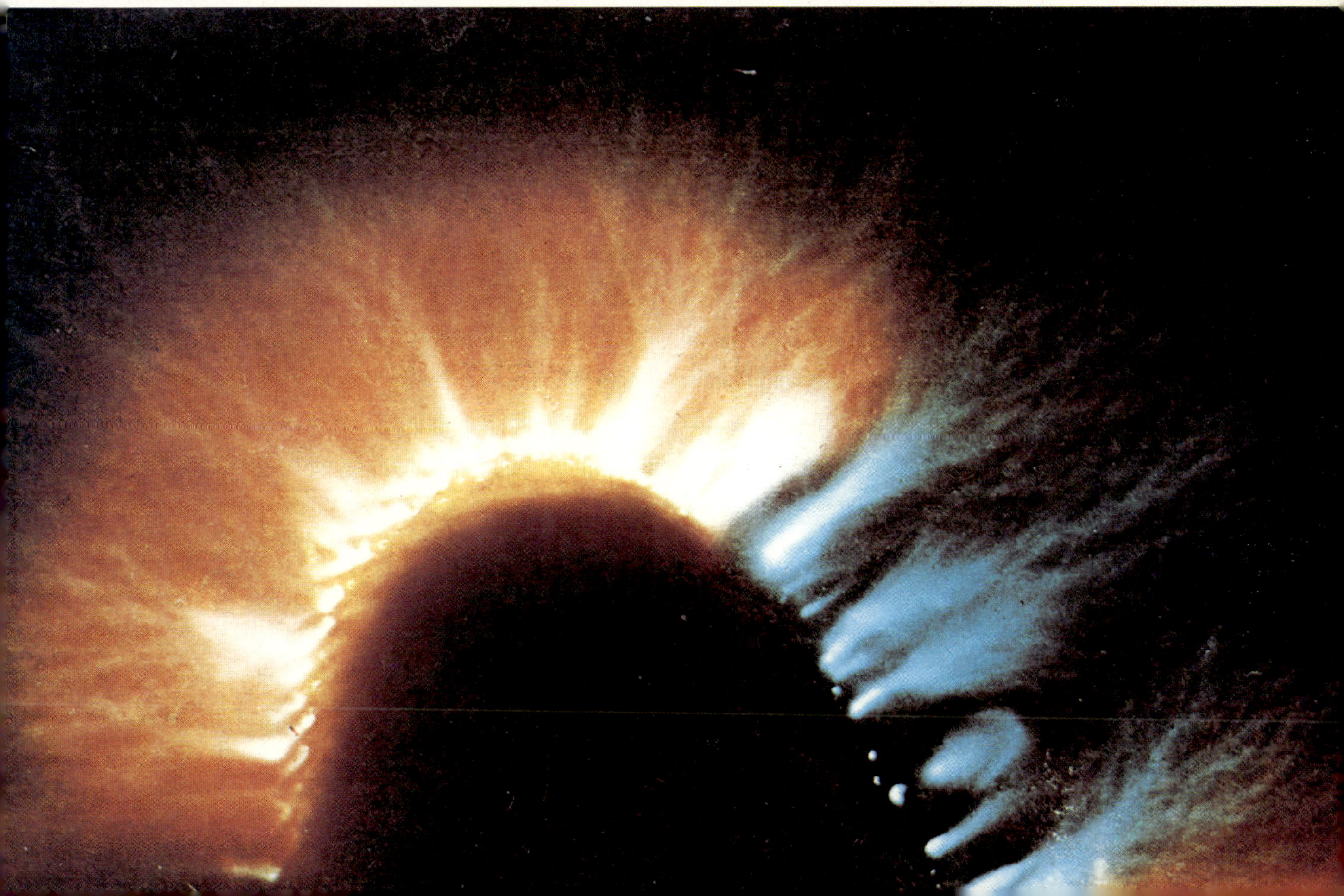

7

Although the theatrical drama of the seance room has mellowed and changed, the seances go on. Spiritualism attracts 20th-century adherents determined yet to prove the survival of the human spirit.

Spiritualism Today

Styles change in virtually all areas of life—from entertaining to child rearing—and Spiritualism is no exception. Today, illuminated trumpets and ectoplasm have disappeared along with gaslight, and table turning is about as fashionable as the polka. Certain aspects of Spiritualism, including its basic beliefs, remain the same, but it has lost most of the melodramatic trappings beloved in the late 19th century.

An experience recounted by Rosamund Lehmann, an English novelist, is typical of many people's first encounter with modern Spiritualism. The author's curiosity about Spiritualism grew out of the death of her

110

"Some mediums are superb entertainers"

daughter Sally. In her quest to discover whether her daughter had survived death Rosamund Lehmann went with a friend to a demonstration of mediumship at the College of Psychic Studies in London. She admits in her book *The Swan in the Evening* that she went to the meeting with a certain sense of guilt because her parents had strongly disapproved of Spiritualism.

The friend who accompanied her also had misgivings, but of a different kind. He told her after the meeting that he had dreaded the possibility of receiving a message from his dead father with whom he had not always seen eye to eye.

Their expectations were similar to those of most people attending a Spiritualist meeting for the first time. However, the very normality of the proceedings seems to put newcomers at ease. Rosamund Lehmann was fortunate in being one of the few people at the meeting to receive a message, and one that she found very convincing. She writes:

"I had heard that the demonstrator was a remarkable sensitive called Mrs. Ena Twigg. She is an attractive, charming looking person, and I saw her with surprise and relief . . . In short, I began to relax. But what followed startled me tremendously. Mrs. Twigg, whom I had never seen before, opened her demonstration by addressing me. Then she described Sally, whom she appeared to see standing behind me; then she put her hands to her temples and said: 'This is a very strange message. . . . Why is she talking about the War God? She is saying Wotan, Wotan, the War God. . . . She is saying she does wish the War God would believe she is alive. . . . Can you understand?' Another pause. 'Oh! Now she's saying I haven't got the name quite right. It's not quite right but it's the only way she could think of to get it through. She is laughing. She says you will understand. Do you understand?' "

The writer was startled and impressed by this message from a complete stranger. The Christian name of her husband—Sally's father—was Wogan, a most unusual English name. It was obvious that, in the spirit communication, one letter had somehow been changed, making the name sound like that of the Norse God of War.

In the course of a modern public demonstration of mediumship or clairvoyance, only about 10 or 12 people at most receive messages. Many therefore leave the meeting with a sense of disappointment, not having heard anything relevant to themselves, and not knowing whether or not the messages received by others were evidential.

To increase their chances of receiving a personal message, those interested can arrange a private sitting. The larger Spiritualist organizations in Britain have special rooms reserved for this purpose, but most mediums give seances in their own homes either in their living room or in a room set aside for spirit communication. Normally the seance room atmosphere is calm and restrained. Apart from the medium describing people invisible to the sitter, and conveying words that she or he alone can hear, the sitting resembles an informal chat. Most mediums now work without going into a trance. Some mediums are superb entertainers, describing the spirits so vividly and poignantly, and conveying the messages with such dramatic

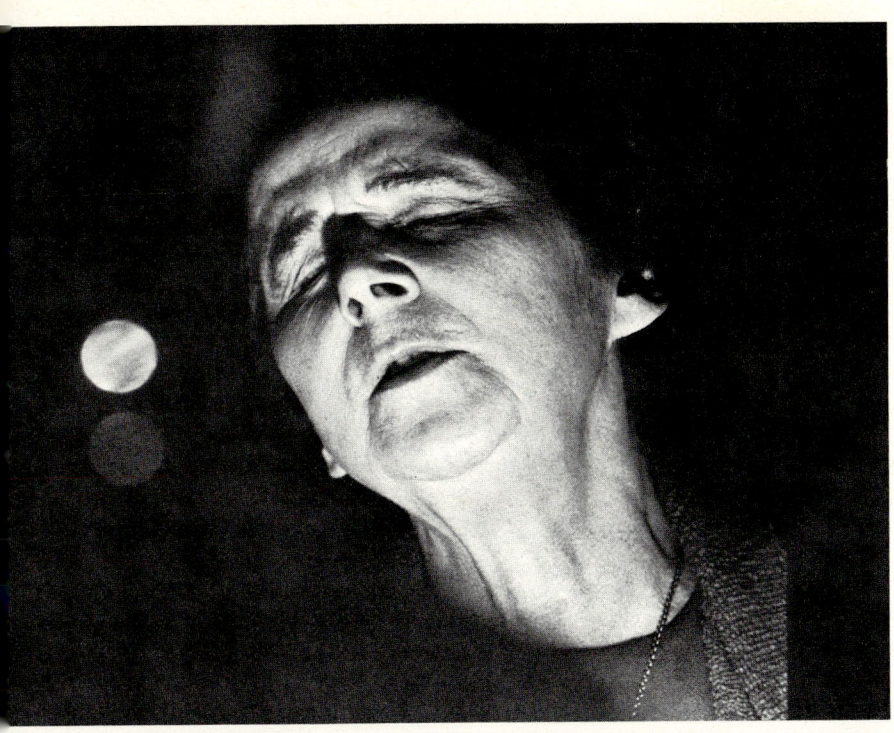

Left: the British medium Mrs. Ena Twigg in a trance. Mrs. Twigg is a minister of the Spiritualist Church and, like any British minister, she can officiate at weddings and at funerals—as well as at seances.

Below: a modern seance, now often called a home circle. These present-day Spiritualists meet weekly to "complete a link" between themselves and the spirit world. The flowers are important because it is believed that "the spirit people like them." Most modern seances do not have showy displays of physical phenomenon.

timing that they can reduce the sitters to tears. The majority of mediums, however, have a matter-of-fact approach, and let the content of the message speak for itself.

Today in Britain mediums can practice their calling with no fear of legal prosecution—provided that they do not do so "with intent to deceive" or use "any fraudulent device." This provision is part of the Fraudulent Mediums Act passed in 1951. Before that time, mediums were liable to prosecution under the Witchcraft Act of 1735. Under that law mediumship itself was illegal so police could raid any seance without prior evidence that fraud was being committed. Spiritualists were understandably upset by this state of affairs. In particular, they feared that mediums in trance could be injured by sudden interference during a physical seance.

The conflict between Spiritualists and the law in Britain came to the boil in 1944 with the trial of Mrs. Helen Duncan. One of the foremost physical mediums of her day, Helen Duncan had been investigated and exposed by the London Psychical Laboratory in 1931. Two years later she was convicted of fraud and given a small fine. It appears that her talents included the technique of swallowing and regurgitating items, and the ectoplasm she produced was shown on one occasion to be chewed-up toilet paper. In spite of her various embarrassments, this medium continued to enjoy great popularity, and many Spiritualists insisted that she could produce genuine phenomena.

Early in 1944 Helen Duncan gave a series of seances in Portsmouth, England. A young naval officer attended one of the seances and received a communication from his deceased aunt, of which he had none, and from his deceased sister, who was actually alive. The man returned for another seance with a plainclothes policeman. During one of the materializations they switched on a flashlight and grabbed the medium, who was veiled in some filmy white material. In the hubbub that followed someone snatched away the vital evidence—the veil—but the medium was arrested.

Helen Duncan's trial provided a little light relief from the war situation. For seven days readers of Britain's newspapers were treated to fascinating headlines such as "Spirit called Peggy liked lipstick," and "Spirit had 20-inch mustache." Despite an able defense financed by a Spiritualist fund, Mrs. Duncan was convicted of fraud and sentenced to nine months' prison.

This was not the end of her career, however. After her release she resumed work, and in 1956 one of her materialization seances was raided by the police. The medium fell ill and was taken to a hospital in Edinburgh. There she died at the age of 59, five weeks after the surprise raid. The death certificate attributed her decease to diabetes and heart failure. Since she weighed 280 pounds, it is probable that her heart would have given out before too long. However, the shock of the police raid may well have accelerated her death.

To Spiritualists it was a clear case of an entranced medium being injured by a sudden withdrawal of ectoplasm into her body. They reacted to Mrs. Duncan's death with a storm of protest. Hundreds of them contributed to a special fund to enable her husband to bring court proceedings against the

Above: Helen Duncan, the British physical medium. This picture, taken during a seance, shows her materializing a hand from her curtained cabinet. During his investigations with the Laboratory of Psychical Research, Harry Price obtained photos of a similar manifestation that was clearly a rubber glove. Right: the rubber doll that masqueraded as Mrs. Duncan's child spirit guide Peggy in some of her fraudulent seances.

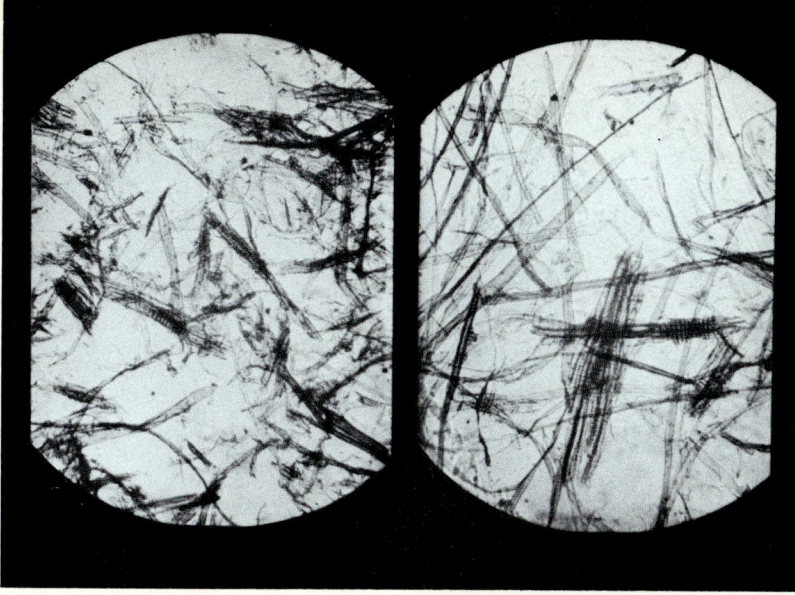

Above: photomicrographs of the "teleplasm" produced by Helen Duncan during a test seance. The teleplasm, on the left, is compared with a control sample of ordinary paper (60% chemical and 40% mechanical wood pulp). The fibers, medullary rays, etc. are identical in both photos.

Right: Peggy the spirit guide again—this time in the shape of a woman's chemise. This Peggy appeared during a seance in 1933. One of the sitters was policewoman Esson Maule, who suddenly grabbed at the spirit as another sitter simultaneously put on the lights. The medium and Miss Maule had a brief tug of war over the garment—the tear is where Miss Maule briefly got her arm stuck through it. The seals were placed on it, with signatures, by most of the other sitters who had been there.

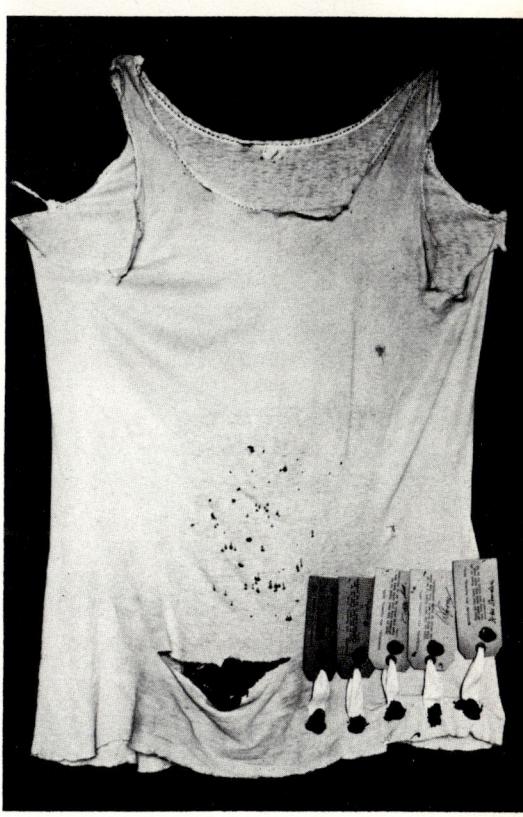

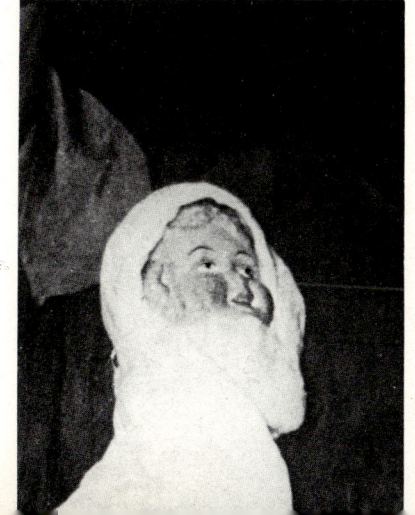

Left: Miss Esson Maule in the hallway of the building in which the Peggy-chemise episode took place. Helen Duncan was arrested as a fraudulent medium and received a sentence to pay a small fine or serve a month in prison.

ĀRI TREMEMBERY - "Cabôclo"
GUIA ESPIRITUAL
FRATERNIDADE ESPÍRITA EVANGÉLICA
São Paulo — Jundiaí
(pintura mediúnica)

Above: a poster for a Brazilian Spiritist meeting showing the Indian spirit control of Joseph Lastorani. In Brazil there are currently many active physical mediums, but since Spiritism emphasizes the importance of service to others, particularly healing, most manifestations are involved with psychic healing.

Right: a series of photos taken during the course of a modern Brazilian seance. A young woman medium apparently produced a complete materialized spirit. The arrows show where the beads were first materialized, and where they appeared on the fully materialized spirit's headdress.

police. On the advice of lawyers, however, the case was dropped. Today, Mrs. Duncan is regarded by most Spiritualists as a martyr. Many attribute the disappearance of physical phenomena to the fear of injury by mediums.

In the United States the legal position of mediums varies from state to state. There is no equivalent to the Fraudulent Mediums Act, although fraudulent psychics are open to prosecution in the same way as frauds in other spheres. In New York and California the courts are tough on mediums. To avoid prosecution, many adopt a religious title such as Reverend.

As a recognized denomination, American Spiritualism is small. The National Spiritualist Association includes about 200 churches with 5000 members, while the International General Assembly of Spiritualists has around 80 churches and 1200 members.

Britain, although a smaller country, has far more practicing Spiritualists. There are more than 500 Spiritualist churches, most of them belonging to the Spiritualists' National Union. This organization was founded in 1890 by Emma Hardinge Britten, one of Britain's earliest mediums and most active Spiritualist propagandists. Its main function is "to promote the advancement and diffusion of the religious philosophy of Spiritualism, on the basis of the Seven Principles." These principles include such generally accepted beliefs as "the brotherhood of man" and "personal responsibility," along with more specifically Spiritualist tenets, such as "the Communion of Spirits and the Ministry of Angels."

Below left: the medium was handcuffed inside a special barred cage. Below right: the woman in trance begins to produce ectoplasm.

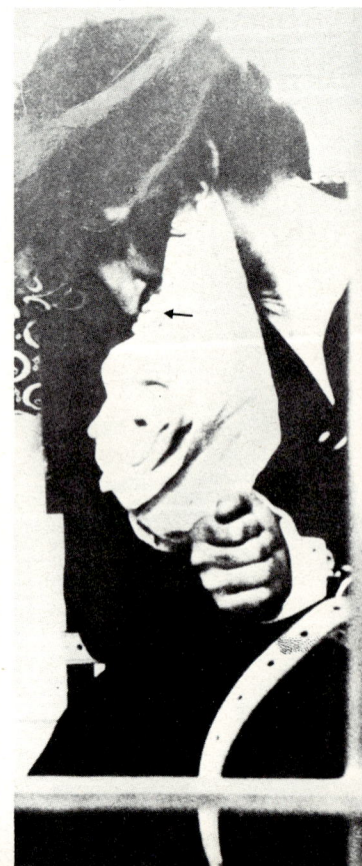

A typical service in a Spiritualist church opens with a prayer by the chairman—not called Reverend in Britain—followed by hymns and more prayers, an address, and a demonstration of clairvoyance. The medium demonstrates his or her psychic talents by pacing the platform and selecting individuals in the audience to whom spirit messages are addressed. The quality of the clairvoyance at these public meetings varies greatly. At its worst it looks like a ludicrous guessing game, with the medium deliberately asking questions or discreetly fishing for information. At its best, as practiced by a gifted medium such as Ena Twigg, it yields some startlingly accurate information. There is no doubt that many people find such meetings satisfying. Every year on Armistice Day, thousands of people pack London's huge Royal Albert Hall to hear the top mediums convey messages from those who died in the two world wars.

This gathering, billed as "the world's largest seance," is organized by the Spiritualist Association of Great Britain. The SAGB is one of the largest Spiritualist organizations in the world. At its headquarters in London's fashionable Belgrave Square, it offers a wide range of activities including seances, lectures, and spiritual healing. The Association produces its own newspaper, publishes books, and sends mediums to the United States, Canada, and a number of European countries.

Although almost every country in the world has Spiritualist associations, Spiritualism has not elsewhere developed to the same degree as in Britain and the United States. The exception is Brazil, where it is said to have some five million followers.

Below: the curtains are drawn over the cage, but the materialized figure appears and accepts a book as proof it is in fact material.

Below: the fully materialized figure appears outside the cage.

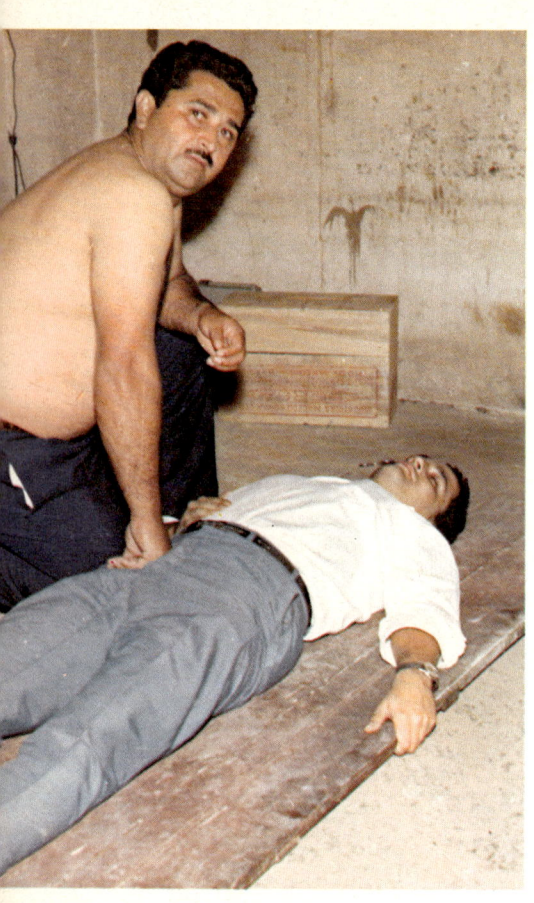

Above: the Brazilian healer José Arigó carrying out an eye operation on a patient. After a phenomenally successful career of psychic healing, Arigó was killed in a car crash in 1971.

In Brazil, as in other South American countries and France, the popular form of Spiritualism is "Spiritism," a set of beliefs formulated by Allan Kardec. A Frenchman whose real name was Hippolyte Leon Denizard Rivail, Kardec began studying Spiritualism in its earliest days. He enlisted the help of 10 mediums in contacting spirits for answers to a wide range of questions. Kardec then distilled and systematized the answers, publishing them under the title *Le Livre des Esprits (The Book of Spirits)*. The 1018 questions and answers in the book cover numerous subjects, from the creation to moral laws. Key passages in the book deal with the various realms of spirit, spiritual progression, and the belief in reincarnation. Not only are souls reborn, according to Kardec, but they also progress by being reborn on more advanced inhabited planets.

A major belief of Spiritism—or Kardecism as it is sometimes called—is that charity is essential for salvation, and the greatest act of charity is to bestow health. This can be achieved by co-operating with spirit entities having appropriate medical skills. This perhaps explains why Brazil, with its large number of Spiritists, is in the forefront of psychic healing.

There are several Brazilian Spiritist hospitals in which medical men and mediums work side by side. The largest of these is the 600-bed Porto Alegre Spirit Hospital, founded in 1926. Like all the other hospitals run by Spiritists, Porto Alegre specializes in the treatment of mental illness. According to Spiritism many disturbances of the mind are caused by spirit entities, and are best treated by trained mediums who can rid the afflicted patient of the obsessing spirit. The medical teams who work with the mediums in such hospitals do not have to subscribe to Spiritist beliefs, and practice orthodox medicine.

The treatment of the mentally ill also led to the founding of Palmelo, the only Spiritist community in the world. Located about 160 miles from Brazil's new capital of Brasilia, the Spiritist village started with one man, Jeronimo Candido Gomide. He built a hut on the site in 1925, and started treating the insane with Spiritist methods. Soon a small settlement grew up around him. Today the town of Palmelo has 2000 inhabitants, plus a fluctuating population of mental patients.

There is nothing startling or revolutionary about the Spiritist treatment of mental disorders. After all, many modern forms of psychotherapy could be described as spiritual healing even though the therapist does not believe the disorders come from spirit entities. But psychic surgery is another matter. In the last few years there have been reports from Brazil and the Philippines, another home of Spiritism, of seemingly miraculous operations performed by untrained people using makeshift instruments or, in some cases, their bare hands.

The most famous of these psychic surgeons was José Arigó, sometimes called "the surgeon of the rusty knife." Before his death in 1971 he operated on thousands of people, using unsterilized instruments such as kitchen knives and scissors. Most of the patients were cured or helped considerably, and there was not a single fatality despite the appalling conditions under which he worked. Arigó was said to be controlled by "Dr. Fritz," a dead German surgeon. Whatever the source of

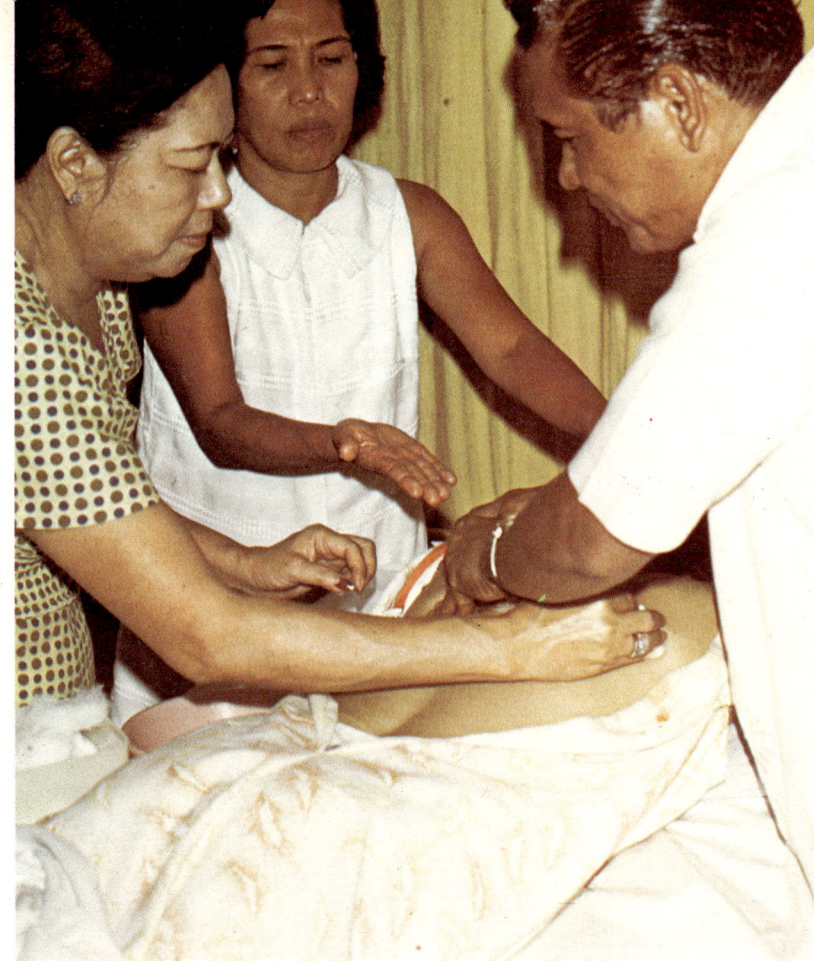

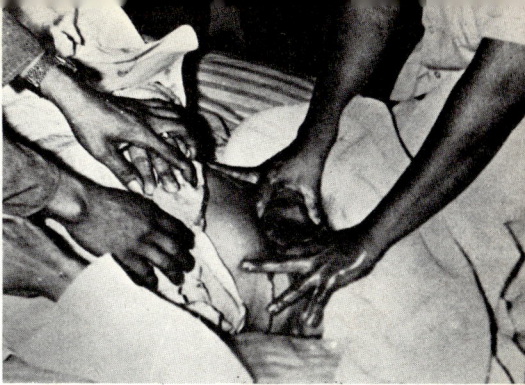

Above and below: Tony Agpaoa, one of the most notable Filipino healers, operating on a malignant abdominal growth. The incision, made with bare hands, took only four seconds. The growth, about the size of an avocado stone, was pulled out, alcohol poured over the wound, and the incision closed. The abdomen, still blood-spattered, shows no scar.

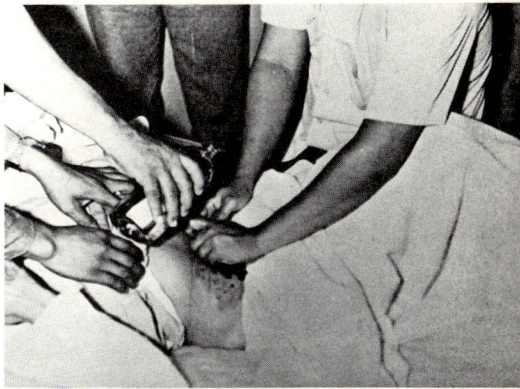

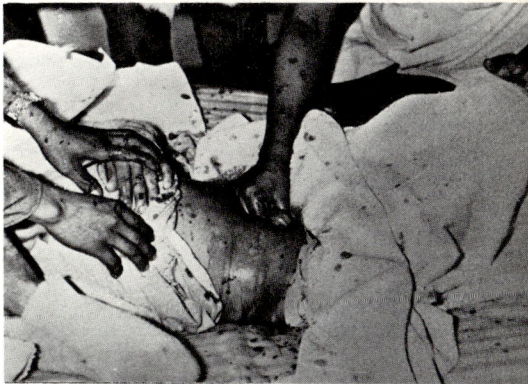

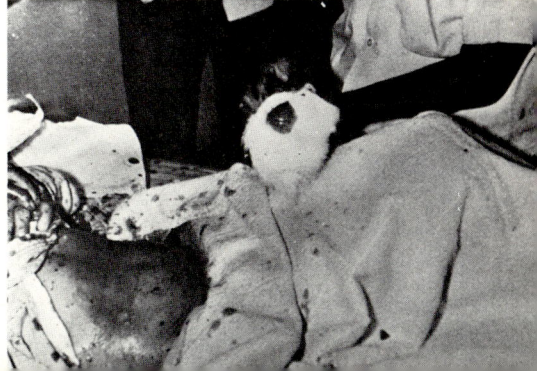

Above: Angelo, a psychic healer, shown working with two assistants on the back of a patient who has lung trouble. The location is Manila, the Philippines, which has now become another thriving center of psychic surgery and Spiritualist healing. There is a long history of faith healing in the Philippines, and today more than 400 healing centers allied with the Spiritualists exist throughout the islands.

Arigó's knowledge, his ability was astonishing. On one occasion a team of doctors studying Arigó presented him with 1000 patients to see if he could diagnose their illnesses. Without touching them, and taking on average just one minute to complete each consultation, Arigó made specific diagnoses and suggested appropriate treatment in each case. He used automatic writing to convey this information from Dr. Fritz. The doctors were able to confirm 550 of Dr. Fritz's diagnoses. The remaining 450 could not be confirmed because the team did not have on-the-spot resources to carry out tests, but in no case was the diagnosis or treatment discovered to be incorrect.

Dr. Fritz has never been identified, but another Brazilian psychic surgeon, Lourival de Freitas, has a very famous control. This is the Roman emperor Nero, although he was not known for medical skills during his lifetime. A woman of Nero's court and a Japanese called "Sheka" also control de Freitas on occasion. The Japanese specializes in certain lung and bronchial operations.

De Freitas is vouched for by Anne Dooley, an English journalist and psychic researcher who suffered from a bronchial condition judged incurable by medical experts. Having watched

de Freitas operate successfully on other people, Anne Dooley decided to let him operate on her. She described the experience in the *Psychic* magazine of February 1973.

The operation began rather unfavorably with Nero controlling de Freitas and indulging in a long-winded attack on the press in general and on the patient in particular. Courageously the fully conscious reporter submitted to having her tonsils removed with a pair of scissors, and to having a cut made in her back. From this incision de Freitas withdrew a large clot of blood.

After a slightly painful but short convalescence, Anne Dooley returned to England and was examined at Greenwich Chest Clinic. The X-ray showed her to be normal.

Even more bizarre than this operation are some of the feats of Philippine psychic surgeons. They work with their bare hands and seemingly open up bodies, remove diseased matter and growths, and mend the wounds.

Dr. Lyall Watson, a British scientist and writer who has watched these Filipino healers at work, offers an interesting hypothesis in his book *The Romeo Error*. While not dismissing the surgery itself as fraud, he believes that much of the blood in psychic surgery is window dressing to make observers believe that the bodies are actually being opened. Analysis of the blood in these operations has yielded some puzzling results. At times the blood is of the same type as the patient's, but at other times it belongs to a different blood group. Sometimes, it has proved to be animal's blood. Watson believes that the healers possess a form of materialization mediumship. He writes:

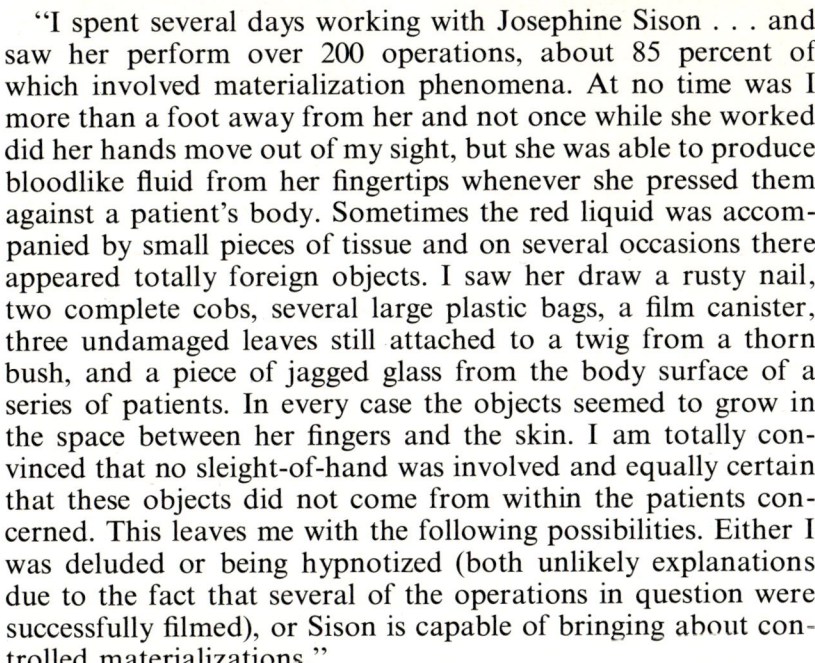

"I spent several days working with Josephine Sison . . . and saw her perform over 200 operations, about 85 percent of which involved materialization phenomena. At no time was I more than a foot away from her and not once while she worked did her hands move out of my sight, but she was able to produce bloodlike fluid from her fingertips whenever she pressed them against a patient's body. Sometimes the red liquid was accompanied by small pieces of tissue and on several occasions there appeared totally foreign objects. I saw her draw a rusty nail, two complete cobs, several large plastic bags, a film canister, three undamaged leaves still attached to a twig from a thorn bush, and a piece of jagged glass from the body surface of a series of patients. In every case the objects seemed to grow in the space between her fingers and the skin. I am totally convinced that no sleight-of-hand was involved and equally certain that these objects did not come from within the patients concerned. This leaves me with the following possibilities. Either I was deluded or being hypnotized (both unlikely explanations due to the fact that several of the operations in question were successfully filmed), or Sison is capable of bringing about controlled materializations."

Here we have the history of Spiritualism repeating itself: a scientist sets out to investigate strange and suspect phenomena, and ends up vouching for their authenticity. The reaction among Western Spiritualist healers to such gruesome surgery has been skeptical, and in some cases hostile. When Lourival de Freitas gave a demonstration of his methods before some British healers at the Spiritualist Association, he was prevented from continuing by the alarmed members of the audience.

The European spiritual healers, however, share with the psychic surgeons the belief that they are merely channels through which the spirits of doctors do the actual healing. Harry Edwards, possibly the world's most famous healer today, believes that a band of medical men—including Louis Pasteur and Lord Lister—direct his healing from the spirit world. "There is such a wide diversity of diseases healed," he says, "that each case must be a planned treatment. There must be an intelligence capable of truly diagnosing the cause of the sickness and possessing the knowledge how to apply the corrective forces necessary to bring about the healing. These healing intelligences must possess a superior knowledge to man. . . ."

Harry Edwards treating a patient suffering from back trouble by laying on of hands. Edwards' technique, basically, consists of keeping his eyes shut to get attuned to his spirit guides, until he can feel the power flowing through his body. Then the healing can commence. He does no manipulation. Apart from the gentle laying on of hands, the most he does is a slight, rocking movement over the affected area of the patient.

Above: Rosemary Brown with one of the scores she claims were dictated to her by the dead great masters of music. This particular piece, "Study in C♯ minor," was dictated by Chopin. Liszt, who is her spirit guide, has dictated more music to her than anyone else, and the closest runner-up is Chopin. Mrs. Brown, who is an untutored musician, writes: "Much of his new music is too difficult for me to play properly—I stumble through it, just getting some idea of how it should sound."

The supposed superior knowledge of spirits continues to be a hotly debated point between believers and skeptics. The communications received from spirits over the years have on the whole been banal and trivial. There have been cases of spirits apparently conveying detailed and accurate information, as in the R101 case, but even such messages as these do not necessarily support the idea of superior intellectual development on the "other side." In fact, communications allegedly received from the spirits of distinguished thinkers, such as scientists Thomas Henry Huxley and Sir Oliver Lodge, have been noticeably inferior to their earthly communications in both content and style.

While editor of the occult magazine *Tomorrow,* F. Clive-Ross was one of Spiritualism's sternest critics. He wrote in 1963 that one of the strongest arguments against Spiritualism was that little of significance had been communicated, "although the welter of rubbish has been stupendous." He went on to issue this challenge:

"According to Spiritualists the spirits of great composers also survive, and it should be a fairly simple matter to communicate some music. Cannot 'Silver Birch' [a then well-known spirit guide] ask Beethoven for a new symphony, Wagner for a new opera, or even an aria from Puccini, Verdi, Donizetti, Gounod, or Bellini? The great writers have been silent, so now let us see whether the great composers can do any better. Silver Birch enunciates long-winded platitudes readily enough, so here is his opportunity to produce something likely to convince a great many people of the truth of Spiritualism. It need not be anything very elaborate; just one of the latest compositions by any of these composers from the spheres where, the Spiritualists tell us, they continued to work and 'progress.' "

At the time this was published, newly widowed Rosemary Brown was struggling in poverty to bring up a young son and daughter. She had been psychic since childhood, and could remember a vision of an elderly gentleman who told her that one day he and other great composers would give her beautiful music, and teach her how to play it.

Years later she came across a picture of Franz Liszt, and recognized him as her mysterious visitor. In 1964 Rosemary Brown began to write music—not just simple tunes, but well-developed compositions in the styles of Liszt, Chopin, Debussy, Rachmaninoff, Brahms, Bach, and Beethoven. Most of these are piano pieces, though some are for orchestra. Having had only a few piano lessons, she finds some of the piano music too difficult to play herself. A recording entitled "Rosemary Brown's Music" was released in 1970. On one side it features Mrs. Brown playing the simpler pieces; on the other side the renowned pianist Peter Katin plays the more complex music.

An observer who watched Rosemary Brown writing some of the music was amazed at the speed with which she wrote. She says that the music has already been composed when it is dictated to her. Some of the composers communicate in English but, she says, "Liszt tends to go off into a stream of German when excited—or French." The medium's schoolgirl French is barely adequate to understanding her French-speaking composers. When Chopin speaks Polish, she tries to write it down phonetically and gives it to a Polish friend to try to translate.

Reaction from the musical world has predictably been mixed. Many musicians have been greatly impressed with Rosemary Brown's works. Pianist Hephzibah Menuhin said: "I look at these manuscripts with immense respect. Each piece is distinctly in the composer's style." Composer Richard Rodney Bennet was more outspoken: "A lot of people can improvise, but you couldn't fake music like this without years of training. I couldn't have faked some of the Beethoven myself."

Nevertheless, some critics have found the music "less than the best" of which the composers were capable—often more characteristic of their early work than of their maturity. Spiritualists counter by saying that the point of the communication is not so much to add to the world's treasury of music as to give proof of survival. An introduction to the recording, supposedly dictated by the late musicologist Sir Donald Tovey, gave this view:

"In communicating through music and conversation, an organized group of musicians, who have departed from your world, are attempting to establish a precept for humanity, i.e., that physical death is a transition from one state of consciousness to another wherein one retains one's individuality. . . . We are not transmitting music to Rosemary Brown simply for the sake of offering possible pleasure in listening thereto; it is the implications relevant to this phenomenon which we hope will stimulate sensible and sensitive interest and stir many who are intelligent and impartial to consider and explore the unknown of man's mind and psyche. When man has plumbed the mysterious depths of his veiled consciousness, he will then be able to soar to correspondingly greater heights."

Spiritualism has come a long way from the rappings in the small cottage in Hydesville. Its manifestations in the modern world are extremely varied—from matter-of-fact messages through a fully conscious clairvoyant to gruesome operations by a psychic surgeon in France. Healing in one form or another is an important part of Spiritualist activity in most countries, but apart from this common concern, the movement has little overall unity. An International Spiritualist Federation exists, but it has not been able to unite the movement. One dividing factor is whether or not mediums should take money for their services. Another is the belief in reincarnation, which is vital to Kardec's Spiritist school of thought but largely rejected in Europe and America. Some believers say Spiritualism is a religion, and others call it a way of life. Spiritualism, then, is thriving in disarray. And since it does not have a world leader— relying instead on the often conflicting teachings of spirit guides for its philosophy—the possibility of its ever growing into a world religion of major importance seems remote.

Spiritualists throughout the world have in common a belief in life after death, and a desire to demonstrate that many forms of communication with the world beyond are possible. To interested outsiders the question is: has sufficient evidence been amassed or are we still waiting for a communication that will decide the case once and for all?

Beethoven Writes his Tenth Symphony

The English medium Rosemary Brown has produced quantities of music she claims has been dictated to her by the great masters of music, who have chosen this way to prove that their spirits survive. One of her special favorites is Beethoven, and the two of them are engaged on a project that is taking years: the Tenth Symphony. It is an enormous choral work, like the great composer's Ninth Symphony.

In writing this new work Beethoven will be able to hear it, according to Rosemary Brown. In her autobiography *Unfinished Symphonies*, she says that his deafness is gone. "Those human ills and frailties disappear once we reach the other side," she writes. The spirit Beethoven is a less stormy person than he was in life, but he is still awe-inspiring. Rosemary Brown was so much in awe of him at first that little conversation took place. She received his music by a kind of telepathy, slowly catching his ideas in writing.

Now Beethoven works much more directly, dictating several bars for one hand, and then going back to fill in for the other. "After all," says the medium, "they know already what they are going to tell me to write, and it is simpler to keep to one line at a time."

8

It all began in a small cottage in the town of Hydesville, New York, with two little girls and an unseen force trading raps. From that first communication believed to be with the spirit world, Spiritualism is now an idea encircling the globe.

Sifting the Evidence

Spiritualism has now been a flourishing belief for more than 125 years. From its noisy, melodramatic beginnings to its present mainly low-key manifestations, it has intrigued, baffled, convinced, and comforted millions of people, while many others have dismissed it as utter nonsense. If no longer news, it at least remains controversial.

If a person is a thoroughgoing skeptic, it is easy enough to refuse to consider the possibility that any part of the self survives bodily death—let alone communicates with the living. For one thing, such ideas seem to contradict present scientific knowledge. Moreover, a few of the more tawdry hoaxes

"Some of the most astonishing phenomena ever witnessed"

Below: Daniel Dunglas Home, the one medium who was never proved fraudulent in the physical phenomena he produced. He never tried materializations, but his levitations were legendary—and no one, ever, proved he was cheating.

perpetrated by some mediums will suffice to reinforce the cynic's belief that the whole Spiritualist case is a tissue of lies and delusions.

Those who start to examine Spiritualism objectively, however, will soon find themselves bewildered by conflicting evidence. They may be amused and disgusted in turn by the hoaxes and by the pathetic gullibility of some of the followers, but they may also discover cases that seem so genuine they are on the point of believing. Then they come across an explanation of how the material communicated could have been obtained by the medium either through telepathy with the sitter or from sources within the medium's subconscious mind. Once in a great while, they will find a case that seems inexplicable except in Spiritualist terms.

Logically, one such case is all that is needed. The American psychologist and philosopher William James made this point when he said in a lecture: "To upset the conclusion that all crows are black there is no need to seek demonstration that no crow is white; it is sufficient to produce one white crow; a single one is sufficient." Once it is proved beyond the shadow of a doubt that in a particular case a communication or phenomenon originated from someone who has died, we have proof that survival is a fact. For convinced Spiritualists, the skies are full of white crows. For a skeptical investigator, such cases are so rare that he is more likely to file them away as "unsolved" rather than to accept them as proof of the existence of spirits.

Among the many physical mediums, the outstanding apparent white crow was D. D. Home. All of the others that were investigated—Mrs. Guppy, Florence Cook, Eusapia Paladino, Helen Duncan, to name a few—were caught in fraud, sometimes over and over again. The faithful would stoutly maintain that these mediums produced genuine phenomena as well, but for a critical investigator, their chronic cheating—often well planned in advance—casts strong doubt on the allegedly genuine occurrences. Not so in the case of D. D. Home. All psychic investigators acknowledge the fact that Home was never detected in fraud.

Time and time again in good light Home produced some of the most astonishing phenomena ever witnessed. The most thorough investigation of Home was done by Sir William Crookes, who also investigated Florence Cook and her materialized spirit Katie King. Crookes devised several tests for Home including a test of his power to make an accordion play by itself.

Crookes built a cage that was open at the top and bottom and would just fit under a table. He bought a new accordion to rule out the possibility of Home's using one of the self-playing models then available on the market. During the test seance, the cage was moved out from under the table and the accordion was placed inside it. The medium picked up the accordion at the opposite end to the keys, and held it with his thumb and middle finger. Adjacent sitters placed their feet on top of Home's, and the medium placed his free hand on the top of the table. The cage was moved back toward the table as far as Home's arm would permit. Soon the accordion began waving about curiously inside the cage. It played a few notes and then a simple tune. "But the sequel," reported Crookes, "was still more striking, for Mr. Home then removed his hand altogether from the accordion,

. . . and placed it in the hand of the person next to him. The instrument then continued to play, no person touching it and no hand being near it."

An even more bizarre psychic concert by Home was reported by Lady Crookes, the wife of the scientist. During a seance held in a London house, she was sitting somewhat apart from the other sitters, facing them. Home, holding an accordion, stood in the doorway leading to the adjacent room. Then, according to Lady Crookes:

"The accordion was immediately taken from his hand by a cloudy appearance, which soon seemed to condense into a distinct human form, clothed in a filmy drapery, standing near Mr. Home between the two rooms. The accordion began to play (I do not remember whether on this occasion there was any recognized melody), and the figure advanced toward me till it almost touched me, playing continuously. It was semitransparent, and I could see the sitters through it all the time. Mr. Home remained near the sliding doors. As the figure approached I felt an intense cold, getting stronger as it got nearer, and as it was giving me the accordion I could not help screaming. The figure immediately seemed to sink into the floor to the waist, leaving only the head and shoulders visible, still playing the accordion, which was then about a foot off the floor. Mr. Home and my husband came to me at once, and I have no clear recollection of what then occurred, except that the accordion did not cease playing immediately. Mr. Serjeant Cox was rather angry at my want of nerve, and exclaimed: 'Mrs. Crookes, you have spoilt the finest manifestation we have ever had.' I have always regretted that my want of presence of mind brought the phenomena to so abrupt a termination."

On the face of it, we might conclude that Lady Crookes was deceived by her will to believe in supernormal phenomena. Likewise her husband, brilliant and honest scientist though he

Below: Home's own accordion, which would play by itself during his seances. Sometimes music would even be heard when there was apparently no instrument present in the room at all.

Above: the cage that Crookes devised and the accordion that he bought as a special test of Home's powers. Home was to hold it only by the non-playing end.

Left: Home with the accordion. In spite of all the controls, including the sitters keeping his feet under their own, it played.

Above: the nurse Stella Cranshaw, known as Stella C. Although she was for a time a superb physical medium, she was barely interested in the phenomena she produced, and was unenthusiastic about psychical research. She did not appear to believe, personally, that the peculiar manifestations which had gone on in her vicinity since her childhood had anything to do with spirits. When she began the experiments, she was 21. During the five years that she was intermittently tested, her powers, and her interest, waned noticeably. After the last series of tests in 1928, she married, and apparently gave up the use of her unusual powers.

was, was a staunch Spiritualist. The other sitters were not necessarily trained observers. Might it not be, then, that their desire to believe in the supernatural, coupled with Home's charismatic personality, created a collective hallucination? Many sane and intelligent people have been known to hallucinate, and for several people to experience the same hallucination simultaneously is not unheard of, although rare.

The sheer bulk of the evidence in favor of Home, however, speaks strongly against hallucination. Dozens of witnesses independently left written testimony of astounding events apparently caused by Home. It was not uncommon for heavy pieces of furniture to rise several feet in the air, for example. One witness reporting such a case asserted that he had to use all his strength to push a levitated table back onto the floor. Perhaps even more astonishing is the report that when tables moved about in the air, the objects lying on them remained undisturbed.

Less spectacular, but perhaps even more convincing for that very reason, were certain other experiments conducted by Crookes in which Home, by merely placing his fingertips in a glass of water resting on a board, was able to cause apparent weight fluctuations in the board. The fluctuations were measured by scales on which one end of the board was resting.

Such experiments convinced Crookes of the existence of a "new force" which Home possessed. Unfortunately, the scientists who were critical of Crookes' investigations and conclusions disdained to check his results with experiments of their own. Had they done so, they might have helped to establish without doubt Home's possession of supernormal powers. Even without their corroboration, however, Home's case continues to challenge the skeptics.

Though no other medium has demonstrated the powers of the new force in such a dramatic and colorful way, there have been some physical mediums whose manifestations have been subjected to rigorous tests. One of these was Stella Cranshaw, a young British nurse, usually referred to in research as Stella C. She was discovered in the 1920s by Harry Price, a well-known psychical researcher, to whom she reported during a conversation on a train that she sometimes experienced breezes in closed rooms, saw objects move apparently by themselves, and occasionally saw blue sparks—a very rare psychic phenomenon. She agreed to be investigated by Price and his team at the National Laboratory of Psychical Research in London. Price conducted several tests on Stella C. in the 1920s. They involved ingenious equipment and stringent controls. One piece of apparatus was a fraud-proof seance table. It consisted of two tables, one of which fitted inside the other. In the top of the inner table was a hinged trap door which could be opened only from the underside. Between the legs of the inner table was a shelf on which small musical instruments, such as a harmonica or a bell, could be placed. The sides of each table were enclosed with wooden trellises, and as an extra control, the legs of the inner table were wrapped with a length of gauze. The investigators thus made sure that no one could surreptitiously gain access to the objects inside the inner table.

Stella C. and the sitters sat around this table, two of the sitters

holding her hands and feet. After she went into a trance, activity began to occur within the center table. The bell that had been put inside rang, and the harmonica therein played. Most remarkable of all, a red light flashed in the telekinetoscope, a device designed by Price. This was a sensitive piece of apparatus containing a battery and a small lightbulb that was turned on by pressing a telegraph key. To insure that the key could not be pressed by a person, Price covered it with a soap bubble and, to prevent the soap bubble from drying out and breaking, with a glass shade. After the seance the bubble was discovered still intact. The light had been turned on by some invisible force. This force that seemed to emanate from Stella C. was also capable of more vigorous activity. On one occasion it levitated the seance table, and at another memorable seance, it completely demolished the table.

Was Stella C.'s power that of telekinesis—the movement of objects by an immaterial force? Telekinesis is a well-established psychic phenomenon that is thought by many modern scientists to account for a great deal of poltergeist activity. Most psychical researchers regard it as a power exerted by living humans rather than proof of the existence of spirits. It seems plausible that Home and Stella C. could have produced genuine physical phenomena through their own powers, and that spirits are not needed to account for them.

How do we account for materializations, though? Many cases can be dismissed as fraud, and many others as hallucinations. Even so, the subject has its baffling aspects. In 1929 and 1930, Harry Price conducted a series of seances in his laboratory with the Austrian medium Rudi Schneider. The medium was seated at a table with six observers including Price. All wore metallic gloves and shoes and touched the hands and feet of their neighbors. In front of each person was a red lightbulb, which remained lit as long as no one broke the circuit. If anyone were to remove his hand or foot, the light would go out. Price also searched Rudi before each seance. In spite of the rigid controls, Rudi time and again produced materialized hands and arms. Some of these

Above left: the musical toys and instruments that were played by psychic forces at Stella C.'s experimental seances.

Above: the fraud-proof table made by H. W. Pugh. The center flap could be opened only from underneath. It did open several times during the seance, and two of the sitters, placing a silk handkerchief over the open flap, felt fingerlike forms moving under the handkerchief. Below: the solid wood table that Stella C.'s forces reduced to fragments during another seance.

Above: a reconstruction of the materialization of a hand from the cabinet while Schneider was under full control. Price is sitting in front of the medium. Price wrote about him: "Never, in the recorded history of any psychic, have phenomena been witnessed under such a merciless triple control of medium and before sitters of such repute."

Above: the Austrian medium Rudi Schneider with Harry Price, demonstrating how electrical control functioned. The left arm of the end sitter was connected to the circuit by a metal plate screwed to the chair arm. In practice, the feet were not loosely slipped into the "socks" as here, but were tightly tied into place with special tapes.

limbs were only partial, missing the thumbs. At one sitting the observers saw a misshapen leg of a "pale chocolate color" emerge from the curtained cabinet and rock the table that stood in front of it.

Price's extensive notes on this series of seances constitute one of the most impressive documents on physical mediumship in the history of psychical research. But even these notes leave doubts. There is an allegation supported by photographic evidence that Rudi had one hand free during a seance in which, for some unknown reason, Price had not used the electrical control. Instead he had relied merely on holding Schneider's hands during the test. Price accused Rudi of fraud, and the whole investigation blew up in a personal quarrel.

The materialization case rests on the existence or nonexistence of ectoplasm. This peculiar substance is believed by Spiritualists to issue from the mouth, pores, and other body openings of the medium. The psychical investigator Schrenck-Notzing pronounced it to be "a material, at first semifluid, which possesses some of the properties of a living substance, notably that of the

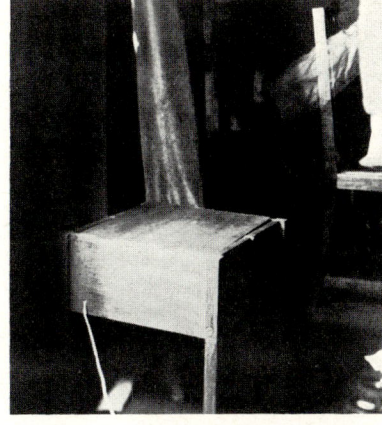

Above: the famous photograph showing Rudi's free arm, taken automatically during a seance. Harry Price, an influential investigator, had defended Rudi Schneider before this photograph appeared. Their relationship became strained as a result of it. Below: Willi Schneider, Rudi's brother, and a medium in his own right, with a faked cloth phantom.

power of change, of movement, and of the assumption of definite forms."

Dozens of investigators have testified to the reality of this substance, and to its ability to assume the appearance and texture of living flesh. Dozens of other investigations have discovered that ectoplasm consisted of chewed-up paper, cloth, and other materials regurgitated by the medium while apparently in a trance. The mysterious disappearance of matcrialization phenomena in the past few decades casts considerable doubt on the existence of this apparently miraculous substance.

With some relief one turns from ectoplasm to some of the more intellectual aspects of the survival question. For, irrespective of the reality or illusion of materialized limbs and flying tables, the central question is the possible existence of a personality independent of the body. If such a personality or mind, as distinguished from the physical brain, exists, its survival of death is logically not only possible but probable.

Most scientific evidence does not support such a theory. In his book *Psychical Research Today*, the psychiatrist and psychical researcher D. J. West cites the "evidence that our thoughts and feelings are entirely dependent upon the state of our brains. A deep anesthetic or a blow on the head will temporarily put an end to all mental activity. The administration of drugs that act upon the brain can cause confusion, change of mood, hallucinations, peculiar thoughts, delusions, and changes of character. Permanent changes of personality or destruction of faculties to the stage of idiocy are caused by disease, injury, or surgical operation. Where is the cherished independence of mind in the face of such evidence?"

This is a difficult question to answer. These facts cast serious

Precisely what ectoplasm looks like and behaves like appears to vary a bit between mediums, and even the same medium may discover that the manifestations appear to be different depending on his or her emotional state. If the ectoplasm is suddenly withdrawn back into the body of the medium—for example when a light is abruptly turned on— the medium is sometimes found to be bruised where the ectoplasm appeared to recoil with something like the force of a snapped elastic band. Of course, whether or not ectoplasm exists at all is a much disputed point. There is considerable proof that Helen Duncan's ectoplasm, for example, was yards of regurgitated cheese-cloth, with the same frayed spots visible at each materialization. Left: Kate Goligher, the Irish medium, levitating a table with the help of rodlike ectoplasm. Right: Margery Crandon at a seance producing dark ectoplasm. Below: Eva C. forming ectoplasm through a veil covering her mouth.

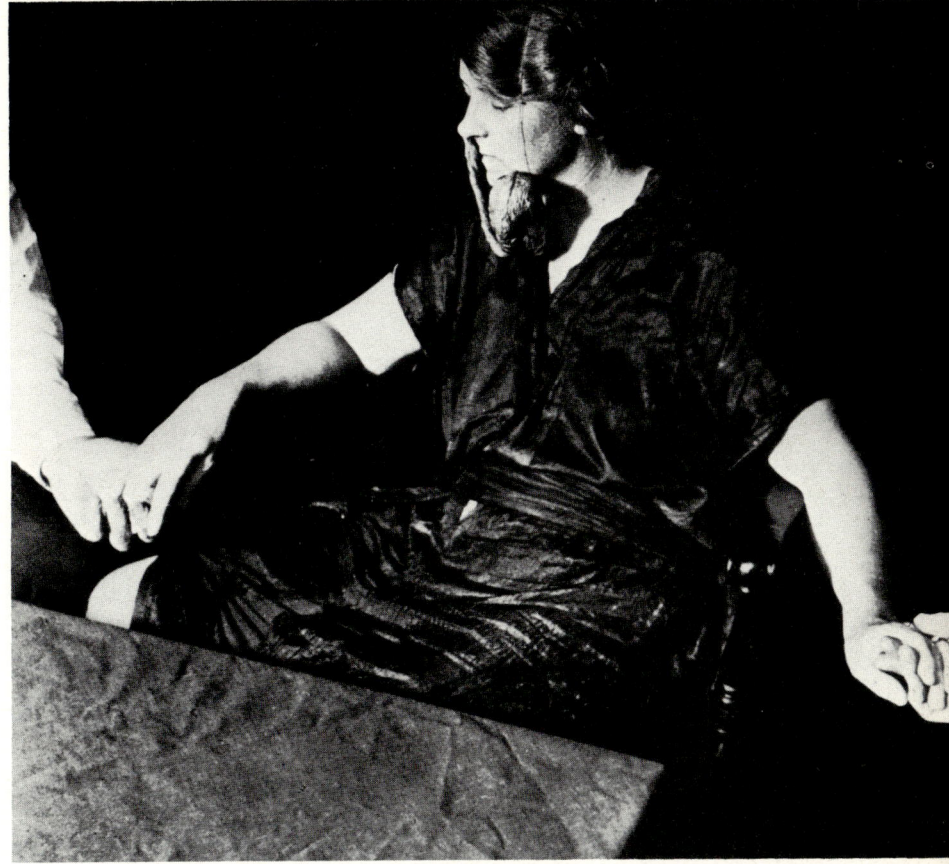

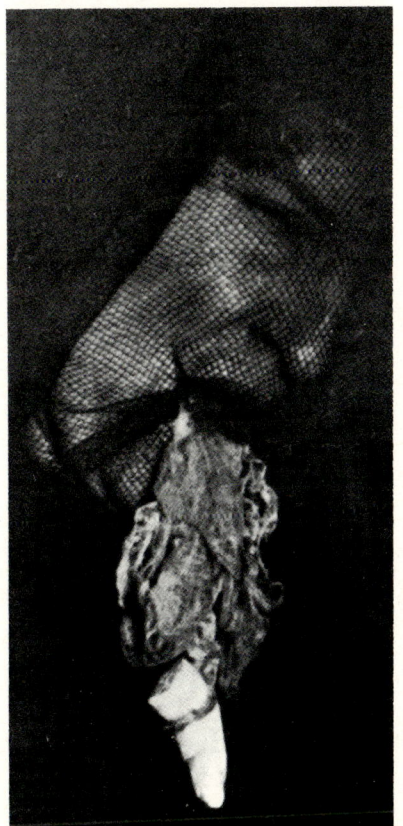

doubt not only on the survival theory, but also on extrasensory perception, which is now a well-established phenomenon. If people can gain information that bypasses the normal sensory media, then there must be something in the brain—subtler than any part or process yet detected—capable of transmitting and receiving such information. It could be that the permanent changes in personality caused by physical injury are only apparent changes, alterations of a superficial nature that do not affect the essential person, or soul.

Relevant to this question is the phenomenon of the OOBE, or out-of-the-body experience, reported by many people. These are experiences in which the person, usually lying unconscious, has a vivid impression of leaving his own body and looking down on it —or of traveling some distance away from it. Some of these experiences can be explained as hallucinations. In other cases, the things seen are later verified. An American woman named Mrs. Wilmot experienced an OOBE while sleeping restlessly because of worry about her husband, who was crossing the ocean in stormy weather. She seemed to leave her body, travel over the water, and alight on a steamer. She found her way to a cabin, entered, and saw her husband lying on his berth. Above him was a berth slightly set back in which another man was lying. She kissed her husband and left.

When she awoke Mrs. Wilmot made detailed notes of what she had seen, describing the cabin and the berth above her husband's. Later her description was found to be correct. Even more extra-ordinary, however, was the fact that, on the following morning

Above: William T. Stead, British editor and convinced Spiritualist. His automatic writing began with messages from a dead journalist friend, but he soon discovered he could receive messages from living friends as well. Oddly, the image of a sinking ocean liner occurred frequently in Stead's writings, and in 1893 he wrote a fictional story about the collision of a great liner with an iceberg in the Atlantic. Stead himself was on the maiden voyage of the ill-starred *Titanic*, and was one of the many drowned.

at sea, Wilmot told witnesses he had seen a vision of his wife and that the vision had kissed him. That was not all: the cabin mate had also seen the woman and had teased Wilmot about his female visitor.

Whatever one may think of materializations and apparitions, the capacities of the human mind—particularly the subconscious mind—seem greater than we can account for by today's scientific knowledge. For example, consider the talents of William Stead, a British journalist of the 19th century. Stead had the gift of automatic writing and used this method to communicate with his living friends. It saved them from having to write letters to him, but they were not always happy about Stead having access to their secrets. Stead himself told this story of one such embarrassed correspondent:

"A friend of mind . . . had spent the weekend at Haslemere, 30 miles from London. She was to lunch with me on the Wednesday, if she had returned to town. On the Monday afternoon I wished to know about this, so taking up a pen I asked the lady mentally if she had returned home. My hand wrote as follows: 'I am sorry to say that I have had a most unpleasant experience, which I am almost ashamed to tell you. I left Haslemere at 2:27 p.m. in a second-class compartment in which were two women and a man. At Godalming the women got out and I was left alone with the man. He came over and sat by me. I was alarmed and pushed him away. He would not move, however, and tried to kiss me. I was furious and there was a struggle, during which I seized his umbrella and struck him with it repeatedly, but it broke, and I was afraid I would get the worst of it, when the train stopped some distance from Guildford. The man took fright, left me before the train reached the station, jumped out and took to his heels. I was extremely agitated, but I kept the umbrella.'"

Stead then continued: "I sent my secretary immediately to the lady's house with a note in which I expressed my regret for the assault she had suffered, adding, 'Calm yourself and bring me the man's umbrella on Wednesday.' She replied: 'I am sorry you have learnt of what happened to me, because I had decided not to speak of it to anyone; but the umbrella was mine, not his.'"

One of the most complex cases of telepathy ever recorded appeared at first to be a detailed message from a spirit. It took place during some sittings that Dr. S. G. Soal, a mathematician at London University, had with Mrs. Blanche Cooper in 1921–22. She was a direct voice medium who conversed normally with the sitter when the voice, which seemed to emanate close to her, was not speaking. The voice would seldom speak for more than a minute or two at a time, and there would sometimes be a pause for as much as a quarter of an hour before the communication would resume.

During one sitting Dr. Soal heard the voice of a man claiming to be a boyhood friend named Gordon Davis. Soal remembered him, but thought that he had been killed in World War I. The tone of Davis' voice and his characteristic speech mannerisms were more or less as Soal recalled them. Davis described various incidents from their schooldays and the circumstances in which they had last met. At the following seance, Davis showed concern for his wife and child and asked that a message of consolation be sent to them. Unfortunately, he was unable to give their address. At this point, one of Blanche Cooper's spirit guides took over and said that Davis was describing the house to her. "He says something about a funny dark tunnel—it's to do with the house."

The guide continued with the description mentioning "five or six steps and a half" to the door of the house. He said there was something resembling a verandah in front of the house, which was not on a "proper street" but on one that was "like half a street." He mentioned the letter "E" but seemed unable to determine its significance. Inside the house were some pictures of "glorious mountains and the sea," curious vases and saucers, two brass candle-sticks on a shelf and "a black dickie bird" on the piano.

The earlier part of Davis' communication relating to his youth was already known to Soal, and could be explained as telepathy between sitter and medium. But the parts of the message relating to the house could not be confirmed immediately. If Soal could prove the description of the house to be accurate, the communication would presumably be evidence for survival, for only the deceased Gordon Davis could plausibly have imparted the information.

Three years after the seance Dr. Soal verified the description. Instead of proving life after death, however, the case raised more perplexing questions. To begin with, Davis was still alive. Dr. Soal found him living in Southend, a seaside town in Essex. His house was one of a row of houses on Eastern Esplanade (the "E's"), facing the sea ("half a street"; English usage considers a street to include the buildings on both sides). Six steps led up to the front door, but the bottom step was only a thin slab ("five or six steps and a half"). At regular intervals between the houses was a covered walkway ("funny dark tunnel") leading to the back garden. Across from Davis' house on the other side of the street was a seaside shelter ("something resembling a verandah"). Inside the house Soal found the pictures of mountains and sea, the two brass candlesticks, and a black figure of a bird sitting on the piano. In short, every detail communicated in the seance was correct except one: Davis was still alive.

The Gordon Davis case has a final strange twist to it that makes it even more astonishing. At the time Dr. Soal received the message, Davis was not living in Southend. He had inspected the house three days before the first communication, but he and his family did not move into it until nearly a year later. The furnishing of the house described in the seance had not been planned in advance by Davis, but had come about partly by chance.

It would seem from the evidence that Blanche Cooper's psychic faculty had been able to rummage in the subconscious mind of a man she did not know existed, and not only produce his voice and correct information about his past but also see the environment in which he would live in the future.

The feats of which the subconscious mind is capable—and the tricks it can play—are illustrated by another communication that Dr. Soal received through Mrs. Cooper. A communicator announcing himself as John Ferguson claimed to be a brother of James Ferguson, a former schoolfriend of Dr. Soal. John Ferguson gave an address, the date, place, and manner of his

Automatic Writing from the Living

Unlike most automatic writers, who received their messages from the spirits, the 19th-century British journalist William Stead got messages from the living—and saved them the bother of writing themselves. He would ask mental questions and his hand would write the answers automatically—sometimes learning more than the friends wanted him to.

Once he had arranged a lunch engagement with a woman who had been out of town over the weekend. He mentally inquired whether she had returned to London yet, and his hand wrote a long note. It described an unpleasant encounter she had had on the train. According to the message, she had found herself alone in a compartment with a strange man. He came over, sat close to her, and when she tried to push him away, attempted to kiss her. Struggling furiously, she thumped him with his umbrella, which broke. Then the train unexpectedly stopped and the man took flight.

When Stead sent his servant to his friend's house with a note condoling her on the assault, the woman was taken aback. She replied, "I had decided not to speak of it to anyone." She added, "The umbrella was mine, not his."

Above: Dr. Samuel Soal and his wife. Dr. Soal has studied many aspects of the paranormal for much of his career, and his series of seances with the medium Mrs. Blanche Cooper—which unquestionably produced evidence of some kind of psychic communication—are a remarkable episode in psychic research.
Below: Mrs. Cooper, who received the "message" from Gordon Davis.

death, and a great deal of additional information. Soal did not remember that James Ferguson had a brother, but after each communication he speculated about the man's existence. He found that these guesses emerged as facts at the next sitting, and so, over a period of several weeks, the hypothetical John Ferguson, as visualized by Dr. Soal, confirmed the sitter's impressions through the medium.

On investigating, Soal discovered that John Ferguson did not exist, alive or dead, and that the details of his life and manner of death were therefore false. "It is interesting to note how rapidly John Ferguson disintegrated as a personality once his statements about himself had been disproved," wrote Soal. "For more than eight weeks he had been sustained by the emotional interest of the sitter, but immediately that interest had evaporated he became a confused and feeble ghost who disappeared almost as suddenly as he had come on the scene."

Probably the most common dramatization of the subconscious mind is the spirit control or guide. For the most part they are American Indians, Chinese philosophers, or anonymous monks. Most of them are patently the imaginings of the medium's subconscious, and yet they seem to play an important role in collecting and conveying supernormal evidence. The gifted medium Mrs. Leonore Piper, whom William James considered his "one white crow," had a succession of colorful spirit guides. They included an Indian girl with the unlikely name of "Chlorine," the English actress Mrs. Siddons, the poet Longfellow, and Johann Sebastian Bach. For most of her career Mrs. Piper's regular control was Dr. Phinuit, a French physician. His knowledge of medicine and command of French were minimal. Despite the obvious phoniness of her control, Leonore Piper produced some of the most convincing, well-documented communications in the history of Spiritualism. Later in her career Mrs. Piper's spirit guide was a known person, George Pelham. His repeated ability to correctly identify anonymous sitters unknown to Leonore Piper was strong evidence for his spiritual existence.

It is conceivable, of course, that Leonore Piper was gifted with extraordinarily acute ESP, and that she was able in some mysterious way to ferret out the sitter's correct identity. Such an explanation can be used to account for many presumed spirit messages.

What is needed to establish evidence for an afterlife that cannot be explained as telepathy or the workings of the subconscious is information that is not known by living people, or that appears to originate only with the communicator. The first requirement poses yet another problem. If the information is not known by living people, it has to be on record somewhere in order to be corroborated. Since some mediums have demonstrated the ability to read the contents of sealed envelopes, it becomes impossible to prove that recorded information in any form has not been inspected by the medium's psychic faculty. A typical example is the book test related by Sir William Barrett in his preface to the Reverend Drayton Thomas' book *Some New Evidence for Human Survival*. At a seance with Mrs. Gladys Osborne Leonard, Barrett received a message supposed to be from Frederick W. H. Myers, a former president of the SPR.

"There were some books on the right-hand side of a room upstairs in your house in Devonshire Place. On the second shelf four feet from the ground, in the fourth book counting from the left, at the top of page 78, are some words which you should take as direct answer from him [Myers] to so much of the work you have been doing since he passed over."

Gladys Leonard asked for the name of the book, but the communicator was unable to give it. He said, however, that while "feeling" the books on the shelf, he got a sense of "progression," and that close to the test book were "one or two books on matters in which Sir William used to be very interested, but not of late years. It is connected with studies of his youth."

The medium had never visited Barrett's home, and the scientist had no idea what book was fourth from the left on the specified shelf. On returning home he found that it was George Eliot's *Middlemarch*. In the first line at the top of page 78 were the words "Ay, ay. I remember—you'll see I've remembered 'em all." Barrett regarded this quotation as singularly appropriate, for since Myers' death, much of Barrett's work had been concerned with the question of survival after death, and in particular whether the memories of friends continued once a spirit had left the body. Close at hand on the bookshelf were two volumes of *Heat and Sound* by Dr. John Tyndall, to whom Barrett had been an assistant when young. This may have been the reference to "studies of his youth."

It could be that Myers' spirit had somehow been able to study the books on Barrett's shelf, as claimed, or that Myers while alive had examined the books, and was now communicating what he remembered. Even so, many researchers would prefer to interpret this case and other such book tests as examples of clairvoyance on the part of the medium.

The most complex and perhaps most convincing evidence for survival is contained in what are known as the "cross-correspondences." These are an extensive collection of scripts taken in automatic writing by a group of women who came to be known as the "SPR Automatists."

Soon after the death of F. W. H. Myers in 1901, his friend Mrs. A. W. Verrall began receiving messages in automatic writing from a communicator claiming to be the spirit of Myers. Some of the messages were in Greek and Latin, though the standard of scholarship in these messages was inferior to that of both Myers and Mrs. Verrall. Then Mrs. Leonore Piper also began receiving automatic writing allegedly from Myers, containing references to topics appearing in Mrs. Verrall's scripts. Mrs. Verrall's daughter then began receiving scripts from Myers alluding to topics in the writings of both her mother and Mrs. Piper. A writer living in India and using the pseudonym "Mrs. Holland" also began receiving scripts from a communicator claiming to be Myers. He asked Mrs. Holland to send the scripts to Mrs. Verrall, and gave her the necessary address. Apparently doubting the accuracy of these instructions, Mrs. Holland sent the scripts to the SPR. There researchers found that the new scripts contained allusions to the other scripts already received.

Over some 30 years the SPR received thousands of pages of

Above: Mrs. Gladys Leonard became a celebrity when she made the first communication with Sir Oliver Lodge's son Raymond, who had been killed in World War I. She was also involved in a psychic experiment with Sir William Barrett in which the spirit of F. W. Myers, one of the founders of the Society for Psychical Research, led Barrett to a particular book he owned. Mrs. Gladys Leonard's powers were apparently heightened by the presence of her husband.

Above: Frederick Myers, brilliant psychologist and long active psychical investigator who helped found the Society for Psychical Research. Judging by the number of mediums who claim to have contacted him, he is apparently one of the most enthusiastic spirit communicators. His description of the soul's progress after death is supposed to be contained in a work taken in automatic writing by medium Geraldine Cummins.

Opposite: a mezzotint by James Tissot of a double materialization he claimed to have witnessed at a seance. The girl had been dear to him in life, and he welcomed her reappearance as certain proof —to him at least—that she had survived the mysterious and inevitable passage through death.

scripts from the automatists. Although the mediums realized that the messages might constitute proof that Myers had survived, they were unaware of the overall pattern of the communications. It was the researchers at the SPR, patiently combing through the masses of unrelated and often trivial material in the scripts, who detected the cross references and pieced together this intellectual jigsaw puzzle. Part of a quotation from the classics would be found in one script, another part in one of the other scripts, and the meaning behind the reference in still a third script. The related references would all appear within a fairly short time span.

Most of the messages are extremely complicated, containing roundabout and obscure literary allusions. An unusually simple example involved a laurel wreath. While in trance one day, Leonore Piper repeated the word "laurel" several times. The following day, again in trance, she was apparently controlled by the spirit of Myers and said, "I gave Mrs. Verrall laurel wreath." Examination of a script from Mrs. Verrall dated three weeks earlier revealed the phrases, "Apollo's laurel bough," "a laurel wreath," "corona laureata," and similar references. Three weeks after Mrs. Piper's trance utterances, Mrs. Verrall received a script containing these words, "Laurel leaves are emblem. Laurel for the victor's brow." The SPR investigators gradually came to the conclusion that the cross-correspondences might be part of a purposeful design on the part of Myers and, later on, of other departed psychical researchers who communicated scripts, to prove survival. There was no reference to such a plan in Myers' writings, but conceivably he could have devised it after death.

Other explanations for the cross-correspondences are discussed by H. F. Saltmarsh in his study *Evidence of Personal Survival from Cross-Correspondences*. He points out that in view of the character of the people involved and the 30-year span over which the correspondences occurred, "the hypothesis of fraud is so fantastic that it need only be mentioned to be dismissed." The possibility that corresponding quotations from classical sources should appear in these scripts at the same time by mere chance was "abstractly possible," but in his opinion had little to recommend it as a theory. The only alternative to the survival explanation is that the automatists had somehow established an extremely high level of ESP without realizing it, and were conveying messages to each other under the assumed personality of Myers.

In this case the ESP hypothesis is almost as great a strain on the reason as the belief that Myers and other spirits devised and communicated a long series of rather obscure messages as a means of signaling their continued existence. To some students of the cross-correspondences, the explanation of spirit communication is more plausible.

If we consider this case along with some of the other highly evidential cases such as the communication of data on the R101 disaster, we approach a situation in which the evidence for survival—slight though it is when weighed against our present scientific knowledge, and buried as it is in masses of phony evidence—becomes very convincing. For most people, however, absolute certainty about life after death is something that may be approached but never attained—at least not in our lifetime.

Picture Credits